RETIRE DOWNTOWN

RETIRE DOWNTOWN

The Lifestyle Destination for Active Retirees and Empty Nesters

KYLE EZELL

Andrews McMeel
Publishing, LLC

Kansas City

This book is dedicated to the millions of Americans
who already know and love downtown living
and for the millions more who are just discovering it.

06 07 08 09 10 11 BBG 10 9 8 7 6 5 4 3 2 1

Library of Congress Cataloging-in-Publication Data
Ezell, Kyle.
    Retire downtown : the lifestyle destination for active retirees and empty nesters /
Kyle Ezell.
        p. cm.
    ISBN-13: 978-0-7407-6049-5
    ISBN-10: 0-7407-6049-1
    1. Retirement—United States. 2. Retirees—United States—Life skills guides. 3. City and town life—United States. I. Title.

HQ1063.2.U6E95 2006
646.7'9091732—dc21

                                                                                    2006045994

www.andrewsmcmeel.com

www.retiredowntown.com

Attention: Schools and Businesses

C O N T E N T S

Part Two: Twenty of America's Best Retirement Downtowns   69

PREFACE

From the time I was five years old, I have been a city fanatic. I sketched "dream plans" on poster boards I purchased with my allowance instead of buying comic books or toys. I studied cities' growth and decline as a teen with a collection of dozens of atlases and hundreds of maps, and I analyzed downtown skylines. I never lost my fascination for cities, especially their downtowns. Over the years as an urban planner I realized that, especially in middle America, a great number of people don't appreciate the center cities. Some couldn't care less about the fate of our downtowns.

Today, downtowns and center-city neighborhoods are finally getting a closer look, although the overwhelming majority still prefer suburban, and now "exurban," living. I believe that more Americans, particularly baby boomers, would choose downtown living if they truly understood the convenience, community spirit, and joy that it could bring to their lives. Walking, using public transit, knowing many neighbors, enjoying a tight-knit community, shopping on Main Street, and other "city" things are basically foreign ideas to many Americans since most, for a variety of reasons, have never experienced city life.

This became even more clear one day when I was walking in downtown Columbus and spotted two women, probably in their fifties, who looked lost and bewildered. I asked them if they could use some help with directions, and they told me they were waiting on someone who was having eye surgery and had decided to take a walk to find a cup of coffee. I told them to follow me to the coffee shop.

As we walked, they commented that they hadn't been downtown in fifteen years, and were amazed by the changes, saying, "It's clean, it's beautiful, and I can't believe it, but *I feel safe.*" They were floored by the pedestrian activity and were surprised by the new condominiums, restaurants, and stores. "I would actually consider living here," one of the women added. "It really seems like fun, but I've lived in the 'burbs for most of my life and I wouldn't know where to begin looking."

About that time, these women were amused by a young woman buzzing up the streets of downtown Columbus on her scooter, hair waving in the wind. It occurred to me that millions of others just like them would be open to at least contemplating downtown living. This book was written to introduce the mature generation to the kind of exciting city lifestyle that they have avoided (until now) and present a clear alternative to a golf course, beachfront, or mountaintop retirement community.

I use this material in downtown-living seminars for empty nesters and retirees to talk about cities' history, issues, and opportunities. Held at lifelong-learning venues and contracted by downtown developers, these fun and educational seminars are reaching many people who otherwise would have never considered an urban lifestyle.

As an urban planner, I realize that there has to be a tipping point for urban living to catch on in Topeka and Peoria. I believe that it is going to happen in every city—not just the big ones. This book is a manifestation of my life's passion.

A C K N O W L E D G M E N T S

Thanks to the following Ruppies for either contributing their written stories or graciously (and often enthusiastically) agreeing to be interviewed.

Betina Bartels, Cincinnati, Ohio
Bill and Peg Balzer, Atlanta, Georgia
Cecelia Muhammad, Atlanta, Georgia
Charles Harbour and Dr. Sheryl Davis, Memphis, Tennessee
David and Sigrid Knuti, Madison, Wisconsin
Deborah McLarney, Omaha, Nebraska
Dr. Melvin and Leslie Hershkowitz, Providence, Rhode Island
Dr. Morgan Lyons and his wife Martha Harris, Los Angeles, California
Ed and Phyllis Gabovitch, Indianapolis, Indiana
Ed Hinshaw, Milwaukee, Wisconsin
Elton and Gladys Boykin, Louisville, Kentucky
Gary Ferraro and Lorne Lassiter, Charlotte, North Carolina
Gene Holcomb, Memphis, Tennessee
Gerry Pighini, San Jose, California
H. G. and Vickie Godbey, Denver, Colorado
Howard and Suzanne Senter, Oklahoma City, Oklahoma
Ian and Jo Lydia Craven, Asheville, North Carolina
Jack and Peggy Houser, Denver, Colorado
Jacqueline Brown, Atlanta, Georgia

Jerry Ade and Cheryl Ross, Portland, Maine

Joan D'Agostino, Providence, Rhode Island

Joan Korte, San Antonio, Texas

Joanna Athey, Austin, Texas

John and Meg Harkins, Philadephia, Pennsylvania

Judith Jossa, Edmonton, Alberta, Canada

June Varney, Milwaukee, Wisconsin

Larry and Susan LeVieux, Austin, Texas

Lee and Tony Junker, Philadelphia, Pennsylvania

Lucia Gelotte, Miami, Florida

Lynn Phelps, Madison, Wisconsin

Maggie Olmstead, Austin, Texas

Marcia Rosenzweig, Providence, Rhode Island

Merrill and Polly Moter, Louisville, Kentucky

Mert and Gary Michael, Boise, Idaho

Patti and Mark Clark, Atlanta, Georgia

Paul and Lynn Sedway, San Francisco, California

Paul and Pat Dravillas, Chicago, Illinois

Rose Cooper, Charlotte, North Carolina

Sandy Duffy, Milwaukee, Wisconsin

Sharon Leicham, Memphis, Tennessee

Steve McClary, Columbus, Ohio

Tom and Bobbie Haig, Madison, Wisconsin

Vera and Terri Stauffer, Indianapolis, Indiana

Vick Haak, Austin, Texas

Wylene Carol, Colorado Springs, Colorado

Zoe Johnstone, Columbus, Ohio

Thanks to the following downtown development, real estate, and communications professionals for their assistance in research:

Anita Woo, Communications Director, Downtown Seattle Association

Angela Rosa, Bluestone Development, Omaha, Nebraska

Anthony McDermid, TA Parchiteure, Oklahoma City, Oklahoma

Barb Gibson, City of Denver, Colorado

Beth Kosley, Executive Director, Downtown Partnership of Colorado Springs

Beth Nichols, Executive Director of Downtown Milwaukee BID # 21

Bill Cooper, "the Loft Expert," Los Angeles, California

Bridgett Rogers, Johnson City Development Authority, Tennessee

Carla Pritchard and Sandra Rose, Chattanooga Downtown Partnership

Carol Schatz, President and Chief Executive Officer Central City Association
of Los Angeles

Carolyn Murray, Hunt Commercial Real Estate, Buffalo, New York

Dave Lopez, President, Downtown Oklahoma City Inc.

Dean Jones, Real Estate Applied Logics, Seattle, Washington

Hal Bastian, Vice President, Director of Economic Development, Downtown
Center Business Improvement District, Los Angeles, California

Janis M. Beitzer, Executive Director, Portland's Downtown District, Maine

Jeff Beals, Host of *Grow Omaha* radio program

Jennifer Hanson, Communications Manager, Indianapolis Downtown, Inc.

Jennifer Tinker, Visitor Center and Volunteer Coordinator, *Centennial
Olympic Park*

Jim Chappell, President, San Francisco Planning and Urban Research
Association

Joanne Gonzalez, Vice President Creative Services

Karen Hundt, Chattanooga Hamilton County Regional Planning Agency

Kâren Sander, Executive Director, Downtown Boise Association

Kate Peterson, Housing Program Manager, Downtown Denver
Partnership, Inc.

Laura Libby and Nicole Hernandez, Historic Denver

Lee Warren, Sr. Vice President of Marketing, Memphis Center City
Commission

Lisa Tabion Martinez, Director of Marketing and Outreach, Downtown
Sacramento Partnership

Loretta Carroll, Carroll Communications, Omaha, Nebraska

Louisville Central Area, Inc.

Marc Conte, Director, City of Columbus, Downtown Development
Research Office

Meredith Joy Creative Consulting, Columbus, Ohio

Moira Quinn, Senior Vice President of Communications, Center City Charlotte

Molly Alexander, Downtown Austin Alliance

Paul Bonneville, CEO, Columbus Retrometro

Richard Orr and Wilma Sothern, Central Atlanta Progress

Robert B. Monnat, Chief Operating Officer, Mandel Group, Inc., Milwaukee, Wisconsin

Dr. Robert Scarfo, Associate Professor, Landscape Architecture, Washington State University–Spokane

Scott Knies, Executive Director, Rick Jensen, Communications Director, Downtown San Jose Association

Shane McDevitt, Center City Charlotte Realtor

Tom Fortin, Urban Loft Ventures, Columbus, Ohio

Tony Giarratana, Giarratana Development, LLC, Nashville, Tennessee

Ty Tabing, Executive Director, Chicago Loop Alliance

Yami Roa, Miami Downtown Development Authority

Are You a Ruppie?

Retired urban people, or "Ruppies," know the secret for staying young has a lot to do with where people choose to live. Downtown is their fountain of youth.

Ruppies keep themselves mentally and physically fit by staying active. They remain vibrant and sharp by finding quality part- or full-time jobs and also enjoying meaningful volunteer positions. Ruppies dance at nightclubs, relax or read poetry at coffee shops, walk to downtown grocery stores, browse through fresh farmer's markets—and best of all they can use public transportation. Their downtown location offers a fabulous lifestyle, and they can live it with the same vitality as their younger neighbors.

Ruppies are the new yuppies. They're the coolest and hippest among America's mature population, and one of the largest and most financially influential demographic groups. But unlike yuppies, young urban professionals still associated with the 1980s and raw consumerism, Ruppies are more concerned with fully experiencing life. They quickly become a part of America's cities, and experience the myriad facets of downtown living: culturally, socially, and economically. Ruppies are interesting, hyper-involved, and giving individuals.

Retire Downtown is the first Ruppie handbook, providing a timely look at the major retirement trend for today's retirees and empty nesters who refuse to give in to growing "old." In this book, 80 million potential American Ruppies can explore twenty of America's best downtowns and dozens of target retirement neighborhoods and learn how to achieve their own fun-filled, convenient downtown lifestyle.

If you are thinking about retirement, or are already retired, or even if you are a not-yet-retired empty nester contemplating a lifestyle change, you have great potential to become a Ruppie if you have ever asked yourself the following questions.

They expect me to move where?

Traditionally, retirees may have been expected to seek out a warm place with a structured environment, perhaps at an adult or a retirement resort community. But now that you've retired, you deserve to do it your way: play just as hard as you have worked.

Are the kids finally gone?

For millions of people who moved to a quiet, out-of-the-way location to raise their children, a newly empty nest makes moving downtown and becoming a Ruppie a viable option. Now that your children have grown and may have even started their own families, why pay higher school taxes or have big backyards with tree houses? It's time to put yourself downtown where the action and fun lives.

What are we going to do with these extra rooms?

Many retirees and empty nesters now have too much space—empty rooms, attics, or basements. Stop paying utility bills and cleaning these areas—be a Ruppie and begin your own extraordinary downtown life.

Can I finally throw this junk out now?

If you're like most empty nesters, you are probably surrounded by a lot of extra stuff that's simply not needed anymore. Empty your closets and pass those memories along to your family, or else to charity. Don't be held hostage to the past. Start a new future: fresh and exciting, in your new stylish downtown digs.

How are we going to keep from being bored?

Don't be bored. Stay energized and engaged. The right downtown offers new opportunities, new kinds of activities and experiences, and new people in your life.

Isn't it time I made some new friends?

Downtown is home to diverse age groups in an array of colors and cultures. You'll be surrounded by other Ruppies, but you'll also live among younger people who can and will help keep you young.

Do we have to keep driving all the time?

One of the most important arguments for living a downtown lifestyle is gaining freedom of mobility. Even faced with age-related problems, you'll never have to worry about fending for yourself. You'll have access not only to food and medical services but also to recreational transportation. More than most people, you'll enjoy the freedom from worry about the cost of gasoline, which is sure to rise over the years, and you'll take pride in your independence. After all, a big part of staying young is the ability to take care of yourself—and you can certainly do this if you live downtown.

This book shows you how to achieve your own fun-filled Ruppie lifestyle by exploring each of the following categories:

Living: You'll understand special real estate amenities and the types of downtown housing. You'll also discover how to find downtown educational opportunities including continuing education classes, community colleges, and universities.

Volunteering and employment opportunities: You can find meaningful volunteer options in downtown and other ways to stay active and help others at the same time. Since offices, shops, and corporations are there, you might even consider keeping busy in part-time or even full-time employment.

Playing: You'll learn where to find downtown's most notable art and culture offerings. You'll find ample opportunity to get healthy, and enjoy your leisure time. Drink a beer and eat a brat at spectator sports venues. Browse libraries and bookstores. Sample an array of nightlife venues, or simply feed the birds in city parks and spend time in the urban outdoors.

Shopping: Whether mom-and-pop or full-line grocery stores—you'll get acclimated to them. You'll frequent city and farmer's markets, retail and specialty shops, or one-of-a-kind antique stores.

Getting around: You'll learn how to take advantage of the city's public transportation system: ride the bus, take a train, or hail a cab. You can even get on a bike. Or rediscover walking—for enjoyment and for your health, and never be a slave to gas prices again!

This book also showcases the twenty best downtown retirement cities in America, including the most dynamic, distinctly different, sunbelt, and four-season cities. There are also downtowns to watch that currently have superior lifestyle amenities either available or upcoming, and that especially cater to the fast-growing Ruppie population.

If you are or will be retired, please read any of the many retirement books that are available for financial advice or other areas of interest to you. Understand your benefits and pensions and become an expert in Social Security and Medicare. Then find the fountain of youth and become a Ruppie. By retiring downtown, you'll experience the most fulfilling, young-minded, and exciting life possible.

PART ONE

LIVING IT UP IN DOWNTOWN

Living Downtown

Joan D'Agostino, who worked in downtown Providence for twenty-three years, witnessed the terrible results of the urban flight years. Downtown had deteriorated after people left the area, and it remained that way up until the late 1990s. That's when the buildings in the central city were spruced up, and downtown was well on its way to becoming an artists' haven.

When Joan's youngest son moved out of the nest, she was a fifty-something mother who lived in North Providence. Instead of staying in the suburbs, she sold her condo and moved to downtown Providence. She now lives next to her church, and faces one of Providence's main shopping corridors. Since Joan has become an urbanite, she's close to stores, can visit her friends, and has no regrets.

As the chief of program development for the Rhode Island Department of Elderly Affairs, Joan has a different perspective and knowledge about the many benefits of downtown living. In speaking with various individuals, she's noticed that some people in their forties and fifties may seem older than they are, while others in their eighties and nineties appear youthful and vibrant. She attributes this difference to a lack of interaction and involvement in life. In other words, some people don't embrace life in all venues and Joan believes that where they choose to live plays a big role.

After Joan's father died, her ninety-six-year-old mother, Catherine, lived alone in North Providence. Joan persuaded her mother to relocate to an apartment directly across the street from her, and the move turned out to be the best thing for Catherine.

Her mother now walks to her hairdresser to get a manicure and even takes the trolley to have lunch with her good friends. She is more youthful and more independent than most inactive middle-aged people. Joan believes that a pedestrian-friendly neighborhood with nearby public transit, many places to explore, and other youthful-minded individuals can make all the difference.

In the next ten years, tens of millions will plan for their retirement—and then finally retire. Deciding where to live during retirement tells a lot about a person's values—especially how they'll spend precious time. For active mature folks like Joan and Catherine, location becomes more important than ever, and the best location is in cities and towns that are preparing an extraordinary setting within their urban cores.

Downtown is for the too-young-to-be-old retiree. It's for people who want to live a dynamic, productive, and meaningful life during their retirement. After all, the fifties are now the new thirties and the sixties the new forties, and basically downtown living is for those who refuse to retreat from the world. Living in a city's downtown is not just for retirees, it's also the perfect move for empty nesters who are ready to downsize and move to a smaller place.

One's age doesn't require doing stereotypical retirement things. There are just too many enjoyable experiences to encounter and problems to solve. It's time to discard those suburban fifty-five plus retirement community brochures and discover a downtown lifestyle in any city—whether it's in the middle of a hometown or thousands of miles away. Get ready for your new life in downtown.

Downtowns are the new retirement resorts

Cities either have or are building full-service communities within their downtown cores. Although some cities offer more than others, downtown areas are now morphing into fabulous places to retire. Center cities have reestablished their historic theaters, offering Broadway shows, plays, opera, and old movies. As more people move downtown, social clubs and neighborhood associations are coming into prominence. There are numerous shopping opportunities, gourmet dining facilities, health and fitness clubs—and the list goes on. Although not technically resorts, downtowns are great locations for people who want a challenging, diverse lifestyle.

The following are the four primary incentives to become a practicing Ruppie.

1. **Youthful influences will help to keep you young.**

    Historically, urban environments have been thought of as communities for younger, hip singles or couples just starting out. It's still true. Many families in their twenties and thirties without children don't need yards, playgrounds, or schools; consequently, downtown areas suit their current needs better than suburban ones. Young adults are also drawn to diverse downtown neighborhoods filled with coffee shops, bars, music and art venues, and educational facilities. These young people provide their city with a vibrant, creative outlook and spirit. Their presence is a good reason why downtown is an ideal place to retire.

    Ruppies understand that living in the right location—not plastic surgery or pills—is the most overlooked secret to staying young.

2. **The mix of people will make you (or keep you) worldly.**

    Living downtown provides opportunities to experience different cultures and be part of a diverse mix of residents. Downtowns also have ethnic restaurants galore, not to mention unique festivals and fairs. Learning and sharing with your new neighbors guarantees that you'll expand your horizons.

3. **You'll find downtown living to be exotic.**

    Suburban, small town, or rural countryside residents are in for a treat, because downtown living is indeed exotic. Sure, your chosen downtown is probably in the same country and even in the same county. But a lifestyle full of walking, using public transportation, riding bikes, and eating at outdoor cafés sounds a lot like Europe or Asia. It's an exotic change for people accustomed to suburban communities in today's cul-de-sac and drive-through culture. "Downtown resorts" represent an escape from the ordinary that many retirees and empty nesters can genuinely get excited about.

4. **You'll gain a quick downtown community.**

    It goes against conventional wisdom, but even in the biggest cities, urban neighborhoods act similar to small towns. As soon as a newcomer settles in, they can readily meet their neighbors. Downtown living provides more opportunities to interact than in the suburbs, and many people find this idea unbelievable until they experience it for themselves.

Wylene's urban community

■ Wylene Carol, a retired school teacher who relocated to downtown Colorado Springs, is a model subject for someone who found community. For instance, her neighbors call to say, "Hi, Wy, if you want your windows washed, I'll be happy to do it. I'm going to repel from my terrace, so if you see me at your windows don't be alarmed." Everyone knows that ladders nauseate Wylene, so sometimes it's "Hey, Wy, it's Sally. Mark's on his way down to replace the light bulb in your office area." Another neighbor might stop in, "Hey, there. I just wanted to know how you liked the wine I dropped off last week. It's the least I can do for all the help you've been." Everyone in the building is "in it together."

Wylene's neighbors know what's happening in one another's lives and are there to provide help and comfort. For instance, if someone has surgery or a baby is born, a get well or a congratulations card is sent. The neighbors know who's changing jobs, who recently got a divorce, and any other important news.

Wylene is often asked to mind the store while a neighborhood store owner runs an errand or makes a dental appointment. Everyone, including the UPS man, knows that 95-pound Wylene has trouble with heavy items, so heavy packages are hauled up to her loft and left waiting for her inside even though it's not policy to enter private residences. Everyone signs for one another when a package comes, since the UPS man knows everyone's first name anyway.

Like Wylene, if you retire downtown, you too can find this kind of downtown family. ■

Face your city phobia

People may say that you're crazy when you tell them that you are planning to retire downtown. Even though many downtowns are no longer the ravaged, abandoned, crime-ridden, X-rated places of the past, a lot of your friends may experience "city phobia" from harboring preconceived impressions about the city that aren't valid today.

Downtowns are not the crime-laden areas they once were. Police records show that they are now among the safest neighborhoods in many cities, and some residents are trying to make this fact known. For example, a group in downtown Miami called "Citizens on Patrol" helped change the perception of that area. When they found statistics kept by the Miami Police Department indicating a very low crime rate—much lower than the surrounding city and even the suburbs—they enlisted the assistance of the media. The *Miami Herald* and local television stations got the word out, and the group helped contribute to the booming residential renaissance that downtown Miami is enjoying today. Still, similar perception problems remain in cities.

Too many people remain apprehensive about going to, much less living in, downtowns because of crime, years of overall deterioration, and urban flight. Now, because of enhanced security and safety improvements, entertainment venues, and, suddenly, new downtown housing, people are starting to rethink their decisions.

If you move downtown, anticipate a lot of questions from family and friends about your new city home. For example, when H. G. and Vickie Godbey moved from the southeastern Denver suburbs to Lower Downtown ("LoDo") twelve years ago, their friends were concerned about their safety. Even today many of them ask, "Aren't you afraid?" and "Do you still like it there?" Vickie explains to them that she walks to the gym under the bright LoDo lights and feels perfectly safe. Bellmen and valet parkers are out on the sidewalk and many pedestrians' eyes are on the street. H. G. also says that they feel safe as can be when walking, shopping, and going to the nearby restaurants and bars.

Downtowns are safer than they used to be, but not all of them. In fact, there are still neighborhoods in many local downtown areas that are unsafe or less than ideal. Some people enjoy tackling challenges and becoming urban pioneers: they're the first people who move into a still-ravaged or empty area and start the ball rolling for a change for the better.

Fifty-something native New Yorkers Jerry Ade and Cheryl Ross became urban pioneers in a downtown Portland, Maine, neighborhood that was crime-ridden. It was here, however, that they saw something magical and were determined to become urban developers. They wanted to transform the city into a safe, fun, and exciting place.

They bought a nearby 1800s roundhouse, a 40,000-square-foot building, and converted it into offices and warehouses, and also bought other less impressive buildings in an endeavor to redevelop other empty parts of the area. Cheryl and Jerry called attention to the area's crime and worked hard to build up their neighborhood. Their risk paid off. Now they have more friends and fun times in Portland than they ever did in New York. They're active in the community, participate in downtown meetings, and have the most jam-packed social calendar that they can remember.

Cheryl's advice for people reluctant to relocate to cities is to confront their fears, be cautious, and then open up to change. There will always be the unanticipated, but clinging to fear would have precluded the Ades from experiencing a most interesting life.

Confront your city phobia head-on. Find out downtown's crime rate for yourself by calling the local police department to ask them for crime statistics. Ask them how this rate compares to other areas of the city, and which crimes occur more frequently. Be prepared to find out how safe the area really is.

Unexpected urban lifestyle destinations

Life as a retiree in Manhattan or San Francisco, although amazing, is very expensive and therefore unrealistic for the majority of retirees. You don't have to move to a large city to experience vibrant urban living. Hundreds of cities could be used as examples, but for now let's consider Oklahoma City, Oklahoma. Howard Senter and his wife, Suzanne, who once lived in places like New York and San Francisco, now consider downtown Oklahoma City their idea of heaven. It's safe and close to the movies, the theater, the art museum, and the library.

In 1991, Dr. Melvin Hershkowitz, who had lived most of his life in New York, and for twelve years in Georgetown, Washington, D.C., moved with his wife, Leslie, to downtown Providence, Rhode Island. His friends couldn't understand how he could adjust to living in a smaller town like Providence. But the Hershkowitzs enjoy going to the theater, the movies, the symphony, and all the various shops, and tell everyone that Providence is a small city that offers a big-city lifestyle.

Sioux Falls, Little Rock, Tacoma, Durham, Grand Rapids, Shreveport, Spokane, you name the city—something great is either going on or is coming soon. Take a closer look at your local city's downtown—an overlooked "mini Manhattan" is probably waiting to be discovered.

Choose a downtown

Retirees seeking an urban lifestyle have plenty of choices. However, many people can't bear the thought of not living near their children or grandchildren. That's why it's a good idea for them to remain in the area. They can then have the best of both worlds: experience their hometown downtown as never before and enjoy quality time with their family.

Grown children and parents will enjoy the city for shopping, eating out, going to the theater and concerts, and attending various sporting events. Families will also have fun establishing new downtown traditions—perhaps inviting the family to see the holiday lights and splendor of the city, or the fireworks on New Year's Eve. They might choose to volunteer together at charitable organizations as well. Children who work downtown can meet their hip urban parents for lunch or plan an after-work walk with them. If the children live in the nearby suburbs, their parents' new city home could be the novelty that keeps variety in everyone's lives.

Retiring to a local downtown enables you to keep obligations and commitments, such as caring for elderly parents or other family members, especially if one or both parents are in a nursing home, or otherwise in need of daily assistance. In addition to having family nearby, many people like to stay close to their friends. Not only can you invite friends over for poker or bridge games, but you can also go out for a night on the town.

Out-of-town downtowns

Some retirees may just choose to live downtown in another region. Maybe the level of downtown development in a particular local city is not satisfactory and a bigger, more finished city is preferable. Or perhaps a local downtown doesn't provide the kind of full-service experience that's needed yet.

Maybe your out-of-town downtown search is to relocate to a desired climate. Some people enjoy warm weather but live in a cold climate, while others can't do without four distinct seasons. Fortunately, there are great downtowns in every region and with every type of climate. Perhaps children, grandchildren, or good friends in another city will be able to send information on downtown living prospects and local urban amenities.

Or, if you live in a region where real estate and property taxes are high, consider moving to a less expensive place. There are areas in the Midwest and South that offer high standards of living, low property taxes, and comparably low-cost downtown housing, thereby allowing you to stretch your retirement dollars.

Ruppie neighborhoods

Downtowns are made up of vastly different neighborhoods and districts. The following are some general categories.

Downtown core

Downtown cores, the very center of a city, are the oldest sections where stately government buildings, such as the city hall or a state capitol building, are normally located. In addition to public squares, old historic movie theaters, hotels, and banks, this part of the city also has the tallest buildings and widest sidewalks, which at times can resemble sections of Manhattan in New York City.

Industrial and warehouse districts

Some downtowns formerly housed industrial plants and huge warehouses. Today, many of these areas have been cleaned up, revitalized, and turned into some of the most revered neighborhoods. Plants and warehouses here were built with high ceilings designed to keep goods and workers cool in the summer and to allow machinery and merchandise to be stacked. Because of their wide-open floor plans, these buildings have now become trendy places to live and are among the most chic neighborhoods with an array of shops, cafés, and five-star restaurants. SoHo, in New York's lower Manhattan, is considered a famous model district.

Historic neighborhoods

Historic residential neighborhoods flank downtown cores in every city.

These were the city's original suburbs, home to the wealthy professionals who wanted to be close to the city but still have the amenities of the country. Historic single-family homes or town homes are often spacious, with big lawns and backyard gardens. Streets are often lined with shade trees that were planted during the days when the homes were constructed, and the parks are often the most magnificent in the entire city. In many cities today, the older historic architecture is protected by a historic zoning ordinance— a local law prohibiting the alteration of any building's exterior without a review by a board appointed to approve the designs. Historic residential neighborhoods offer a quieter kind of city life with front porches, birdbaths, and lots of charm. The Garden District of New Orleans or Washington, D.C.'s Georgetown are good examples.

Entertainment districts

Entertainment districts are for those retirees who want immediate access to fun and action. Many city neighborhoods are characterized as entertainment districts, such as a "brewery district," where microbreweries and pubs dot the landscape and a freshly brewed beer is easy to find. Or perhaps an arts district that features a wide variety of art galleries and fine dining. Other district themes can include nightlife, live music, or sports. Think about New York's Times Square as an extreme example of an entertainment district.

No man's land

Some areas of the city will not be as well maintained as the others, and may have vacant properties, unkempt and/or boarded-up buildings, and certain properties overrun with weeds and trash. These neighborhoods, called "no man's land," have less people because there are fewer opportunities for individuals to live and work there full time. But if you look closer you'll see urban pioneers (like Jerry and Cheryl) working hard to make these neighborhoods livable. Although retiring to this kind of neighborhood is not for everyone, over time, the rewards can be very gratifying.

Determining which neighborhood is right for you

Start at a home that you're considering buying or renting and walk down the street. What do you notice that you would never see from your car? What kinds of businesses are you passing? What is the condition of the residential buildings? Is there a mix of homes and businesses? Are there places to purchase food? A drug store? Restaurants? Coffee shops? A pharmacy? List all the services and destinations that are within walking distance of the place where you want to live. Then determine which neighborhood provides the most convenient and pleasant walking experience and make a good, informed decision.

It's also important to know your activity-tolerance quotient. What level of noise, crowds, and commotion can you handle? Find your tolerance level by visiting as many downtown neighborhoods as possible, and then move to the one where you feel comfortable. Don't forget to talk to the people who live there. Ask them questions about the area and ask yourself if you would like to be their neighbors.

Usually, if steady streams of people are engaged on the street and involved in a variety of activities, the surrounding neighborhood is a great place to live. Pay attention to streets where people are walking, shopping, jogging, walking dogs, and talking with their friends. This is a high-quality, fun, and safe downtown community.

Downsize to downtown

For millions of retirees, downsizing to a smaller place usually coincides with fewer maintenance demands and unanticipated problems. It's the opportunity to live simpler, and for Ruppies this idea has become very popular.

Center City, Philadelphia, residents John and Meg Harkins recently downsized. They moved from a suburban house full of items they didn't need when they became urban dwellers. Their new place had no attic or basement and they had accumulated "tons of stuff" over the years. Needless to say, the Harkins held several huge yard sales.

Be forewarned: There is a difficult aspect of downsizing—smaller living spaces in downtown are often more expensive than larger suburban homes. Are you ready to pay more money for less space? Judith Jossa, a real estate agent, sells downtown lofts in Edmonton, Alberta. She explains the financial advantages in downsizing to a new smaller living space in downtown to retirees and empty nesters. There will be no more upgrading, modernizing, or maintenance expenses. Judith then shows retirees who are giving up their big houses and lawns for small city spaces that they are paying for the entire neighborhood, not just their home.

Go ahead and downsize, enjoy a clutter-free, simplified life, and understand that most homes or apartments will be smaller and likely more expensive, at least in dollars per square feet. It's rarely possible to have the best of both worlds, but it is very possible to love the downsized life in downtown.

The hippest retirement housing

There are four major styles of downtown housing that retirees can choose: condominiums, apartments, full-service hotels, and single-family homes.

Condominium living— the most popular downtown choice

Condominiums are buildings or complexes with multiple housing units that are owned by a group of property owners. Note, the common sections, such as the grounds and the building structure, are jointly owned by the tenants, and the homes within the structure are owned by individuals. Exterior maintenance, such as mowing and painting, lawn care, or trash pickup, is taken care of through a maintenance fee that is paid by all condo owners—something retirees can certainly appreciate.

Many residents also like the instant community afforded in condo living and the opportunity in their condominium to attend various get-togethers, functions, and/or parties. Most condos can be categorized as follows:

High-rise towers are eight stories and higher and offer some of the most luxurious amenities, including a terraced balcony. They were once found only in the largest cities, but are now springing up even in smaller cities across the country.

Mid-rise towers, between five and eight stories, are either older structures, such as office buildings, that have transitioned into residential uses or new buildings built on empty lots in the downtown area. The new structures are often much wider than high-rises (such as ones built on entire city blocks) but can have the same number of housing units. Some have a main entrance, and others even offer individual ground floor entrances for those units at street level.

Sometimes high-rise and mid-rise living is inspired living, as is the case with Charles Harbour and his wife, Dr. Sheryl Davis, in downtown Memphis. Their penthouse allows them to enjoy jam sessions coming from the Peabody Hotel across the way, listen to the Mud Island concerts, watch people dancing, or soak in the spectacular views of the Mississippi River.

In Milwaukee, Ed Hinshaw, a retired local news personality, considers his twenty-sixth floor view a stunning work of changing art. He can see thunderstorms approach, the new Calatrava Music Hall, a marina with hundreds of

Downtown Nashville's Signature Tower (left) will be the Southeast's tallest at 1,040 feet and the third tallest building in the United States. Four hundred condominiums and a luxury hotel will be complete in 2009. (Giarratana Development, LLC, Nashville, Tennessee)

boats, and several parks. Since both Charles and Ed's wife, Victoria, are authors, the high setting is perfect for creative thinking.

Low-rise buildings are one- to four-story structures that come in a variety of architectural styles—from sleek modern lines to historic and faux-historic designs. Low-rise buildings can be one hundred years old or brand-new, with varying price points and lifestyle amenities. Like mid-rises, these structures can have a main entrance, individual first-floor entrances, or both.

Town homes and row houses are usually two- to four-story connected buildings typified by a "stoop" (staircase leading up to the front door of each unit). Because town homes and row houses are smaller developments, they usually do not offer the extra amenities (such as indoor gyms and spas) found in mid- and high-rise luxury condominiums. (Some are not condominiums at all, but attached "fee simple" homes where each town home owner's property line is the walls.)

All of these condominiums usually offer one or two spaces of either underground or secured parking, and most require the buyer to pay extra for them.

The following is a list of typical condominium amenities found in new and updated structures. Not all condos (especially the low-rise and town home variety) will offer the entire list of services, since all of the amenities will also depend on the price of the unit and the maintenance fees collected.

- Heated indoor and/or outdoor swimming pools
- Dry cleaning service
- Weight and exercise room (with fitness instructors)

The interior of Carlyle's Watch, an eight-story mid-rise condominium in downtown Columbus completed in 2006. Special features include floor-to-ceiling walls of windows, an open floor plan, sky deck, sound-deadening insulation, and a ten-year tax abatement. (Tom Fortin, Urban Loft Ventures, LLC, Columbus, Ohio)

- Large balconies and terraces with spectacular views
- Gourmet kitchens with top-of-the-line appliances (such as Sub-Zero refrigerators)
- Granite or marble countertops in kitchens and bathrooms
- Luxury baths with whirlpool tubs
- Rooftop common spaces
- High-speed elevators
- Gardens and contained open spaces
- Concierge services
- Building security guards
- Covered or underground parking
- Wireless Internet and other built-in technology
- Grocery delivery service
- Tennis courts
- TV/movie rooms
- Community/party rooms

Apartment living

Apartments are for free-minded downtown retirees, especially those with hurried lifestyles. They offer no-worry maintenance, including interior upkeep. If a problem arises, it's just a call to the landlord—with no out-of-pocket expenses incurred. In addition, renting provides the option of testing out a downtown neighborhood (or city living in general) before making any long-term commitment.

Apartments can be town homes or high rises of any height and size, and, like many new condominiums, new apartments in most downtowns are being constructed in the middle of the action and in high-profile urban locations. Rental homes are usually a major part of urban redevelopment plans because their residents stimulate sidewalk activity and local businesses. New downtown apartments are often located near restaurants and entertainment destinations, or above storefronts—perfect for action-loving retirees. A few are also designated exclusively for retirees.

The following is a list of typical apartment lifestyle amenities.

- Twenty-four-hour maintenance hotline
- Twenty-four-hour security

- Free parking, often in garages and underground
- Swimming pools
- Weight rooms
- Community rooms
- Balconies
- Rooftop common spaces
- Gardens and contained open spaces
- Concierge services
- Wireless Internet and other built-in technology

Hotel living

More and more downtowns are providing hotels as an option for downtown retirement living. Luxury hotels offer month-to-month agreements or year-long leases, similar to apartments. Some are even selling rooms as a micro-condominium or offer co-op opportunities.

Whether renting or buying, hotel living provides all the luxury services of being on a permanent vacation in the middle of a vibrant city. This idea is still relatively new, but as baby boomers age and demand for downtown retirement increases, hotels will become a viable option.

Major benefits of hotel living include:

- Daily cleaning service
- Turndown service
- Room service
- No utility bills
- Parking included
- Twenty-four-hour security
- Broad-based amenities, including swimming pool, workout facility, restaurants, bars, and concierge services

Single-family homes

The stand-alone home is the alternative to condos, apartments, and hotels. Some retirees who choose downtown living don't want to downsize every-thing in their lives, and want a little grass for themselves (and their pets), or a spot to maintain a small vegetable garden. Although terrace and rooftop gardens are possible in condominiums and apartments, single-family homes offer a small area to garden and some require only minimal time to maintain. These small yards can also have patios for entertaining. This type of home will most likely be found outside of the immediate downtown and in the surrounding historic neighborhoods.

Many Ruppies can't resist the lure of these neighborhoods with their beautifully preserved houses. Some nimble woodworkers and pre-servation enthusiasts are attracted to these homes because they enjoy the structural rehabilitation work on old houses. Others with no interest in refurbishing may choose new homes in historic neighborhoods because they are normally built with the most efficient heating and cooling systems.

Go green

Costs for home heating and cooling are forecasted to rise in the coming years. Protecting the earth's environ-ment is also on the minds of many Americans these days. If you are concerned about these issues, you will likely have an opportunity to live in a "green" building when you retire downtown.

Sustainable homes are the wave of the future because they're designed to use windows to capture the sun's natural light instead of light bulbs. Some green buildings in downtowns offer garden or grass rooftops to

Personalizing your pad

■ If you live in an urban loft today, you might assume that the interior décor will be minimalist and stark like those found in New York's SoHo. But when Vick Haak moved to downtown Austin, he hired a designer to replace the light wood floors and cabinetry with rich mahogany tones. The stark-white industrial-chic walls were too much and he didn't want angular modern furniture. So he hired a leading area interior designer to implement a faux finishing on many of the walls and columns, and brought in furni-ture that fit his tastes. To top off his personal loft space, Vick installed a colorful three-piece art collage with light blue, emerald green, and yel-low circles, oblong rectangles, tri-angle shapes, and neon lights. Similarly, Deborah McLarney's new Omaha Old Market district town home is constructed with modern interiors that call for "loft-style" furniture. Since Deborah had lived in a historic house for years and collected antiques, she proudly displayed them in her town home. Like Vick and Deborah, you should also be yourself when you become urban! ■

refract solar heat. Solar panels, special water runoff and water recycling features, clean interior air systems, and reused building materials are other examples of green technology. Living in a green building could be a great way to save money on energy bills and set a good example for your grandchildren!

General downtown housing costs

Real estate prices vary tremendously depending on location. For instance, in large cities like New York, Boston, or San Francisco, prices will naturally be much higher than Des Moines or Tulsa. Major cities are target destinations for many people from all over the continent and the world. Since demand is often higher than supply, the price is also higher.

Smaller cities in the southeastern United States, and especially in the Midwest, will have much more reasonable downtown housing prices. Keep in mind that smaller downtowns in Middle America are quickly improving, and now offer amenities comparable to those offered in larger cities but at much lower costs. For instance, in Columbus, Ohio, and Indianapolis, Indiana, it's possible to find a comfortable, new 1,000 to 1,200 square foot condominium for around $250,000, while that same unit could cost $800,000 or more in San Francisco. Average rents usually correspond to a specific region and a city's general cost of living.

If you can't afford the bigger cities' rents and real estate prices, and are willing to look for the right city in the right region, you'll eventually find your targeted prices. Explore the downtown Web sites and their real estate links in chapters 6 through 25 and in the appendix for examples of available urban homes, including amenities, rents, and sales prices.

The rest of this book will provide you with many ideas and suggestions about downtown living.

Working, Volunteering, and Educational Opportunities in Downtown—and Not Growing Old

Cecelia Muhammad, a retired nurse who lives in downtown Atlanta, frequents the new multipurpose senior facility up the street from her home where she takes computer training and line dancing classes. She's also a community volunteer for AARP, an assistant in the information booth for Centennial Olympic Park, president of the local Toastmaster Club at the senior center, and secretary of her building's tenants association. In addition, she's a community health advocate with the Avon Breast Foundation at Emory and Grady hospitals, is a program chair for the East Side Council on Aging, and also sits on a volunteer board to plan for a transit rail line extension.

Since she loves the theater and any kind of musical concert, Cecelia also decided to volunteer as an usher for the Atlanta Symphony Orchestra and the Rialto Theater. In both venues, she meets and greets show goers, directing them to their seats. Then she sits down and watches the orchestras, plays, dancing, and all kinds of cultural events. One of her favorites is African drumming.

As a retired nurse, Cecelia's professional skills remain current through her volunteer nursing at the Department of Homeland Security, keeping her professional license active. She believes that her full life is God's reward for her thirty-eight years of dedicated nursing, and that's one of the reasons why she remains a nurse.

With her high activity level, you'd never guess that Cecelia was pushing seventy. She's active, young-minded, free-spirited, and engaged. Moreover, she's taking advantage of the educational opportunities that her downtown offers. She is growing her mind and spirit every day in downtown Atlanta. It's a fulfilling and go-go kind of life.

Downtown: The epicenter of possibility

Cecelia demonstrates the varied activities that a downtown lifestyle provides. She is a shining example of how Ruppies can keep their minds sharp, become involved in the community, and keep their soul fed. You too can put your talents to similar use and do, move, learn, help, and create with the same gusto as Cecelia.

Many people fear having nothing to do after they retire. Downtown is the epicenter of possibility, and there is no excuse for having a lack of purpose. Of course, a retiree who lives outside of downtown can have a wide variety of work and/or volunteer opportunities, but downtown dwellers can pick from a broader spectrum of human services and civic organizations, activity centers, and cultural establishments. Downtown is the ideal environment to delve into a purposeful, stimulating, and satisfying life.

Become a student again

You might be familiar with the growing retirement trend of living in "university-linked retirement communities," or ULRCs. These are retirement developments located near, or sometimes on, a college or university campus. Downtown is the ultimate ULRC. Here, retirees have the advantage of being close to college and university campuses and continuing education centers. Whether you want to pursue a college degree or just want to learn something new, there is a wide variety of courses available. There's no commuting or parking concerns since the school will be close by.

Many people have always wanted to learn a second language or study subjects such as contemporary art, painting, culinary arts, or history. Some of the most popular classes today keep students abreast of current technology by teaching them how to e-mail, send photos over the Internet, use a digital camera, and create a PowerPoint presentation. There are also how-to classes, home decorating, nature photography, acting, starting your own business, or painting.

Classes for downtown retirees are affordable: An increasing number of universities provide free classes for older students. The Ohio State University offers Program 60, which gives Ohio residents over the age of sixty free tuition. Similar programs are found across the country for sixty-plus students who want to become part of a college community and expand their intellectual horizons.

In addition to courses at your downtown college campus, you may also want to take advantage of the many social activities available. Colleges have theater and music departments that offer inexpensive shows and concerts. Many universities also have museums that host traveling expositions from time to time.

Downtown retirees often undergo a metamorphosis. Doctors may become art students. CEOs of large companies may try their hand as writers. Schoolteachers may turn into homebuilders, lawyers may become landscapers or nurses, and salespeople may even morph into actors. These life-changing opportunities allow new skills to be tapped, barriers to be broken, and roles and expectations to be redefined.

For some of you, getting a degree or obtaining another degree will be in your future. Lucia Gelotte started out as a New York fashion model in the 1950s, transitioned into designing, and then spent most of her adult life creating one-of-a-kind evening wear for local New York performers. Then she became a psychologist who specialized in adult women's self-esteem issues. But when Lucia decided to retire to downtown Miami, she wanted another career change and enrolled at a local university for a masters degree.

After a year and a half, Lucia moved to downtown Miami, where she teaches executives in the Miami corporate community. She makes personal visits to their offices to hone the skills of leaders who are proficient in intermediate English, and teaches them the vocabulary of business English. Because Downtown Miami is an international business center, Lucia teaches Cubans, Latin Americans, and Brazilians Spanish-to-English and Portuguese-to-English. She also teaches people from China and Europe while learning much about their different cultures.

Marcia Rosenzweig from downtown Providence, Rhode Island, is a former language teacher who lives directly across from the library. She enjoys taking computer classes, especially the eBay classes inside the gorgeous historic library building. She and her husband, Fred, have a collection of autographed baseballs they wanted to sell, and the classes taught her how to download photos, do comparison studies of other sellers, and manage all of the intricacies of the eBay selling game. Marcia also enjoys taking Microsoft Office and keyboarding classes to sharpen her computer skills.

Whether it's time to change directions like Lucia or Marcia, living in downtown offers a wide variety of educational opportunities. There's no limit to what subject downtown students can study and what they can to do with their new acquired knowledge.

Get on the education seminar circuit

It's amazing who will show up in the city: You can find famous and infamous authors, politicians, inventors, activists, and innovators. For instance, a *New York Times* best-selling author in the middle of his thirty-city book tour happens to have a book-signing stop just three blocks away. Or the governor speaks at the nearby university, or a movie star might talk to students in a downtown theater. All kinds of "teachers" are always showing up for your learning enjoyment.

Join a downtown book club

Book clubs are also mind sharpeners, and are as easy to join as walking to the library and looking at the postings for clubs seeking new members. Librarians will also be able to provide opinions and advice on the best book clubs. New and old bookstores will have a variety of informational reading lists and activities that are currently available.

Delve into your faith

Downtown will have the highest concentration of religious institutions and religious diversity. Buddhist, Baptist, Bahá'i, or any other religion will more than likely be in the area. Since downtown locations represent the city's first settlement, the historic houses of worship are usually more majestic than even the mega churches and other huge new monoliths that have recently been built.

Volunteer downtown

Volunteering is as much a part of urban living as Cosmopolitan martinis. Initially, most retirees become engaged in a wide variety of volunteer roles. Logical places to begin are at the local offices of the United Way, Volunteers of America, Red Cross, Salvation Army, Goodwill, or other nationally known organizations. There are also homegrown community organizations, faith-based agencies, and community foundations to investigate.

Gladys Boykin lives in downtown Louisville and volunteers for a foundation for the blind by sitting on a panel that selects students to go on trips to places like London or Mexico, and considers the students inspirational because they refuse to be handicapped by their disability. She also serves on the board of the Louisville International Cultural Center to pair up employers with visitors from Russia, China, and other countries. Her husband, Elton, enjoys his work as a member of Louisville's Downtown Residents' Association to help to make his city a better and safer place to live.

The issues that deeply affect you tell you where you should focus your time and energy. What makes you mad, sad, upset, or irritated? For many, a lot does—that's why so many downtown residents volunteer. For example, did your elderly parents need companionship or special care? Has a member of your family needed crisis counseling or help overcoming an addiction? If you live downtown, you can find organizations where your own personal experiences may help others. Where can you leave your thumbprint? What kind of impact will you leave on your new neighborhood? With will and courage, you can cause something really fantastic to happen.

The following are the major volunteer categories.

Volunteer downtown developers

■ Center City, Philadelphia, residents Lee and Tony Junker volunteer for a group called the Friends of Center City Retirement Community. They know that most downtown retirees are newcomers from outside the city, but long-time city dwellers know how good they have it and want to remain. The Junkers and three hundred others are working to find a location for a new city center retirement community so they can *stay* in downtown, the neighborhood they've helped improve during their adult years, and enjoy the fruits of their labor. They want to build a place where locals can downsize with their friends, and still continue to walk to cultural events and restaurants. They're working hard to find a location in the middle of the city for a retirement community, not an independent living or healthcare facility, but a place just for retirees. As downtown living gains popularity and as the country's baby boomers age, look for more of these downtown retirement options. ■

Children's Services: People who love children can lend a hand in after-school care programs, such as telling stories, reading books, teaching and tutoring, and leading group activities and games.

Aging Issues and the Elderly: Being in a mature age group themselves, retirees understand the tremendous needs associated with aging. Volunteering in nursing homes, assisted-living facilities, and senior centers that aid the aged, is one way to help. Many elderly people live alone and need help with meals and mobility, or perhaps desire company. Others would really like someone to read to them or help them with errands.

Drug and Alcohol Abuse: Volunteering in centers that lend a hand to people battling addiction is a huge challenge, but the need is enormous. Various organizations and agencies will appreciate volunteers, especially those who have a background in substance abuse prevention and intervention.

Housing: Some people can't afford housing, including families with children. One of the most popular forms of urban volunteer work is working with Habitat for Humanity. This group uses volunteer construction workers and donated materials to build homes for needy families. Homeless shelters always need volunteers, too.

Jack and Peggy Houser, retirees in downtown Denver, work with their neighbors to support a variety of service providers who help the homeless. Their primary role has been with the Denver Rescue Mission, in its "New

Life Rehabilitation Program." With the help of their downtown church, Trinity United Methodist, they serve 250 free lunches, three days a week.

Families: Too many families in the city have been ravaged by domestic violence, substance abuse, mental illness, poverty, and hunger. Volunteers can help through any number of social service agencies. They can assist one or more families with short-term needs or long-term recovery, and may even be able to "adopt" a needy inner-city family.

The Disabled: Many people were born with or acquired a physical or developmental disability. Volunteers can help them get from place to place, assist with household chores, and provide company and companionship.

Prison Population: Those with experience in education or faith-based initiatives can volunteer for reform programs, public speaking opportunities, and teaching and learning seminars, and provide company and support to prisoners without family or friends. Some corrections volunteer programs assist ex-convicts in settling back into the community.

Disaster and Emergency Services: It's possible to become a volunteer who assists in future weather-related or civil emergencies. Agencies such as the Red Cross and Salvation Army prepare and train volunteers to help people when they need it the most.

These needs categories only scratch the surface. Find out much more about special needs and leading organizations for volunteers—and volunteer whenever you can. Remember that people who don't volunteer do not connect with their neighborhoods nearly as much as involved residents.

Help out with health care

Downtown retirees find hospitals to be fulfilling places to volunteer. Health care volunteers are provided specialized training in a wide variety of programs and services.

Volunteers in the patient-care units make people feel more comfortable. They bring books or flowers, fluff pillows, help people get changed and get in and out of bed, answer patient calls, and give hand rubs. Some patient-care volunteers also play with children or rock them to sleep.

Become a downtown ambassador

People with outgoing personalities who enjoy talking to others can become a downtown ambassador. In almost every city, downtown ambassadors are working in important roles to make the downtown area more user-friendly and welcoming. There are programs that employ teams to keep the area clean and safe, including property and landscape upkeep, sidewalk sweeping and cleaning, graffiti removal, high-pressure washing, painting, and picking up trash. They also provide social services for those in need, especially homeless people, and are responsible for many positive changes that have occurred in city downtowns.

Help out with hospitality

Another excellent way to nourish an extroverted nature is by volunteering in the hospitality services. Downtowns are normally the surrounding region's hub for hotels and conventions. Depending on the size of the city, there are usually at least hundreds of thousands of visitors each year, and the industry is always looking for volunteers to help out with their guests.

Typically, cities have a visitor's center where volunteers advise conventioneers and tourists and provide a variety of services to the city's "customers." Visitors seek information on various entertainment venues, the quality and cost of local restaurants, hotels and other accommodations, and special things to do in the downtown area.

Most convention centers cannot have too many volunteers. They need people to hand out packets, and to help make reservations for restaurants, theaters, and concerts. Convention centers also need "hall floaters" and "room monitors," making sure that the conventioneers are taken care of during their meetings.

Become a civic leader

Downtown is the perfect location for civics junkies. Instead of merely staying current on issues found in the daily newspaper's local section, they can be in the story and then read about themselves. Government agencies might appreciate your help, and it's easy to find out what various positions are available for any level of government.

Gerry Pighini, a retiree in downtown San Jose, California, is an excellent example. As a Hewlett-Packard retiree, he traded his high-tech skills for a position on the San Jose's Downtown Housing Implementation Group, offering a year of service to study ways to entice more people to move downtown. Because downtown residents had to drive to outside locations, the committee's greatest success was attracting Zanetto's grocery store.

Besides serving a one-year term on the Santa Clara County Civil Grand Jury, attending public openings and ribbon-cutting ceremonies, city hall council meetings, and public hearings, Gerry also served on the Guadalupe River Park technical committee. Downtown residents now enjoy a new three-mile walking and biking trail and park because of the committee's dedication.

Lynn Phelps works with Capitol Neighborhoods, Inc., a group on the forefront of guiding new development and influencing the design of new buildings in downtown Madison, Wisconsin. He helps ensure that buildings and developments blend in with the existing historic neighborhood. The group holds meetings with groups who often had divergent opinions of the developers, and champion historic preservation and structural aesthetics. Lynn's work with Capitol Neighborhoods is a big part of why Madison is the beautiful city it is today.

Both Lynn and Gerry are as busy, if not busier, than they were in their full-time work. And, as Gerry says, "What you don't get paid in dollars, you'll consider yourself amply compensated with good feelings and accomplishment."

Assist inner-city schools

Inner-city school systems are, almost without exception, home to the poorest students. They also are woefully underfunded, with substandard facilities and materials. Many schoolchildren come from disadvantaged homes and single-parent families, and are more likely to drop out of school, and perform poorly on standardized tests. Inner-city schools desperately need help.

Programs, especially the arts, have suffered because of a severe lack of funding. Schools especially need volunteers who can assist in music, theater, and visual arts. They also need after-school tutors in all academic subjects, and coaches and assistants for their sports teams. Volunteers can also help in the cafeteria, hall, library, or playground. Some schools even seek volunteers for summer activity programs and day camps.

Inner-city school system administrations also call for volunteers to help register students for classes and assist in workshops and placement tests. Fund-raisers like cookouts and community raffles are frequently understaffed. Some assistance is even needed to help fix up classrooms, renovate buildings, and maintain playground parks.

Downtowns are epicenters of opportunity for implementing ideas that can make huge changes in people's lives. How will you engage yourself by improving your new home in the city?

The retiree's land of opportunity

People who need to find a job in their retirement years can find a local job and put themselves inside of the city's action—the urban environment can make working downtown really special.

Would you ever want to work full-time again? Retired downtown residents often find that they can't resist going back to work. The typical mid-sized city downtown has between 25,000 and 100,000 employees working in every sector of commerce.

Since downtowns remain a leading center of finance and government, there are plenty of job opportunities at banks, insurance corporations, financial centers, and in government at the local, state, county, and federal level. There are other areas like the service industry, including tourism and food service, that also could be investigated.

Finding a job now can be as easy as taking a walk. With a leisurely stroll, it's possible to pick and choose the work setting, make educated comparisons among several options, and take your time to find an enjoyable job.

Find extra cash anytime

Odd jobs are the kinds of jobs a person might not have considered before. They're perfect for people who are not the corporate type, or who don't want or need a full-time job, or who just want some additional spending money.

With plenty of businesses searching for people and individuals who need assistance, downtown residents can have their choice of jobs. They can consider babysitting for a night, watching a pet for a weekend, or being a house-watcher for a few days. Or perhaps they'd like to become a part-time nanny, a driver for a wealthy family, or a dog-walker. There are even part-time personal assistants, paid companions, or handypersons. Downtown is a part-time job smorgasbord.

Odd jobs in downtown can also be found with ease. Check postings in neighborhood newsletters, city papers, and fliers plastered on apartment and condo associations' bulletin boards. Putting up advertisements at coffee shops, grocery stores, or even on light poles can work too.

Remember that every downtown has an office for temporary employment services. Temp agencies will place you in several positions, allowing you to sample all kinds of interesting jobs. Downtown retirees can explore the spectrum of employment and make extra cash while doing it.

Start a business

Without even realizing it, your personal skills and hobbies could turn into an unexpected job. Everyone possesses some level of creativity, and has something that they love to do more than anything else. Those skills can be turned into profit as unexpected opportunities present themselves.

Downtown Milwaukee resident June Varney found this out. She grew up on a Potowanami Reservation in northern Wisconsin in a high unemployment environment. As a child, her clothes came from the church's clothes bin, and she had to learn to sew the mismatched pieces with a treadle sewing machine. Later on, she learned to make her own clothes. She worked in sewing shops for most of her life and became a master at her craft.

Flash forward to a few years ago when June and her husband Tom decided to downsize to a condominium in downtown Milwaukee's Historic

Third Ward District. When her sewing machine needed repairs, she happened to meet a woman who asked her if she could sew. Instantly, June was in business—she lived in a place where nobody sewed. June is now the premier seamstress for trendy women's stores in her artsy neighborhood, and sewing is not just her livelihood, it's also her social outlet.

You might have a specific service that just so happens to be one of your hobbies. Downtown is the place where serendipity can and does happen on the street, in a restaurant, or on an elevator.

Downtowns everywhere are working hard to increase their full-time resident populations and opportunities for commerce. Over the next decade, it's likely that thousands of new city dwellers will be moving into the downtown of their choice and creating new markets for all kinds of goods and services.

It's inevitable that residents might find necessary services that are not offered. Maybe walking along an empty storefront will manifest the need for a local coffee shop or a clothing store. Ingenious talents and hobbies may turn into businesses, such as cooking, making pottery, painting, or sewing.

Try checking with the city's economic development offices for start-up funds in special downtown neighborhoods, and explore tax incentives for new businesses. Try the downtown neighborhood business association or any other organizations that support and grow local businesses such as a business incubator, an organization that nurtures small private businesses by providing office space and equipment, and financial, accounting, and legal services.

Volunteering and working in downtown will fulfill you and satisfy your spirit.

3

The Ruppie's Downtown Playground

Ed and Phyllis Gabovitch had been commuters to downtown Indianapolis their entire lives. As their children grew and matured, so did the downtown, and eventually they decided to become enthusiastic urban dwellers. Now they can frequent the variety of fifty restaurants—all within easy walking distance of their home. When dining out, they run into neighbors and friends and end up chatting the night away. They can eat well and walk off the pounds, or head to the senior center for serious exercise, just a block away. It has an exercise room provided by the National Institute for Fitness and Sport and prescribes a fitness program for each participant. The Gabovichs eat without guilt—a new experience for both of them.

They also enjoy attending a wide variety of cultural activities, all close by. Watching the Fourth of July fireworks display from their living room window is one of their most enjoyable experiences.

Phyllis and Ed are happy and thankful to live in a place that features unlimited ways for them to spend their days and nights. This chapter shows you how to achieve an action-packed existence—but in your own way, and in your own city.

Live in a creative atmosphere

Downtown living is creative living, even for those people who consider themselves unimaginative. A stimulating urban environment is all that's needed to discover a special, individually creative talent, and downtown living provides a place that is so extraordinary that it can attract and produce artists. It's the drastic change in scenery, a change in habits and patterns, and especially being around other creative people that cultivates this creative spirit.

Downtown Atlanta retiree Jacqueline Brown can morph into an artist anytime she walks to the local senior center down the street from her condo. Finding many options for creating handmade art, including ceramics, mosaic tiling, and quilting, Jacqueline is most fond of the center's card-making class where participants learn to craft greeting cards for every occasion and for special people in their lives. They make congratulatory cards for weddings, family and friends' birthdays, graduations, and other important events. Ms. Hall, the teacher and master card maker, shows everyone how to turn paper into unique pieces of art.

Jacqueline's prime downtown location is coveted by her friends, who drive from suburban Conyers and other suburbs to downtown Atlanta to meet for a walk down to the center for a fun-filled afternoon.

Living downtown means having a creative spirit similar to downtown Austin "retiree" Maggie Olmstead. She's sure that no one literally retires to her city and finds that retirees who move to places such as a traditional Sun City–style retirement resort are much different people than downtown Austin folks. She cherishes the fact that downtown Austin attracts artists, writers, and people who need a more diverse environment, committed to being engaged, involved, and connected.

These creative individuals are more interested in computers and coffee shops than golfing, and eminently engaged with the community. Creative Maggie plans on living to be at least 100, and was inspired by a recent editorial by Liz Carpenter that stated, "At 102, I am going to declare victory and leave." Maggie thinks that this affirmation is what all creative retirees should declare!

Gaze in galleries and browse in museums

With so many artists in cities, it's no wonder that downtown neighborhoods are speckled with art galleries. Whether it's a famous artist's premier or the opening of a local painter's abstracts, galleries offer entertainment and intellectual value.

In most galleries, everyone is invited. In fact, the success of an artist's showing has as much to do with attracting a diverse crowd as the sales level of the art. Mixing with the patrons at the gallery is entertainment by itself.

Sharon Leicham, a resident of the South Main Arts District in downtown Memphis, takes the local trolley down to the neighborhood's myriad art galleries. On the last Friday of every month, she joins her friends and neighbors, and thousands of visitors, to enjoy music, street performers such as "strolling musicians," and art flicks at the outdoor movie events. Memphis' art-trolley tour is unusual, but it's certain that the downtown of your choice will offer a way to mesh art with community.

Urban stimuli

■ When former Moscow and Budapest residents David and Sigrid Knuti want to feel young, they walk down State Street—a street in downtown Madison, Wisconsin, that they consider as lively and creative as any in Europe. They enjoy the theaters and political taverns, and the University of Wisconsin commons, where anyone can become part of a political rally or listen to an impromptu rock concert. State Street teems with people of all ages, races, and creeds and offers shops, coffee houses, and taverns for everyone. The Knutis love the State Street Brats, which offer an irresistible Wisconsin grilled bratwurst on a bun. They also join the party that fills the street after 10:00 p.m. on weekends. On a recent visit for a late-night beer on a football weekend, they felt very much at home as many respectful students greeted them like long-lost grandparents. Just like the Knutis you'll thrive on the variety of activities and interactions in downtowns that force stimulation and creativity. ■

Art museums, like galleries, rotate different artists' works—for example, photographs taken by a famous photographer one month, then a collection of paintings, followed by glass-blown objects from a world leader in ceramics. History museums, usually in a historic structure or house, immerse you in times past with period interiors and artifacts, while natural history museums display exhibitions of biodiversity such as a wetland habitat or one of Earth's extinct creatures, such as dinosaurs.

It might be argued that museums are more educational than recreational, but investigating what's new at museums is pure entertainment. A downtown location will offer museum choices and you'll likely be able to walk to most of them. For instance, consider the options that Phyllis Gabovich's downtown Indianapolis location provides her grandchildren when they visit. She can walk with them to the White River Gardens butterfly exhibit, or to the Canal Walk and the Indiana State Museum, or to the Eiteljorg Museum to view western and Native American art, or to the NCAA Hall of Champions to pay tribute to past and present student athletes with interactive exhibits.

Museums aren't just for schoolchildrens' field trips, and galleries aren't reserved for the upper crust. When you visit these places, you'll realize their universal importance.

"Broadway" down the street

Imagine being able to walk to the opera or a show. Think of it, Broadway could be just down the street from your home. New city dwellers quickly find out how incredible it is to be able to dress up, hail a cab, or even walk to a show.

People who appreciate the performing arts should consider living in the downtown theater district. You'll probably be near restored historic performing arts halls, and/or old movie theater buildings, known as movie "palaces," that were once popular in the early- to mid-1900s.

Your city theater might have a concentrated area of major performing arts productions and, like Broadway, offer nearby restaurants. After the performance, you may go to a favorite bar or lounge to recap the experience, and drink an after-the-show cocktail.

Let music fill the air

There are a variety of music events offered on any given day in the city. The following are frequently held music events and/or venues offered in downtown:

- Intimate neighborhood park concerts are held during the summertime. Musicians often play to small crowds, and these concerts are almost always free.

- Most city downtown organizations designate one night a week (mostly Fridays) for a weekly music concert, attracting local, regional, and national musicians who play a variety of genres to packed downtown crowds.

- Music festivals are day- or weekend-long events featuring musicians and groups, usually tied to a particular musical genre. Most cities will have an open-air amphitheater or pavilion that provides acoustical canopies for local music festivals.

- Symphony or pops concerts are popular year-round in symphony halls and during the summer at festivities in large outdoor amphitheaters or in riverfront parks.

- Arena concerts allow you to catch both current and beloved music stars as they make a stop in your city.

- Music clubs and bars provide a different musical experience. You can pick rock tonight and Americana tomorrow night, then follow it up with jazz, instrumental, hip-hop, and country.

- City markets regularly schedule local musicians, especially during the weekend, to serenade you as you shop for fresh produce and specialty items.

- Sidewalks in the city have musicians singing for change or just to express themselves.

Living in theater

- Bill and Peg Balzer are board members of an Atlanta theater group, Theatrical Outfit. Because of their love of theater, they moved to a condominium in downtown Atlanta. They can now take the MARTA train to the symphony, several theaters, and art galleries, and have dinner after the show. They enjoy frequenting a twenty-four-hour New York style diner next to their building to fill their post-show late-night hunger pangs. As former suburbanites, the Balzers love their downtown location that so easily allows them to get their theater fix. ■

As a new city dweller, it's important to understand that music is not only in the concert halls and nightclubs—the city is a symphony itself. Sandy

Duffy of downtown Milwaukee enjoys the steady monotone of Lake Michigan's foghorns combined with the hum of freeway traffic, church bells ringing, buses whooshing, and seagulls crying, along with thousands of other city sounds that make her downtown so special. Every city's downtown plays its own individual song.

Establish your favorite hangout

One of the greatest misconceptions about moving to cities is that urbanites are cold and distant. Some people believe that means getting lost in the uncaring, fast-paced, and hard-core urban jungle—but this is not true.

The irony of becoming a downtown resident, even in a big city, is that, compared to moving into a car-oriented suburban community, residents are small villagers. Because of the city's close quarters, you'll meet and interact with new friends and familiar faces in a variety of places and shops. Sometimes these can even become an extension of your home. Popular hangouts include coffee shops, libraries, bookstores, bars, and parks.

Urban coffee shops

Coffee shops offer much more than a good cup of joe or a morning muffin. They have become the hub of everyday neighborhood conversation and the birthplace of ideas. People of all ages come together to discuss current events, read newspapers, and catch up with friends.

Workers or students on the go might stop for a quick cup of coffee. People establish their own patterns, and within their self-prescribed coffee time is when they meet new sets of coffee shop friends and acquaintances. Perhaps they'll meet their breakfast club during the opening hour, their pick-me-up bunch after lunch, or join their nighttime crew for a poetry-reading session or a live music hour.

Libraries and bookstores

Just being inside the historic halls with their high ceilings, beautiful light fixtures, and stone floors (not to mention the great smells of old books) makes browsing aisles, reading books, and checking them out so much fun. For those who relish reading and want to meet others who read, there's no better place than the main library for variety, diversion, and atmosphere.

Retiring downtown could also place you in the proximity of independent bookstores. Some might be cozy, similar to the feeling of a mom-and-pop coffee shop. These stores have more used, rare, and out-of-print books than you could ever read in a lifetime. There could also be big-chain bookstores such as Barnes and Noble or Borders.

Your local pub or bar

Many pubs and bars are long-established (even historic) fixtures of the city. The following provides a list of the major types of neighborhood bars.

- *Pubs* originated in Britain and is short for "public house." Most local pubs have an Irish or German theme with traditional dark wood walls and darker beer. You might not be able to resist ordering a serving of traditional fish and chips.
- *Sports bars* cater to fans who like to watch different games on a varied number of television sets. The walls may be adorned with athletic uniforms, logos, or banners of the favorite local sports teams. You can eat a casual game-day variety of food, such as chicken wings, popcorn, hot dogs, and nachos.
- *Lounges* serve mixed cocktails such as martinis or chilled fruit daiquiris. You can mingle with a more sedate and sophisticated crowd with background piano music and occasional live singers here.
- *Wine bars* may also be a combination gourmet coffee and wine bar, and the fancy ones even allow cigar smoking

An unusual urban hangout

■ When you retire downtown, you could find yourself discovering unusual ways to have fun. Gene Holcomb of downtown Memphis and his airport pals enjoy formation flying and gentleman's aerobatics over the Memphis skyline at a most unusual hangout—the Dewitt Spain Airport. Instead of a coffee shop or neighborhood bar, you'll find Gene and friends putting up a "four ship formation" or two. ■

inside enclosed humidors. If you seek swank crowds, a wine bar could be your new hangout.

▤ *Gay bar* is a blanket name for a bar that serves the gay and lesbian population—but anyone is welcome. Some bars feature drag queens who perform in shows, but mostly they're just like other bars where people congregate.

▤ *Ethnic bars* cater to a specific group featuring that culture's music and drinks.

▤ *Holes in the wall* are "what you see is what you get" kinds of bars. They're often very small and nonpretentious and fun experiences for people who don't come in every day.

Of course, the best part is if you have a little too much to drink, you won't have to worry about driving home. You'll just start walking, hop on a bus, or hail (or call) a cab to drive you safely to your doorstep. Besides, you wouldn't drive a few blocks to get to your pub in the first place. People who don't drink alcohol should consider going with friends to some of these establishments and ordering a Shirley Temple, just for the experience of getting to know the new neighborhood!

Catch up with friends at the park

Every city dweller needs a place to spend time in natural open spaces within the shade of mature trees and grass under foot. Some parks are huge like New York's 843-acre Central Park, with elaborate bike trails, walking paths, horse-back riding, bridges over streams, open fields, and even embedded restaurants. Other parks are tiny, sometimes called "pocket parks," and are good places to rest your feet and watch the world go by. Regardless of the size, these beloved oases can become one of your prime hangouts. The following are only a few of the most popular ways that you can enjoy them.

Dog walking

Besides being loyal companions who provide extra security, dogs are especially fun to walk through city neighborhood parks. Walking your dog will become just as much of a social event for you as it is for your dog. On any given day, dog owners meet in the middle of their neighborhood park for doggie playtime.

Rose Cooper's advice to anyone moving to a downtown environment is to understand how dog-friendly it can be. She says that a lot of her friends think it must be hard on her little Pomeranian to live in Uptown Charlotte, but it is actually a joy. Walking along downtown sidewalks, Rose and her Pom make friends with everyone from business people to panhandlers. She's never felt uncomfortable walking her Pom along Uptown's sidewalks or even taking her dog to the park at night. Rose considers Uptown to be a very friendly and safe place. She also likes the "scoop the poop" plastic bag dispensers placed throughout the park for dog owners.

Birds of a feather

Bird watching, or birding, is a very popular activity in city parks. Cities are havens for many types of birds and they thrive in an urban environment. Depending on the climate, you'll see grackles and starlings, white-winged and mourning doves, gulls of all kinds, robins, blue jays, crows, and hummingbirds. Cities even have red-tail hawks, such as New York City's Pale Male and his mate Lola, that soar among trees and skyscrapers. And of course, let's not forget the most quintessential of all city birds, the pigeon, waddling among pedestrians and scavenging for food.

Bird watching allows city dwellers to meet some of the most conservation-minded folks around. You can even join them in working with the city parks department to place bird boxes on posts and trees to encourage more birds to nest there. In many cities, there are bird walks with signs explaining which kinds of birds are frequently seen, their physical characteristics, what they eat, and their migration path.

Yes, you *can* go clubbing

Living downtown means having a potpourri of ways to be entertained at night, and never having an excuse for being lonely or bored. Whether high action or a relaxing night with friends, or a combination of both, the city is the place to be.

Although nightclubs are often frequented by twenty-somethings, every now and then a night on the town, especially to a dance club, will provide the jolt you need and the fun you deserve, regardless of your age. Hit the dance floor, then surprise your friends when you "nail" the latest steps. These are also cabarets, comedy, and live music clubs around, so you can take your choice of what downtown has to offer.

Dine out on the town

Cooking is a popular hobby for retirees, but even if you don't like to cook, you will certainly appreciate eating out. Dozens of kitchens surround the average city dweller, so they can leave the cooking responsibilities to the chefs.

If you frequent a neighborhood restaurant, the owner may eventually know your name, you will always have a seat, and you may even get a complimentary dessert since restaurant owners pay attention to loyal, familiar customers.

A reservation to a good restaurant is the start of a fun night out, perhaps before going to a club or a movie. Simply walking up many commercial corridors in the city is like browsing through a vast menu. You can choose Chinese, Japanese, Middle Eastern, Mexican, French, Italian, and other specialties. (It's always possible to grab a burger or a hot dog too.) Dining al fresco has also exploded in popularity and provides a festive fresh-air atmosphere.

See a flick

Downtown movie theaters are making a rousing comeback today. Entrepreneurs in some cities have restored historic single-feature movie houses back to their original grandeur, and they are now showing art flicks and independent movies. Other cities have, or are building, first-run movie theaters, luring people to downtown with a new form of entertainment. These multiplex theaters have the latest high-tech designs and sound systems and feature stadium seating, leather rocking chairs, and bars that allow moviegoers to order a drink and have sushi before or during the show.

These impressive new movie theaters often play the same movies as the theaters in the strip malls, but being able to walk to a local movie theater is a true luxury.

Enjoy festivals, parades, and special events

Downtown is festival central, with numerous year-round choices for organized entertainment. It's always time to celebrate the city and its people, so it's easy to understand why retiring downtown is perfect for individuals who can appreciate these special entertainment venues.

Do you love a parade?

Downtown parades are particularly amazing because they use the backdrop of the city skyline and the most celebrated streets. One of the best examples of parade people are native New Yorker Joan Korte and her ex-military husband, Roland, originally from rural Nebraska. They moved into a condo directly on the famed San Antonio Riverwalk and never miss their city's most unusual river parades. Throughout the year, Joan and Roland have a bird's-eye view of the floating barges from their balcony that faces the Riverwalk.

Visual art festivals

Downtown art festivals feature local and nationally known artists' booths—often hundreds of them—all situated in a major park, plaza, or blocked-off street. Craft lovers can browse past woven baskets, pottery, wood carvings, handmade quilts, tapestries, or jewelry.

Explosive celebrations

For generations, Independence Day and New Year's Eve have centered around pyrotechnic displays and are usually choreographed with a musical score.

First Night and Independence Day celebrations are free and usually family-oriented. Kids will love the storytelling, puppet shows, musicians, and balloon sculptors. Grandchildren will not be able to wait to spend the First Night with you, and then spend the night at their "city grandparent's" place.

Enjoy the holidays

During the winter holidays, many downtowns are transformed into a veritable winter wonderland—even in warm-weather cities. People of all faiths appreciate the festive decorations from Thanksgiving until New Year's Day.

Some cities celebrate this season with a Festival of Lights, where carolers sing and the *Nutcracker* plays in the theater nearby. The city hall or another prominent location may host a lighting of the city's Christmas tree, while Santa Claus sits on his chair welcoming kids and grown-ups alike.

Although downtowns have not been the primary retail shopping areas since the suburban malls took over decades ago, downtown merchants still hold contests for best winter window decoration in the retail districts. Downtown's Christmas, Hanukkah, and Kwanza parades during this time make a great afternoon excursion for the entire family—and so do those for Chinese and Jewish New Year's Day, Cinco de Mayo, and many other holidays.

Explore cultural heritage festivals

Cultural heritage festivals are enlightening, real-life testaments to our various ancestors who immigrated to this country.

Since these festivals celebrate cultural heritage, they always showcase rich traditions, especially music and dance. There may be clogging at Irish festivals, or pow-wows that feature chants and singing with drums at Native American festivals, or Mariachi music at Mexican festivals. Like all other festivals in downtown, the cultural variety provides many food vendors for visitors to sample native fare, such as a falafel in a Middle Eastern celebration or *doro wat* (hot and spicy chicken stew) at the Ethiopian festival.

Since downtown living provides a multitude of options for entertainment, one may inadvertently overlap another. For example, Merrill and Polly Moter, from downtown Louisville, passed an Oktoberfest, a German festival, as they went to dinner. On the way they noticed that B. B. King was playing at a theater across the street. They bought tickets to the show, headed back across the street to the festival, and greeted some friends who just happened to be there. Since they had an hour until B. B. King, they browsed the food vendors' booths and picked out some German beer and brats, then sat down with their friends and enjoyed the cultural festival, proving that "distractions happen" in downtown.

Exercise and pamper yourself

There are a variety of options for city residents to become healthier both physically and mentally. The following is an overview of downtown gyms, sports, and health spas.

Choose a downtown gym

Downtown gyms are similar to other gyms with free weights, weight machines, stair-climbing machines, step or spinning classes, and yoga and Pilates studios. Some may even have enclosed squash courts and swimming pools. What makes the downtown gym special is configuration and location. Instead of the strip mall gym's flat, predictable horizontal layout, you could have a dramatic view of the bustling city as you stretch or walk on the treadmill. Downtown gyms, like so many other buildings in the city, take advantage of big windows and tall buildings to connect people with the outside environment. It's the urban experience provided by the downtown gym that makes it a brilliant place to work out.

Participate in downtown sports

Do you love jogging, walking, or cycling? What about badminton, lawn bowling, horseshoe, and croquet tournaments? In downtown, you will have numerous opportunities to join a sports club or form one with friends.

Perhaps you'll play kickball, the downtown sport that's sweeping the core areas of many cities nationwide, allowing adults to play like children on statehouse and city hall lawns. Although bowling alleys and golf courses are mostly found in neighboring communities, you can join or set up a carpool for either or both sports.

Even though downtowns are known more for their asphalt and concrete, there will be plenty of opportunities to participate in outdoor sports. You can probably find a place to fish along the city's primary waterway, or in one of the ponds in the parks. Locals can hike on a number of walking trails among native trees and grasses, and some cities even have nature paths within close proximity to downtown that provide a lush, relaxing oasis.

Create an urban obstacle course

Urban environments are excellent places to mix up a cardio workout: For instance, you can combine a high-energy power walk on packed city side-walks with a serene riverfront cool-down stroll. Upper-floor condominium or apartment dwellers can top off their jog in the park with a challenging stair climb. Or perhaps you would prefer to in-line skate to the gym, or to the park, and then rest on a bench, and walk back home. You could also ride a bike through the park. Choose your outdoor activity while exploring the urban surroundings and experiencing city life.

Pick a neighborhood health spa

To keep their skin, muscles, mind, and body in tune, downtown dwellers find their choice of health spas and day spas. Often, the most exclusive spas are located in downtowns to serve the new clientele. You could choose a relaxing Swedish massage with a deep tissue rub down, a hot stone treatment, or a seaweed wrap, or just lose yourself in music and aromatherapy.

Cheer the team on

Attending sporting events is a big part of city life, and you'll have ample opportunity to go to a game or look forward to one.

People in most cities have easy access to professional football and baseball. Stadiums that are home to the National Football League and Major League Baseball will be located downtown or not far away. Some cities also house arena football, NBA, and NHL games. Smaller cities have built new stadiums, and offer minor-league sports venues, such as hockey, basketball, and even lacrosse. Some downtowns have Major League Soccer stadiums, but most of them are a short drive away. Since colleges and universities are almost always located in or near downtowns, residents also have access to collegiate spectator sports venues. The novelty of walking out of the house and seamlessly transitioning into a packed crowd of fans walking to the game will never wear off.

Find out what you can do for entertainment in the downtown of your choice and have a ball.

Shopping in the City

Larry and Susan LeVieux from downtown Austin lived in France for four years during the seventies. They both agree that Austin is now becoming more like Paris all the time. Susan explains that the city is built around the idea of leisure and simplicity: an ease of movement and a variety of nearby destinations—especially shopping. Frequenting Whole Foods, "the world's greatest grocery store," has become a part of their weekend routine.

Every Sunday morning, they walk out of their back door and hop on the Hike and Bike trail for a stroll along Town Lake toward the grocery store, which is only a mile away. Many other walkers and people on a morning bike ride join them on the way, passing ducks and their ducklings, and swans. It's not at all what most Texans experience when on a trip to the grocery store.

Making sure they make it to Whole Foods at eight, the LeVieux's snag a table outside if they can. They know they have to make it early because outside tables are always taken by nine. After they find seats, they order a cup of fresh coffee and a breakfast taco, read the paper, and talk. The experience takes them back to their years in France, where they would gather with friends for breakfast at the city markets.

The LeVieuxs like to get distracted on their walk home from Whole Foods to soak up all of Austin's activities. For example, they'll walk to the farmer's market where farmers from all around the area bring produce, and they'll buy veggies from their friends, who are organic farmers. Then, the LeVieuxs shop, play, walk, and explore the city. They are in love with their simple Austin lifestyle and appreciate every aspect of downtown living.

If you're used to shopping at a suburban-style strip mall you are in for a treat. This chapter points out the tools you need to delight in your city shopping experience.

Shopping's an experience, not a destination

Urban shopping is a lot like life should be: a journey, not a destination. It's not just what you buy, it's also where and how you buy it.

Anyone who's ever been to New York's 5th Avenue or Chicago's North Michigan Avenue, the "Magnificent Mile," understands that shopping in the city is far from a singular act. It's an entertaining event and a different experience every time you shop. Browsing either of these city streets during the holidays is sensory overload. Shoppers can feel the excitement and anticipation of the approaching holidays just by walking down the avenue or looking at the lavishly decorated windows decked out in colorful, rich reds and green velvety fabric, with bright, vivid Christmas lights.

Of course, the holiday season is one of the most amazing times to shop in the city, but even during the rest of the year an urban environment is fun. Few cities have anything to rival the world-famous corridors in Chicago or New York, but just about every city has its own version of extraordinary shopping to experience.

Who are the people in your neighborhood?

Shopping in an urban environment, although unusual in today's suburban world, is actually a throwback to a simpler time. And it's a kind of lifestyle that people can become quickly accustomed to.

One reason shopping is so wonderful is simple—the proprietors' relationships with customers. Many store owners will know your name because they see you almost every day. Neighborhood proprietors are there to take care of their customers because they are also their neighbors.

Main Street shopping

Main Street shopping is in style again as the new old-fashioned way to shop, and urban shopping districts are becoming beloved, special places for consumers to experience.

Shopping in the city's commercial districts is like contributing to a storied history. These old districts were the center of commerce during the horse and buggy days, with mercantile stores, ice block warehouses, feed bins, and corset shops. Smoothly paved streets here used to be dirt roads, concrete sidewalks were once wooden planks, and electric street lights have long replaced gas lamps. Trolley bells rang as street cars packed with people made their way up the middle of the street. Parades celebrating the end of wars and politicians' victories marched here. Every Main Street has a rich past.

History makes shopping in the city special. Streets here were named for the property owners, important people who helped found the city, or landmarks such as parks, churches, or other old structures. Main Streets are substantial. Comparing this to a shopping center in the 'burbs, named for a rolling meadow that has recently been paved over with asphalt to become a parking lot, it's easy to understand why places with rich histories provide a more enjoyable, meaningful shopping experience. When someone asks, "Where did you get that?" your normal response will be as much about the great neighborhood store in the historic district than it will about the item itself.

Main Street shops' large, original windows and their eye-grabbing displays encourage browsing. In display after display, pedestrians get a visual treat and a taste of what's inside. In contrast to the ceiling-to floor "displays" in shopping malls, most are often homemade, designed by the owners and not rubber-stamped by the far-away corporate headquarters.

To lure shoppers out of malls, neighborhood shops may come together to advertise special shopping days and nights. These may even include shopping-focused weekend getaway packages for regional residents in cooperation with nearby hotels. Valet parking is sometimes offered, as are VIP cards with discounts at all participating stores.

Downtown is the most stylish and fun place to shop in San Francisco (Union Square), New York (5th and Madison avenues), and Chicago (Michigan Avenue). Main Street eventually could become *the* place to shop in cities from Bakersfield to Baltimore.

Schlep your stuff

Schlepping is Yiddish for "toting or dragging around," and a quintessentially New York City kind of term. New Yorkers schlep food, household goods, and any conceivable purchase on the subways, up the stairs, on elevators, and on buses. Some also schlep goods on bicycles and motor scooters. Whichever downtown you choose, you'll practice your own version of schlepping.

Outside of downtown, people schlep items from point A to point B and haul a week's worth of groceries home in a car, minivan, or SUV. Outside of the city, carrying things from your home to anywhere and then back again means grabbing your briefcase, purse, lunch, gym bag, emergency snacks, a change of clothes, or anything else, and then tossing them into the passenger seat or the trunk.

For downtown retirees, however, this car-oriented mind-set will have to change. Whether you retire to Manhattan or Boise, learning and developing a knack for hauling personal goods is essential to city living. You'll find that using your car will probably be more of an inconvenience than hoofing it.

Mert Michael found this out when she downsized to a condominium in the middle of downtown Boise, Idaho. She and her husband, Gary, found themselves a few short blocks away from the places they were accustomed to visit by driving their car. Their condominium in Boise was steps away from coffee houses, breakfast bistros, pizza shops, French restaurants, wine bars, and a huge farmer's market, and many other big city-style offerings. Boise's most interesting specialty shopping district was also on their block.

It was weird for Mert in the beginning when she went on shopping trips. She was so used to hopping in her car that her first time shopping, she bought far too many things and couldn't carry them all home because she was used to putting everything in her car. Now, she makes sure to take her L.L. Bean canvas bag before she heads out the door.

A bag is all that's required to schlep. But not just any bag—a schlep bag of your choice.

The science of schlepping

Since a day's worth of needed items can't be carelessly dumped in a bag as if it were a car trunk, plan ahead. The science of schlepping is about anticipating the day, and it is as easy as making a five-point mental checklist:

1. Where are you going and how will you get there?
2. Who are you going to see?
3. What will the weather be like today?
4. What do you know you'll purchase?
5. Is there enough room to carry everything securely?

For example, you might plan an entire day of volunteer work and know that you will take the bus, take muffins to the staff, stand outside on a scorching hot summer's day and eat lunch with your friends in the park, then stop at the city market to purchase dinner before coming home. No problem—the science of schlepping will become second nature once you become a seasoned city dweller.

Everyday shopping

Now that you understand schlepping, it's time to begin finding places to buy food, everyday household items, services, and anything else. It's also important to learn what you can't buy downtown. Depending on the city's size and level of vitality, your ability to find everyday goods and services will vary tremendously.

Urban grocery stores

It's important to live close enough to a grocery store to be able to comfortably carry your purchases home.

Of all things, being able to walk to a full-service grocery store is truly living a city lifestyle, which explains why downtown residents' number one wish is for a new, clean, full-service grocery store. No one wants to move in and have to drive outside of the neighborhood to shop for food—not having a grocery store in downtown diminishes the urban experience.

Some downtown cores have one or a few older, smaller, mom-and-pop grocery stores that are often satisfactory when everyday foods and household goods are needed, but most don't have small grocery stores anymore.

Downtown residents want fresher produce, choice meats, an assortment of ethnic foods, and a variety of organically grown foods, just like their suburban counterparts—they want a *real* grocery store.

Neighborhoods outside of the immediate downtown will likely have a full-service grocery store. However, they're being planned in small city downtowns such as Greenville, South Carolina, and on the way in large downtowns like Minneapolis, and soon will be found in downtowns from coast to coast.

Lynn Sedway of downtown San Francisco is today's example of tomorrow's urban grocery shopper. Living high above the street in an upscale condominium in downtown San Francisco, she purchased a grocery cart that she pushes onto the elevator and then a block down Market Street to buy food. Lynn considers being so close to grocery shopping one of the most luxurious aspects of her life.

It's also possible to shop for groceries in city neighborhoods by calling in an order like you would a pizza. Whether by phone or on the Internet, grocery delivery service makes life easier for people who hate the idea of shopping for food, or don't have the time to go.

The city market

City markets, also called public markets, are similar to supermarkets, but are usually cooperative ventures where individual vendors share space. Each vendor specializes in a particular food category, and their products are sought after by local and regional customers. What keeps the city market relevant today is the uncommonly strong vendor/customer relationship.

City markets usually have the freshest seafood, chicken, and meats. Vendors are passionate about their products because for most of them it's their livelihood. City market vendors know where their meat comes from, and customers can feel confident about asking the vendors for advice.

Some local growers have specialty or certified organic produce. Customers can sample a variety of in-season fruits, vegetables, and whole herbs and appreciate their quality and freshness.

It's worth visiting city markets just for the fresh-baked smells of roasted garlic and Parmesan cheese from the Italian focaccia, the pungently sweet and sour pumpernickel breads, or the salty bagels. Bread vendors stack unwrapped

When a schlep bag isn't necessary

■ Uptown Charlotte Ruppies Gary Ferraro and Lorne Lassiter consider their most dramatic lifestyle change from their old lives in the 'burbs is that they don't have to think too much. This is especially true for planning their meals. In the suburbs, they had to plan what groceries they would buy because the drive to the grocery store was a big deal. In Uptown Charlotte, they can run across the street and purchase cooked chicken, or make a salad at the salad bar, or buy fresh fish to throw on the grill. They'll decide five minutes before dinnertime what they want and walk across the park to get it. And if they forget the mayonnaise, it only takes minutes to run back to the store. They're not dependent on an SUV, or *even a schlep bag.* ■

loaves, allowing customers to choose their favorite, and possibly even take one home that's still warm.

Pastries and desserts are prominently showcased in glass coolers and you can watch the pastry chefs do their magic. Choose from elaborate masterpieces such as tiramisu and marzipan, or hometown favorite doughnuts and cream puffs.

City markets have specialty items. One of the most popular are fresh cut flowers. Depending on the day and the season, customers can choose a bouquet of calla lilies, a bunch of spring daffodils, or a single big sunflower. Markets may also have coffee roasters, ice cream makers, salsa and sauce producers, cheese specialists, wine makers, importers, and sushi booths. Some vendors offer prepared food or even have a restaurant that features the great array of the market's fresh goodies.

City markets also host festivals and special events throughout the year: wine tasting, art, music, crafts, and perhaps street performers.

The farmer's market

Farmer's markets bring the country to the city, and guarantee the ripest produce. Most cities have at least one farmer's market during various times of the growing season. Sometimes they are small gatherings in parks, downtown alleys, or on sidewalks. More often, they are weekend events attracting many vendors and featuring ripe tomatoes, ears of corn still moist with silk, and mouthwatering local fruits.

Joanna Athey, from downtown Austin, has good advice for farmer's market shoppers: Place a few towels and coldpacks in your schlep bag and wrap fragile or perishable foods to protect them on the trip home. One time while at the Austin Farmer's Market, Joanna purchased hard honey jars and a few cranberry orange scones, and realized she was going to end up with "scrumbs" if she put them all in the bag at once. She learned how to carry the delicate desserts, nesting them while shopping, then placing them gingerly on top of the hard items for the trip home.

Disciplining yourself is also important at the farmer's market because you can end up buying too much. Since Joanna never knows how many days she'll eat out, she only takes twenty dollars with her and purchases only three days of fresh food. The farmer's market appreciates smaller bills and change, so her husband, John, puts his spare change in a small change purse that she makes sure to include in her shopping bag.

Street vendors

Grabbing a chili dog or a pretzel on the go with a can of soda is as easy as stepping out onto the sidewalk. You can find fresh flowers, books, or get shoes shined, or even pick a piece of art from the street vendors. From day to day, you never know what's possible to buy.

Most food vendors have versatile rolling carts. Several different heating and cooling compartments can allow a vendor to sell warm knishes, pretzels, hot dogs, or hot sausages, and then pull out a cold soda or bottle of water from a refrigerated section. Because of their assortment of accessories and because they loudly advertise their goods and services to the passing crowd, vendors make the city sidewalks come to life. Enjoy the hotdog!

Specialty stores

Downtown specialty stores focus on a highly specific market and offer limited, specialized goods and services. They're independently owned and operated, and provide a homegrown atmosphere compared to chain stores or franchise operations. Unlike malls, shopping centers, or strip malls, downtown's specialty stores are often located in individual and distinctive buildings, which are full of personality.

City shopping becomes even more special when the alcoves of the business district are uncovered: You can find small shops that have the most incredible items. Some might be knick-knack stores while others could be consignment or antique shops. Whatever they sell, they will usually not have store directories and huge "sale" signs—you'll have to unearth these hidden treasures yourself.

City dwellers will not only discover stores hidden in nooks and crannies, but they'll also find their own little special place inside each store. And even after living in a neighborhood, shoppers will still continue to notice more stores in places that might have been overlooked before.

Sometimes, specialty stores are called boutiques, and imply a more upscale establishment. Usually they're associated with haute couture fashion, such as women's dresses, handbags, or hats. But today specialty stores use the term "boutique" to describe all kinds of products, including motor scooters, cookware, and stationery.

Specialty stores are one of a kind. Independent bookstores have hard-to-find or out-of-print listings that chain bookstores would never stock. A corner hardware store is rare and priceless, and so is a shoe repair shop where the owner knows just what to do. The livelihood of these stores depend on their repeat customers and positive word of mouth, so they go out of their way to cater to them.

Chain stores

Neighborhood residents will also have plenty of conventional chain stores in their shopping districts, especially the restaurant staples, such as McDonalds, Starbucks, and Taco Bell.

Although some shopping purists avoid the chains, these stores can provide the kind of convenience and reliability that most downtown residents appreciate. Good neighborhoods maintain a healthy mix of nationally franchised establishments and the local variety. Many of the chains even conform to neighborhood design standards, by placing their parking in the rear or occupying existing buildings and trying to blend into the surrounding structures. As long as the scales don't tip too far to the chains, the balance keeps everyone happy.

Megastores come to downtown

Currently, very few cities have "big box" or megastores in downtown, but most will be confronted with this issue. The general consensus is that, even if downtown residents have to drive outside of downtown to shop for certain items, megastores are extremely bad for downtown business. New city residents may be in the middle of this argument, and will have to weigh the pros and cons and decide for themselves.

Convenience stores

Residential neighborhoods, just outside of downtown, have many convenience stores—including gas stations. However, these are rare, and you'll probably have to drive to get to most of them.

Some downtown cores are beginning to offer convenience stores for pedestrians only, and these blend in with the city's other stores. Once this occurs, you can consider it a strong indication that the neighborhood is a pedestrian-friendly place. In New York and other big cities, residents may see this type of store on almost every corner, but most cities will probably not have nearly that level of variety.

As more people begin to move downtown and more people are on the sidewalks, the demand for these kinds of convenience stores will grow. Until then, stock up at the grocery store or enjoy the drive.

Downtown malls

The lure of suburban shopping malls has ravaged downtown department stores and small businesses since the 1960s. These large indoor buildings featured up to two hundred stores of every kind and have plenty of free parking. At least one big enclosed mall has been built on every side of most cities.

In the late 1980s, building new downtown malls that resembled those in the suburbs seemed like a great idea, but today, many of these have already closed or are barely hanging on. This is because newer, bigger malls have attracted customers away from the city, and the novelty of going downtown to an older mall quickly wore off.

Downtown malls, especially the large ones, tend to be fading out except in big cities like San Francisco and Chicago. This time, the competition might not be coming from a new mall in the suburbs, but from the street itself: Main Street.

5 Getting Around Downtown

etina Bartels moved to downtown Cincinnati and adopted what she considers to be the most efficient form of transportation—"scootin'." Her three-hundred-pound gas-powered motor scooter can reach speeds up to 75 mph and isn't for the faint of heart. Scootin' became a big part of Betina's new lifestyle, but, more importantly, her vehicle immediately became an adopted member of her family. She even named her "Lana."

One day Betina was driving up a narrow inclined street. As she came around a bend Betina saw a lane to her right and quickly leaned to turn her scooter. Before she knew it, Lana jumped a curb! Her front end was airborne and she wasn't slowing. Betina realized that she was tightly gripping the handle bars and pulled back on the brakes. They came to a stop with Betina's heart in her throat.

Betina started laughing as she replayed the scene in her head—the view of a grandmother hanging on to a bucking scooter. She laughed so hard that Lana was soaked with her tears. A couple deep breaths, a long look at the beautiful city below, and they were off for more fun, still chuckling. But Lana had taught Betina an important lesson that day: When you turn, keep your hands on the brake grips. Betina and Lana established some other rules:

1. No riding in the rain because it hurts;
2. No riding in the dark only because they're sissies; and
3. No riding passively in the lane on a busy day—because they are "badass."

Betina and Lana stick to their rules and explore the historical community overlooking Cincinnati's central business district: the beautiful residences, the parks, and the views of the Ohio River. They also ride through quaint neighborhoods and on the city's narrow streets and cobblestone alleyways adjacent to the river to take advantage of the water's cool breeze on hot days.

Since parking is never a problem, they can make a quick stop at a favorite coffee shop for breakfast and buy groceries at busy local markets. Lana also has a sizable storage area under the seat and a hook above the floorboard to hang bags between Betina's feet. It's very convenient and the extra weight has little effect on how Lana drives. After a quick stop by home to unload, they're off to check out the latest treasures at a local furniture resale shop and art gallery.

Scooters have open access and this leads to conversations at red lights. People are always curious about the cost, gas mileage, the speed, and if a motorcycle license is required. City bus drivers laugh with envy while rooting her on. "You go, girl," they yell from their perched seat.

Find your way around town

Betina is a model for empty nesters who want to kick up their heels and drive something special. When she became an urbanite, Betina realized it was time to make her life "hers," to live outside the box and dare to explore the uncommon. Yet as unique as she seems, Betina epitomizes the typical downtown resident. This chapter presents the most priceless benefit of living in the city: the freedom and the joy of movement. The following are a few distinctive ways of getting around downtown.

Scooters

Riding a motor scooter is an excellent way to go anywhere in the city: They're fun and economical. Scooters are enjoying a huge revival in popularity that coincides with the recent popularity of urban living and economizing during times of high gas prices.

Scooters come in an array of colors and models, from a three-wheel stand-up scooter that resembles a motorized skateboard with a small seat and handlebars to souped-up mini motorcycles. Many are decked out with accessories geared to downtown living, such as big compartments for carrying just-purchased items, and comfy leather seats. Since most scooters can go as fast as cars on city streets they can hold their own in heavy or unpredictable traffic.

They're fairly inexpensive to own and to operate. Eco-friendly electric models are typically powered with a rechargeable 12-volt battery, and gas-powered models usually have a one-gallon tank. Plus, expensive scooters are thousands of dollars less than the cheapest car. Scooters can also be locked in bicycle racks for free, and there are no parking problems.

Faster scooters may require a motorcycle license and driver's training, so it's always wise to take a motorcycle safety course—especially for new riders.

Bicycles

Bike riding is a healthy and extremely economical form of transportation: It reduces stress, promotes weight loss, and builds stamina and strength. And there's always a place to park and lock: If a bike rack isn't available, a tree trunk or a street signpost will do fine.

"City bikes" are the most popular category of bicycles for downtown dwellers today. They are hybrid bikes that are a cross between a mountain bike and a ten-speed one. Low, maneuverable handlebars and tall tires make these models popular with bike couriers because they are both fast and efficient. But it really doesn't matter what type of bike you choose as long as it works for you.

Some cities have designated bike lanes that allow cyclists to ride a safe distance from car traffic, while other cities force cyclists to share the road.

Other ideas

Low-speed mini electric motorcars resemble very fancy golf carts and are becoming popular downtown vehicles and can be used on city streets if the speed limit is less than 35 mph. Although they're more expensive than scooters, they allow the driver and a passenger to ride comfortably together, and are much less expensive to buy and operate than regular cars.

For the truly young at heart, Rollerblades or skates offer an amusing and economical way of moving around the city, but remember elbow, knee pads, and a helmet are recommended. Segways, the stand-up, battery-powered scooter, are also gaining in popularity. These "vehicles" will never need a parking place.

Your way around the city couldn't be easier. Whether it's using a motor scooter, bicycle, Rollerblades, skates, or Segways, you'll discover a whole new world awaits you when you lose your inhibitions.

Insure your mobility and independence

Your mobility around the city is free-spirited fun but it also has a serious side. Most people spend years securing health care and saving money for their retirement. In the same respect, securing how you will shop for food, make it to a doctor's appointment, and travel independently and effortlessly during the retirement years is very important too.

Retiring downtown provides "mobility insurance." It guarantees your mobility to get from place to place with ease and without dependence on another person. Easy mobility characterizes urban neighborhoods because they provide residents an unparalleled freedom of movement and trouble-free access to the places they need to frequent. Your getting around, along with living, working, playing, and shopping, is a package deal.

Too many people planning to retire fail to recognize the tremendous consequences of having too few transportation options. For example, retirees in a rural community may not have thought about mobility insurance. They will be forced to drive to the strip malls, restaurants, or stores that are miles from each other, and also miles from home. If for some reason they become unable to drive, they're 100 percent dependent upon someone else to take them where they want or need to go.

Tom and Bobbie Haig, a high-energy older couple, raised a total of twenty-three foster children and spent thirty-two years restoring and maintaining a barn on a remnant of a Wisconsin dairy farm. They thought they would live the rest of their lives in peace and contentment on their quiet homestead, but after Tom retired he was diagnosed with macular degeneration.

This highly independent man was now immobilized and stuck on the farm because he could no longer drive. Bobbie had to drive him everywhere. Unfortunately, his wife later needed knee implants and couldn't navigate the farm anymore. So, they solved their problem by moving into a condo in downtown Madison, in the heart of the vibrant Capitol Square neighborhood.

Tom is now able to fend for himself. He rides the bus to appointments at the hospital, and appreciates the reliable, convenient service. He walks to several mom-and-pop delis nearby, and shops at a full-service grocery store that's only five blocks away. He goes to the public library and the senior center with Bobbie, and they also like to visit the University of Wisconsin Arboretum's Olbrich Botanical Gardens, which has long paths and gorgeous flowers.

Sometimes Bobbie takes Tom to shop outside of downtown, but they found out quickly that they could get along fine without a car if they had to. They now feel liberated by being active and are insured against immobility and dependence.

Everyone always hopes to fend for themselves, but life doesn't always work out that way. Be prepared and protect your future: Consider moving downtown. You will enjoy increased freedom, and never have to worry about imposing on your children or anyone else to ask for a ride because you will be independent and self-reliant.

Start walking

Walking is fundamental to downtown living. Most people today live in car-oriented suburbs and subdivisions, and have lost touch with (or have never known) the idea of walking for practical purposes. Living in a lively downtown neighborhood provides you with unlimited opportunities to *walk*: to a museum, a bookstore, the library, the pharmacy, or shop with friends—and this is also good exercise and good for you.

The United States is designed for driving. Convenient drive-through windows allow drivers to stay in the car instead of walking into a restaurant. Businesses and department stores are located far apart, making a car necessary for a shopping trip or to run errands. Subdivision dwellers likely have only one access to a main road—and few of these have sidewalks. In other words, you really don't have to walk.

Paul and Pat Dravillas can walk to so many fun places in Chicago's downtown Loop: the Taste of Chicago festival or the Chicago Blues Fest or just to take a leisurely stroll. They might stop to eat at one of the ethnic neighborhoods like Greektown, Chinatown, or Little Italy. The coffee shop is nearby and a good place to read a book, and if they feel like it they could walk to Printer's Row, the Art Institute of Chicago, Chicago Cultural Center, Millennium Park, or to any number of performances at Orchestra Hall.

Walking is possible in all downtowns, even in Los Angeles where Dr. Morgan Lyons and his wife Martha Harris walk with friends through the financial district, past the Richard J. Riordan Central Library, and end up at the Millennium Biltmore Hotel with its elegant and historic lobby. Along the way, they tour the lobbies of several grand old buildings. Morgan says that even now that the downtown has been "discovered," people are pleasantly surprised by the grandeur of the spaces, and how safe and comfortable it is to walk around at night.

When you become a downtown retiree, you'll learn to walk again. It will take practice at first, but you'll soon understand the breathtaking freedom that walking can bring to your life.

Walk for health

We all know that walking is an excellent way to improve your health, but Steve McClary knows this better than most people. The retired city planning director for Columbus, Ohio, decided to take a part-time job at the city's health department. His job was to identify the way people currently live and how to encourage more active lifestyles. Steve came up with some very interesting findings for people thinking about retiring downtown.

Steve found that, even though public health professionals tell us that routine physical activity is necessary to prevent obesity and related diseases such as diabetes, stroke, and heart disease, three out of four Americans fail to achieve the recommended level of physical activity. It's no wonder the latest figures from the Centers for Disease Control and Prevention (CDC) revealed that, in 2002, 64.5 percent of adult Americans were either overweight or obese.

For his report, Steve is compiling evidence to suggest that a city's design and where a person lives in the city can greatly influence the level of routine physical activity in their life. Suburban living in general discourages walking. For suburban residents, most trips, even to buy a newspaper or a quart of milk, require the use of an automobile. In fact, the Federal Highway Administration has determined that one-fourth of all car trips are one mile or less.

In a recent article in the *Journal of the American Medical Association*, men with the lowest levels of physical activity had three to five times the risk of dying of cardiovascular disease than men who were more active. Women who walk ten blocks a day have a 33 percent lower risk of cardiovascular disease. The more you walk, the healthier you'll be, especially if you choose to live downtown.

Good walking shoes: A must

As a city dweller, you need a comfortable pair of walking shoes. They help avoid foot injury, and since feet are now even more important for moving around, preventive maintenance starts with a good pair of walking shoes— one of your most important tools. Before you purchase shoes, remember these must-have features and be prepared to discuss them with a knowledgeable salesperson:

- *Good-fitting shoes* that fit your feet perfectly will be less likely to cause bunions, blisters, corns, calluses, or other injuries.
- *Your arch type* should match your shoes' arches to distribute your body weight. If you have fallen arches, use a proper arch support or insole.
- *Appropriate insoles and padding*, especially in the heel area, will help absorb shock when you walk.
- *Keep your feet dry*. Whether it's sweat or rainwater, clammy and uncomfortable feet can spoil your day. Powder your socks to ensure dryness if you know you'll be walking far. Also, make sure you have a good pair of boots and rubbers to supplement your walking shoes.

If you don't have a podiatrist—find one. Your feet are going to be impacted more than any other body part, and long-term foot health is important to almost all aspects of active urban living.

Downsize to one car

The first chapter featured information about downsizing to a smaller living space and getting rid of unnecessary items—that means transportation too. Perhaps you really don't need that second car in the city now.

Parking your car in downtown can be very expensive, and condominiums and apartments often permit only one car per home. Some condo developments require residents to purchase one parking space, and if a rare additional space for a two-car family is available, expect to pay more. The solution to saving the expense and hassle of trying to store a second car should be to get rid of it. Remember, it's now possible to get around in other, cheaper ways.

In addition to parking space issues, general car expenses are also worth considering. Selling off one car will save thousands of dollars per year on maintenance and upkeep, depreciation, parking fees, registration, insurance, and those unpredictable gas prices.

Some people might even consider going carless. In large cities such as New York, Chicago, Boston, San Francisco, and Philadelphia, not owning a car is a viable possibility. The wide variety of public transportation options—including subways, buses, trolleys, and taxis—can offer a quick method of getting from one part of the city to another. And if a car is necessary for a shopping trip or a retreat to the country there's always the car rental agencies.

In small and mid-sized cities, one car is generally needed, especially for personal emergencies or travel to visit family or friends outside of the city.

Make plans for guest parking

Before your family and friends visit, check out the parking facilities that will be available to them.

Get a downtown parking map and check it out. The map will show meters and the nearby public surface parking, parking garages, or underground parking lots. Find out their costs and time rules, and relay this information to your guests. Knowing when the surface parking lots clear out after rush hour, and when the attendant is no longer monitoring spaces, provides even more options. You could always try to convince your family and friends to try public transportation.

Get to know buses, trains, subways, and cabs

Millions have never used public transportation and see it as a last-resort choice for people who can't afford a car. But they quickly change their minds when they retire downtown, often because, out of necessity, it becomes a key part of their lives.

Public transit offers stress-free rides with good views and fewer hassles than freeway traffic jams. Using public transit also eliminates the need for city dwellers to find parking spaces. Why drive and park when many downtown areas are designated "fare-free zones"?

Riding the bus or train is like watching an independent film where you're the star, surrounded by a huge cast of unusual supporting characters. You won't be able to help but wonder why that man is so tired and snoring, and why his hands are folded upside down as he sleeps, or what big event is waiting for the gaggle of teenage girls who are made up and dressed up. You'll try to uncover the mystery of who that man is talking to and how the young mother can possibly carry that big bag with two babies on her arms. You'll also feel the concern of the businessman in a tie looking flabbergasted at his papers. If you enjoy the sport of people-watching, you'll get a kick out of these rides.

Ride the city bus

Busing can be a convenient, reliable, and inexpensive way to get around town, and a bus stop will never be far from home.

The best way to become familiar with the bus system is by grabbing maps and schedules at the main headquarters or at a customer service center, or on the bus. Transit officials and bus drivers will also answer any questions you may have.

Bus stops will either be designated by a street sign or by their covered shelters. Not all buses service each stop, so knowing which bus lines stop there is important.

Buses have regular pick-up times at every stop, and it's best to be at the bus stop five to ten minutes early. Schedules are sometimes listed on a poster or mounted sign inside the shelters, and can also be found in each route's pamphlet. (This may be located in a dispenser near the bus driver.)

In some smaller cities, you might find yourself waiting longer than you anticipated for a ride. Call your local transit agency and they'll provide an estimated time of arrival. Many transit agencies have buses with global positioning systems that allow them to precisely locate each bus. Buses normally arrive on time, but knowing the hotline number will make a much longer-than-normal wait a little easier to take.

Buses, combined with other transportation modes such as walking or cycling, are excellent ways to move around downtown. Local bus systems can be used as a medium for local travelers. For instance, walking a few blocks, catching a bus for a mile or two, and walking the rest of the way is possible. So is securing a bicycle on special front bike holders on buses, combining two vehicles into one trip.

Love trains

Most transit users prefer trains over buses because they're faster, cleaner, and more reliable. In the sometimes-gritty world of public transit, trains—especially the newer systems—seem almost luxurious.

Some trains, like the Bay Area Rapid Transit (BART) ones in San Francisco, are very comfortable, providing upholstered seating, a quiet ride, and carpeted floors. Salt Lake City's Fast Trax, Denver's DART, and Portland's MAX (and many others) offer clean, modern cars that make riding a pleasant experience. Others, like the New York Subway or the Chicago "L," offer a more bumpy ride and hard plastic seating. In almost any case, urbanites love trains.

Living in an area with an easy walk to a train platform or station is becoming very desirable, especially in cities with new train networks. Booming development is occurring along train stops. New condos and apartments are rising up near the tracks, along with stores, restaurants, and offices.

Riders can purchase one-way or round-trip tickets at an automated machine by using coins and bills, or a prepaid card. Seniors over sixty-five, and sometimes students, qualify for a discount or free ticket. As with bus systems, train passes, including ten-ride ticket books or monthly passes, are popular, and can be purchased online or at the transit system's administrative offices.

The walls of some train stops and stations have artwork, including sculpture, murals, and ceramics. Some of the artwork might celebrate the surrounding neighborhood, with special tiles, painted with names and local symbols.

Patti and Mark Clark and a group of their friends from downtown Atlanta have started what they call the MARTA (Metro Atlanta Rapid Transit Authority) Pub Crawl, where they get together at the central Five Points station and "crawl" on the train from station to station, pub to pub. Someone acts as a host at each stop, choosing the establishment, encouraging fun and conversation, and then it's on to the next stop. MARTA train rides mean not having to stop at just one drink—no one ever has to worry about driving!

Take trolleys and monorails

In the late 1800s and early 1900s, trolleys (or streetcars) were used in all sections of cities. They were eliminated in the 1930s and '40s to make way for the automobile. Downtown trolley lines in some cities have remained intact for nostalgia and historic preservation but also to encourage urban development around the lines.

Some cities are using the romantic aspect of streetcars as marketing assets. Paul Sedway and others from San Francisco's Union Square area are fascinated by the city's use of vintage trolleys from other parts of the world. Original trolleys have been restored and painted in their historic colors, and Paul wonders which one is coming. It could be from Milan, Baltimore, Boston, Cincinnati, Philadephia, or even Brooklyn, a car he may have ridden as a kid. Paul and others enjoy sitting down in the street car and feeling like being transported in time and space to other places around the globe.

Monorails, most often associated with popular amusement parks, like Disneyland or Disney World, demonstrate what high-tech transportation should be as they provide park enthusiasts with a special futuristic experience. Think of Seattle. Its monorail to the Space Needle joins Pike's Market and Mount Rainier as the city's best-known icons.

Hail a cab

Another perk of living downtown is having convenient access to taxis. Cab companies provide on-demand chauffeurs. You will likely need a cab to get to the airport, or to a special event. Here are a few tips for anyone who has never hailed a cab.

In big cities such as New York or Washington, D.C., cab hailers must be a bit aggressive. When you spot a cab coming down the street, stand as close to the curb as possible. Then nod your head, wave your hand, or raise your entire arm up in the air—or yell. In the smaller cities, call the cab company.

Passengers are charged by the distance they travel, plus a flat fee at the beginning—this varies widely from city to city. (It's usually less expensive in the big cities.) The meter on the dashboard displays what is owed at any given point on the trip. And don't forget to tip the cabbie.

It's important to recognize legitimate cab companies from "gypsy cabs." The upstanding companies keep their cabs immaculately painted, have professional logos, and skillfully painted lettering on their cars. They always have "taxi" caps that light up on top of the car, and the meters are clearly visible in the dash. They'll have cab license papers visibly placed, and will provide clear and nonnegotiable rate quotes. Gypsy cabs may not immediately look suspicious, but they are not licensed or regulated. They offer cheaper rides than the competitors, but getting into an illegal cab is not the wisest or safest way to save a few bucks.

Becoming a downtown dweller means having many, if not all, of these transportation options. City people have mobility insurance, guaranteeing their ability to move independently for as long as they choose to live downtown.

PART TWO

TWENTY OF AMERICA'S BEST RETIREMENT DOWNTOWNS

anhattan is the quintessential city living experience, with countless books and neighborhood guides written to highlight its never-ending urban lifestyle options. As is universal with die-hard fans of cities, New York is my dream city. But in part 2, I've decided to show you how, regardless of the city you choose for your retirement, you can find a great city neighborhood to create your personalized, miniature New York City lifestyle.

Twenty city downtowns are featured here where you can take a cab to dinner and a show, use public transportation, enjoy a variety of nightlife, and live in classy urban housing. It's true that the vibrant section of the city you choose won't stretch for miles—in fact, it might only last for several blocks. But choosing the right downtown can give you the sense that you are indeed in a city full of opportunities where you can live like a New Yorker.

Catch the New York Spirit

If you are planning a Manhattan retirement, congratulations! If not, learning more about New York neighborhoods will help you keep the spirit of the Big Apple alive as you establish your own mini-Manhattan lifestyle somewhere else. Here's a New York neighborhood refresher.

Lower Manhattan

Downtown
At the southern tip of Manhattan, Battery Park, the Financial District, and Civic Center neighborhoods blend. Downtown is home of the upcoming Freedom Tower and the World Trade Center memorial, and the entire world is watching as the area is rebuilt. See the Downtown Alliance Web site at **www.downtownny.com** and click "**Live**" for residential information.

Tribeca
This fashionable and expensive downtown neighborhood used to be an industrial district similar to SoHo (see page 71). For more information, see **www.tribeca.org**.

Lower East Side
Roughly between the Brooklyn Bridge north to Houston Street (blending with

East Village), and west of Bowery, the neighborhood known for immigrants is hard to define today—it's one of the most diverse in terms of income, artists, professionals, and people and business of all kinds. New York's Chinatown bleeds into the neighborhood to the west along Canal Street.

SoHo

The original industrial-turned-artist-turned-extravagantly-expensive neighborhood, SoHo is now an iconic boutique and arts district. It's between Houston and Canal Streets, and it borders the tiny yet festive Little Italy neighborhood on the west. See more about SoHo arts at **www.artseen-soho.com**. Little Italy: **www.littleitalynyc.com**.

Greenwich Village

Home to New York University and Christopher Square, Greenwich Village is arguably New York's most famous neighborhood. West Village extends from 6th Street west to the river, and the hip Meatpacking District is sandwiched between the West Village and Chelsea along the Hudson River and West 14th Street. See the Village Alliance for more information at **www.villagealliance.org**.

East Village

Generally east of Broadway and south of 14th Street, the East Village is the setting of Broadway's *Rent*. It's a diverse, interesting side of Lower Manhattan. See the East Village Neighborhood Directory and Free Press for more information at **www.east-village.com**.

Midtown

Chelsea

Roughly between 40th and 14th streets and west of 5th Avenue, Chelsea is known for its young, trendy residents, and it is often known as New York's primary gay enclave. The Hell's Kitchen neighborhood (sometimes referred to as Clinton) blends into Chelsea north of 40th to the Hudson River.

Union Square / Gramercy Park

Tree-lined streets and grand brownstone town homes typify the east and southeast Midtown neighborhoods. Union Square, much quainter than

Times, provides a center commercial district with fresh farmer's markets that the entire city enjoys.

Garment District
East of 10th Avenue and west of 5th, and located between Times Square and Chelsea, this is the very center of fashion and of Midtown.

Murray Hill
Centered on Park Avenue and south of great shopping on 5th and Madison Avenues, this eastern Midtown residential enclave is close to everything. Many homes have close-up views of the Empire State Building.

Uptown
Central Park is the centerpiece of Uptown, separating the two upscale neighborhoods (the Upper East and Upper West Sides) and representing Harlem's southern border.

The Upper West Side
It's one of the most sought-after residential districts with easy access to Central Park, Times Square, great restaurants, and culture. Northward toward Harlem is Morningside Heights, home to Columbia University. See more at **www.nysite.com** and **www.morningside-heights.net**.

The Upper East Side
This area has long been the poshest of Manhattan residential neighborhoods and the home to most of the city's famous museums, such as the Museum of Modern Art, the Metropolitan Museum of Art, and the Guggenheim. See the Upper East Side megasite at **www.uppereast.com**.

Harlem, East Harlem, and Washington Heights
The city's original African American neighborhood, today's Harlem is more diverse while keeping its rich history and authenticity. The Apollo Theater, many museums, and historic brownstones set Harlem apart. Notably, Washington Heights, or WaHi, just north of Harlem, is also newly appreciated for its Manhattan address. For more information, visit **www.east-harlem.com** and **www.washington-heights.us**.

Brooklyn, Queens, and the Bronx offer excellent "downtown" living options as well, as do Hoboken and Jersey City, New Jersey. Find out more:

Brooklyn: **www.digitalbrooklyn.com**

Queens: **www.queensnewyork.com**

The Bronx: **www.ilovethebronx.com**

City of Hoboken: **www.hobokennj.org**

Jersey City: **www.cityofjerseycity.com**

In the following chapters, you'll find downtowns that are excellent choices for Ruppies. There are descriptions of the downtown neighborhoods that you should target, and a Downtown Lifestyle Web Guide. Instead of lists of specific restaurants, shops, and other establishments, there are a wide variety of organizations' Web sites for information on living, volunteering, playing, shopping, and getting around a specific city's downtown. Many Web sites include continuously updated material (including maps) and offer valuable information for future retirees. Please take the time to explore them, especially the downtown and neighborhood organizations that provide local insights and further descriptions of what their areas have to offer.

Dynamic Downtowns

Dynamic downtowns are dream downtowns—the places where enthusiastic urbanites wish they could live if money were no object. They're "finished products," even though they continue to grow and evolve, because they are further along in their development than most other cities. These are the most energetic cities with the tallest skyscrapers, an abundance of retail establishments, and all types of businesses.

In addition to encouraging high-density residential areas, especially high- and mid-rise condominiums, these downtowns maintain their long-established historic neighborhoods. Public transportation works better here because large populations in small areas allow buses and trains to operate more efficiently. Housing costs are also considerably higher in these dynamic downtowns, and worth it!

Enjoy exploring America's four most dynamic downtowns outside of New York: Chicago, Philadelphia, San Francisco, and Seattle.

6
Chicago, Illinois

hicago, located on the shores of Lake Michigan in northeastern Illinois, is the most exciting and dynamic city between New York and San Francisco. It's still called the "Second City," although Los Angeles is now the second largest in America. Chicago retains a bustling New York ambiance, and it's less expensive than Manhattan. Here are five more reasons to entice Ruppies to consider downtown Chicago as a truly dynamic place to retire.

1. Dramatic, world-class waterfront

Chicago residents enjoy spending time in two of the greatest downtown waterfront parks: Grant Park and Millennium Park. Both parks combined span more than a dozen city blocks between Chicago's breathtaking skyline and Lake Michigan. Grant Park is best known for the elaborate Buckingham Fountain built in 1927 and features choreographed spotlights and color displays. The park also has manicured green spaces, a yacht basin, a rose garden, formal gardens, museums, and an aquarium. There's even a bandshell that hosts free evening concerts.

Neighboring Millennium Park is the culmination of ideas from talented designers, architects, artists, and planners where concerts and music festivals are held at the Jay Pritzker Pavilion, an outdoor amphitheater designed by world-renowned architect Frank Gehry. The pavilion's 4,000 seats and expansive stage are framed by large folded ribbons of stainless steel supporting a state-of-the-art sound system. The Crown Fountain uses high-tech LED screens that project human faces with water spouting from their mouths. Gorgeous gardens and innovative sculptures make this one of America's most impressive new downtown parks.

2. High-rise living

Much of Chicago's identity is tied to its tall buildings, most notably the 110 story 1,450-foot-tall Sears Tower, the tallest structure in the United States, and others, such as the 1,127 foot John Hancock Center. In recent years, residential skyscrapers with marvelous views have been added to the city's already inspiring office towers. Within the downtown core and its adjacent neighborhoods, new residential high-rises will continue to join older structures: the proposed ninety-two-story, 1,362-foot Trump International Hotel and (residential) Tower, and the tallest residential tower in the world at 1,458 feet, proposed by the Fordham Company. Because of these projected dense residences, downtown Chicago's population is expected to double.

3. Cosmopolitan Midwest

Chicago is the perfect place for people who want to live in a huge, sophisticated, internationally known area. The city has one of the world's busiest airports, the finest symphonies, operas, and museums—all just a short drive away from the open cornfields and prairies of America's heartland. It's a blend of big-city life and down-home Midwestern sensibility.

4. Art in architecture

Downtown Chicago is known for its beautiful, architecturally detailed buildings. The Auditorium (1889) and the art deco–influenced Chicago Board of Trade Building (1930) are two of many gloriously preserved historic structures. Cruise boats carry tourists on an architectural tour down the Chicago River, floating under the bridges, and through the canyons of the magnificent buildings. New residents will love the city's stunning, intricately designed structures—especially if they're the focal points from a terrace view.

5. The "L"

Train enthusiasts will appreciate Chicago's elevated train, popularly known as the "L." It loops around downtown on steel trellises above the city streets and provides a fascinating ride for commuters and locals.

Target Retirement Districts and Neighborhoods

Downtown Chicago's target retirement neighborhoods are the Loop, the neighborhoods of the Near North Side, and the greater South Loop area.

The Loop

The Loop, the name for the center of downtown Chicago, is generally contained inside the elevated "L" train tracks that form an oval-shaped loop. Full of skyscrapers and one of America's busiest Manhattan-like downtowns, the Loop is the financial and business capital of the Midwestern United States. It also hosts the historic shopping district along State Street between Randolph Street and Jackson Boulevard, the Wabash Jeweler's Row on Wabash Street between Randolph and Madison, as well as one of the largest theater districts in America.

Historically, the Loop has not been a residential neighborhood, but this is quickly changing. New high-rise towers are beginning to emerge, designed to complement the rich architecture of the old existing buildings. Residents can easily walk to shopping and retail stores and to Grant and Millennium Parks—and some of the best city views outside of Manhattan.

Although the "L" train's loop is considerably smaller (between Lake, Wabash, Van Buren, and Wells streets), the Chicago Loop area refers to the area south and east of the Chicago River, west of Grant Park, and north of Congress Parkway. For more information, contact the Chicago Loop Alliance at **www.chicagoloopalliance.com**.

Near Northside Neighborhoods

Near Northside's four primary neighborhoods, the Magnificent Mile, Streeterville, the Gold Coast, and River North, are a collection of luxurious condominiums and apartment buildings and offer world-class shopping and urban living amenities.

The Magnificent Mile

This area, just across the Chicago River Bridge from the Loop along North Michigan Avenue, is primarily a shopping district and one of the most internationally recognized commercial corridors. Check out the detailed architecture of the Tribune Tower (1925), near the Chicago River. This magnificent structure was built in 1922 as a result of the Tribune's international "most beautiful office building in the world" competition. The Wrigley Building is called "The Jewel of the Mile," and its clock tower dramatically lights up at night. To the north are shops, boutiques, and anchor department stores that lure locals and visitors year-round, especially during the festive holiday season with their sparkling Christmas lights and elaborate window displays. Quaint Chicago is between Chicago Avenue and Delaware Place and particularly around the Old Water Tower courtyard, near the stately Fourth Presbyterian Church.

Several expensive residential towers line this fabulous corridor beginning at the Chicago River north to Oak Street. For more information on real estate, shopping, and dining visit **www.themagnificentmile.com**.

Streeterville

Immediately east of the Mag Mile is Streeterville (sometimes called River East), one of the most sought-after and expensive residential real estate areas. Streeterville is anchored by the John Hancock Building, Northwestern University's medical and law schools, the Chicago Museum of Contemporary Art, and the popular Navy Pier and beaches of Lake Michigan.

Streeterville is the area east of the Magnificent Mile, north of the Chicago River, west of Lake Michigan, and south of East Oak Street/Lake Shore Drive. For more information on Streeterville, see the Streeterville Chamber of Commerce Web site at **www.streetervillechamber.org**.

The Gold Coast

The northernmost Near Northside neighborhood is the Gold Coast, a lakefront neighborhood with easy access to Lake Michigan's beaches. It's known for posh high- and mid-rise apartments and condominiums, and also features the Astor Street Historic District, a residential enclave along north-south Astor Street, with charming old homes, town houses, and apartment buildings. The area is also a premier shopping district, particularly along Rush Street, which teems with shops and specialty stores, and on Oak Street, with its exclusive boutiques.

The Gold Coast is west of Lake Michigan, south of North Avenue, east of North LaSalle Boulevard, and a fuzzy boundary north of East Chicago Avenue. Visit the Oak Street Council at **www.oakstreetchicago.com**.

The Clare at Water Tower is a new and exciting retirement option coming soon to downtown Chicago. This first-of-its-kind, high-rise senior living community will be situated on the Loyola University Water Tower Campus in Chicago's Gold Coast. The Clare will provide maintenance-free services and resort-style amenities, right in the heart of it all. The Clare is owned by the Franciscan Sisters of Chicago Services Corporation, sponsored by the Franciscan Sisters of Chicago, and designed by Perkins + Will.

River North

River North, to the west of the Magnificent Mile, is an area similar to New York's SoHo district in lower Manhattan because it once housed industrial warehouses. This area, formerly called Smokey Hollow, is by far one of Chicago's hippest, most popular residential neighborhoods and the hub of art galleries, design stores, entertainment venues, fine restaurants, and hopping nightclubs. What's most exciting about River North is the boom of mid- and high-rise condominiums, with units featuring the dazzling views of Chicago's skyscrapers in the Loop, and the high-rises of Michigan Avenue and the Gold Coast to the east. Residents here can also walk to shopping along North Michigan Avenue, the Red Line subway, the Loop, grocery stores, and the neighborhood's upscale boutiques and specialty stores.

River North begins just north and east of the branches of the Chicago River, west of Wells Street, and south of West Chicago Avenue. Visit the

River North Association's Web site at **www.rivernorthassociation.com** and the River North Resident's Association at **www.rivernorthresidents.com**.

And for information on retail, services, real estate, and more for all of the Near North Neighborhoods, see the Greater North Michigan Avenue Association's Web site at **www.gnmaa.com**.

The South Loop

In recent years, massive development has occurred south of the southern Loop, adding thousands of residents to this old industrial area. The low-rise commercial and warehouse district is undergoing a vertical construction revolution with skyscrapers and mid-rise condominium towers springing up in the blocks around South Michigan Avenue.

Once a center of Chicago's printing and publishing industry, the Printer's Row district along Dearborn Avenue is now a loft and retail district on the area's northern border. The neighborhood is also flanked on its south side by Chinatown, and the Prairie Avenue district's remaining historic homes.

South Loop is adjacent to the mammoth open spaces of Grant Park and the serene docks of Burnham Park Harbor on its east side. The giant John G. Shedd Aquarium and the Field Museum also call South Loop home, both taking advantage of the McCormick Place Convention Center's three million annual guests. Residents here live near the Loop and Millennium Park, and with new grocery stores, movie theaters, and retail stores opening every year, this area is fast becoming one of Chicago's most complete residential districts.

The South Loop is bounded by the Congress Parkway (north), the Stevenson Expressway (south), Lake Michigan (east), and the Chicago River (west). For more information, visit the Greater South Loop Association at **www.greater southloop.org**. Also see the South Loop Neighbors Association at **www.south loopneighbors.org**.

Downtown Chicago Essentials

Ice skating: From November to March, celebrate Chicago's cold and snowy season and head down to Millennium Park's McCormick Tribune Ice Skating Rink to enjoy free evenings of ice skating under the dazzling lit-up Chicago skyline.

Cubbies vs. White Sox: Baseball is big in Chicago and you'll be required to take sides. Will it be the north side's Cubs or the south side's White Sox?

City views: If you decide to live in one of America's best cities for tall buildings, make the view an important element of your decision-making process when deciding on a place to live.

Exploring neighborhoods: There's a lot more to Chicago than the Loop. You can hop on a train or take a cab and visit any one of a variety of different areas. Walk the streets of Lincoln Park, spend an afternoon of taste-testing at the near West Side's Greek Town restaurants, or browse through any other interesting neighborhood.

Comedy and pizza: The Second City Comedy Club has birthed a host of today's stars. Catch tomorrow's celebrities today at this world-famous club in the Gold Coast neighborhood. After the show, enjoy a slice of Chicago-style pizza—the thick-crusted and extra cheesy kind.

General Statistics

Population: Downtown core: 72,843 (2000); City: 2,862,244 (2003); Metro: 9,333,511 (2003)

Terrain: Downtown Chicago's generally flat terrain borders Lake Michigan on the east, and the Chicago River on the west and on the north.

Climate Overview: cold winters/mild summers

Average January high/low temperature: 29/13F

Average July high/low temperature: 80/57F

Average annual total precipitation: 35 inches

Average annual snowfall: 38 inches

Number of cloudy days: 176

Cost of Living: Find out the current cost of living between Chicago and your community by visiting **www.homefair.com** and clicking **"Moving to a New State"** or **"Moving Locally,"** then follow the prompts.

Cost of Housing:

Zip code: 60601, 60602, 60603, 60604 (The Loop); price snapshot: $474,208; sq/ft: N/A

Zip code: 60605 (South Loop, sections of The Loop); price snapshot: $435,330; sq/ft: N/A

Zip code: 60610 (River North, Gold Coast, Near Northwest); price snapshot: $594,663.06; sq/ft: 1,583

Zip code: 60611 (Magnificent Mile, Streeterville); price snapshot: $796,717; sq/ft: N/A

Real estate prices fluctuate. For up-to-date neighborhood housing cost information, input the zip codes above in the Homestore Web site (affiliated with Realtor.com) at **www.homestore.com/Cities**.

Rent Costs: If you want to rent, explore **www.rentnet.com** and also investigate the neighborhood Web sites for current rents and available properties.

Taxes

Property Tax: Varies by location. Please keep up to date by visiting the Cook County Assessor's Office at **www.cookcountyassessor.com**.

Sales Tax: 9 percent for combined local, state, regional, county, and transportation taxes; 1 percent food; 1 percent prescription drugs.

State Income Tax: 3 percent flat rate. Personal exemptions: single: $2,000; married: $4,000; child: $2,000.

Downtown Chicago Retirement Lifestyle Web Guide

Living

The Loop

Visit the Chicago Loop Alliance's Web site at **www.chicagoloopalliance.com** and click "**Business Loop**," then "**Residential Real Estate**" for high-rise and office-conversion housing developments and their availability.

Near Northside Neighborhoods

Magnificent Mile: For luxurious living along and near the Mile, visit **www .themagnificentmile.com**, click "**Professional Services**," then select "**Residential Properties**."

River North: Visit the River North Association's Web site at **www.rivernorth association.com/directory**, then click "**Residential**" or "**Real Estate Brokers**" to find local residential listings.

Streeterville: See the Streeterville Chamber of Commerce's Web site at **www .streetervillechamber.org** under "**Find a Local Business**," then click "**Real Estate**" for an up-to-date listing of real estate specialists.

Be sure to visit the Greater North Michigan Avenue Association's Web site at **www.gnmaa.com**, click "**GNMAA Member Listing**," then "**Search by Category**," then "**Residential Real Estate**." (Real estate listings will also include the Gold Coast neighborhood.)

The South Loop

South Loop: Visit the Greater South Loop Association at **www.greatersouth loop.org**.

For all downtown neighborhoods, also consider contacting a Realtor at the Chicago Association of Realtors at **www.car-realtor.com**.

City Hospitals

*John H. Stroger Jr. Hospital
of Cook County*
1901 West Harrison Street
www.ccbhs.org

Rehabilitation Institute of Chicago
(main campus)
345 East Superior Street
www.ric.org

Jesse Brown VA Medical Center
820 South Damen Avenue
www.visn12.med.va.gov/Chicago

Northwestern Memorial Hospital
251 East Huron Street
www.nmh.org

Rush University Medical Center
1653 West Congress Parkway
www.rush.edu

*University of Illinois Medical Center
at Chicago*
1855 West Taylor Street
www.uillinoismedcenter.org

Health Clubs
– North –

Magnificent Mile: Visit **www.themagnificentmile.com**, and click "**Personal Services**," then "**Fitness Centers**."

River North: Visit the River North Association's Web site at **www.river northassociation.com/directory**, then click "**Athletic Clubs**" for local fitness clubs.

Gold Coast/Oak Street: Visit the Oak Street Association's Web site for specialty services at **www.oakstreetchicago.com/directory.html**.

Streeterville: Visit the Streeterville Chamber of Commerce's Web site at **www.streetervillechamber.org** under "**Find a Local Business**," then click "**Health and Athletic Clubs**" for an up-to-date listing.

Also visit the Greater North Michigan Avenue Association's Web site for the entire Near North area's shopping opportunities at **www.gnmaa.com**, then click "**GNMAA Member listing**," then "**Fitness Services**."

– South –

South Loop: Visit the Greater South Loop Association at **www.greatersouth loop.org** and click "**Merchants and Services**" for up-to-date information.

Volunteering

United Way of Metropolitan Chicago
560 West Lake Street
www.uwonline.org and click
   "**Volunteer**"

American Red Cross of Greater Chicago
2200 West Harrison Street
www.chicagoredcross.org and click
   "**Get Involved**"

Educational opportunities

City Colleges and Universities

Chicago-Kent College of Law
565 West Adams Street
www.kentlaw.edu

Chicago State University
9501 South Martin Luther King Drive
www.csu.edu

City Colleges of Chicago
  (community colleges)
Various locations
www.ccc.edu

Cooking and Hospitality Institute
  of Chicago
361 West Chestnut Street
www.chic.edu

East-West University
315 South Plymouth Court
www.jmls.edu

National-Louis University
122 South Michigan Avenue
www.nl.edu

Northwestern University
303 East Chicago Avenue
www.northwestern.edu

School of the Art Institute of Chicago
37 South Wabash Avenue
www.artic.edu/saic

University of Illinois at Chicago
Harrison and Halstead streets
www.uic.edu

Columbia College
600 South Michigan Avenue
www.colum.edu

DePaul University
Loop Campus,
  1 East Jackson Boulevard
www.depaul.edu

Illinois Institute of Technology
3300 South Federal Street
www.iit.edu

John Marshall Law School
315 South Plymnouth Court
www.jmls.edu

Loyola University
Water Tower Campus,
  820 North Michigan Avenue
www.luc.edu

Northeastern Illinois University
5500 North Street Louis Avenue
www.neiu.edu

Roosevelt University
430 South Michigan Avenue
www.roosevelt.edu

University of Chicago (Hyde Park)
5801 South Ellis Avenue
www.uchicago.edu

Library

Harold Washington Library Center
400 South State Street
www.chipublib.org

Entertainment

Restaurants, Bars, and Nightclubs

– North –

Magnificent Mile: Visit **www.themagnificentmile.com**, and click "**Professional Services**," then "**Dining and Nightlife**."

River North: Visit the River North Association's Web site at **www.rivernorth association.com/directory**, then click "**Restaurants**" or "**Entertainment and Nightclubs**" for current listings.

Gold Coast/Oak Street: Visit the Oak Street Association's Web site for a listing of restaurants: **www.oakstreetchicago.com/directory.html**.

Streeterville: See the Streeterville Chamber of Commerce at **www .streetervillechamber.org**; under "**Find a Local Business**" click "**restaurants**" or "**lounge**" for up-to-date listings.

Entire North Side: Visit the Greater North Michigan Avenue Association's Web site at **www.gnmaa.com**, and click "**GNMAA Member listing**," then "**Restaurants**" or "**Night Life**."

– South –

South Loop: Visit the Greater South Loop Association at **www.greatersouth loop.org** for up-to-date information. Also visit the South Loop Neighbors Association's restaurant directory at **www.southloopneighbors.org**.

Professional Spectator Sports

Chicago Bears (football)
Soldier Field,
   1410 South Museum Campus Drive
www.chicagobears.com

Chicago Blackhawks (hockey)
United Center,
   1901 West Madison Street
www.chicagoblackhawks.com

Chicago Bulls (basketball)
United Center,
   1901 West Madison Street
www.nba.com/bulls

Chicago Cubs (baseball)
Wrigley Field,
   1060 West Addison Street
www.cubs.com

Chicago Fire (soccer)
Soldier Field,
   1410 South Museum Campus Drive
www.chicago-fire.com

Chicago White Sox (baseball)
U.S. Cellular Field,
   333 West 35th Street
www.whitesox.com

College Sports

DePaul University
Lincoln Park Campus (north of downtown, take the Red Line)
Men's and women's basketball, cross-country, soccer, tennis, track and field,
   men's golf, women's softball and volleyball
www.depaulbluedemons.com

Loyola University
Lincoln Park Campus (north of downtown)
Men's and women's basketball, cross-country, golf, soccer, track, volleyball,
   women's softball
http://loyolaramblers.cstv.com

The Performing Arts

Chicago Chamber Orchestra
332 South Michigan Avenue,
   Suite 1143
www.chicagochamberorchestra.org

The Chicago Symphony Orchestra
Theodore Thomas Orchestra Hall,
   220 South Michigan Avenue
www.cso.org

Lyric Opera of Chicago
Civic Opera House,
20 North Wacker Drive
www.lyricopera.org

Joffrey Ballet of Chicago
Auditorium Theatre,
   50 East Congress Parkway
www.joffrey.com

Live Theater

To sample the shows playing in Chicago's theaters, see the League of Chicago Theatres at **www.chicagoplays.com**, then "**theater links**" for the list of member theaters and current productions.

Major Museums

Adler Planetarium and
  Astronomy Museum
1300 South Lake Shore Drive
www.adlerplanetarium.org

Chicago Children's Museum
700 East Grand Avenue at Navy Pier
www.chichildrensmuseum.org

DuSable Museum of
  African American History
740 East 56th Place
www.dusablemuseum.org

Garfield Park Conservatory
300 North Central Park Avenue
www.garfieldconservatory.org

Museum of Contemporary Art
220 East Chicago Avenue
www.mcachicago.org

Museum of Science and Industry
57th Street and Lake Shore Drive
www.msichicago.org

Art Institute of Chicago
111 South Michigan Avenue
www.artic.edu

Chicago Historical Society
Clark Street at North Avenue
www.chicagohistory.org

Field Museum (Natural History)
1400 South Lake Shore Drive
www.fieldmuseum.org

Museum of Broadcast Communications
400 North State Street, Suite 240
www.museum.tv

Museum of
  Contemporary Photography
600 South Michigan Avenue
www.mocp.org

Shedd Aquarium
1200 South Lake Shore Drive
www.sheddaquarium.org

Special Events (Best Bets)

Chicago Blues Festival
June. The largest free-admission
   blues festival in the world held
   at Grant Park
www.chicagobluesfestival.org

Chicago Jazz Festival
Late August/early September
   in Grant Park
www.chicagojazzfestival.org

Chicago Outdoor Film Festival
June. Tuesdays in August in
   Grant Park's Butler Field
www.cityofchicago.org/
   specialevents

Chicago Winter Delights
January/February. Multiple events
   to celebrate winter in Chicago
   including Mag Mile lights, ice
   skating in Millennium Park,
   and many cultural events
www.cityofchicago.org/
   specialevents

State Street Thanksgiving Parade
Thanksgiving Day. State Street from
   Congress to Randolph
www.cityofchicago.org/
   specialevents

Chicago Gospel Music Festival
June. More than 300,000 gospel
   music lovers converge on
   Millennium Park
www.chicagogospelfestival.com

Viva! Chicago's Latin Music Festival
August in Grant Park
www.cityofchicago.org/
   specialevents

Chicagoween
October. Halloween fun in Civic
   Center Plaza at Washington
   and Dearborn streets
www.cityofchicago.org/
   specialevents

New Year's Eve Fireworks
   at Buckingham Fountain
December 31.
www.cityofchicago.org/
   specialevents

Taste of Chicago
June/July. World's largest celebration
   of food in Grant Park
www.cityofchicago.org/
   specialevents

Movie Theaters

900 North Michigan Cinemas
900 North Michigan Avenue

Loews Cineplex
600 North Michigan Avenue
www.enjoytheshow.com

Navy Pier IMAX Theatre
600 East Grand Avenue
www.imax.com/chicago

Gene Siskel Film Center
164 North State Street
www.siskelfilmcenter.com

AMC River East 21
322 East Illinois Street
www.amctheatres.com

Loews Cineplex Esquire
58 East Oak Street
www.loewscineplex.com

Favorite Downtown Parks

Millennium Park
201 East Randolph Street
Featuring art, architecture, concerts, gardens, ice skating—the most exciting urban park in America.
www.millenniumpark.org

Grant Park
331 East Randolph Street
Grant Park is attached to Millennium Park and features Chicago's most important museums: the Field Museum of Natural History, Shedd Aquarium, the Chicago Art Institute, and Buckingham Memorial Fountain and surrounding gardens.
www.chicagoparkdistrict.com

Lakefront Harbors
Chicago's miles and miles of shoreline, pathways, docks, piers, and beaches are accessible to all downtown neighborhoods.
www.chicagoharbors.info

Navy Pier
600 East Grand Avenue
A peninsular amusement park with a mammoth ferris wheel, fireworks every
    summer evening, an IMAX theater, Shakespeare plays, a children's museum,
    and a shopping district.
www.navypier.com

Shopping

– North –

Magnificent Mile: Visit **www.themagnificentmile.com**, and click "**Professional Services**," then "**Shopping**."

River North: Visit the River North Association's Web site at **www.rivernorth
association.com/directory**, then click any number of links for specific
retailers and services. "**Catering/Retail Food**" provides a listing of grocery stores.

Gold Coast/Oak Street: Visit the Oak Street Association's Web site for an
extensive listing of shops, boutiques, and services: **www.oakstreet
chicago.com/directory.html**.

Streeterville: Visit the Streeterville Chamber of Commerce at **www.streeter
villechamber.org**; under "**Find a Local Business**" click any number of
merchants and services for updated information. For groceries, click
"**Deli/Supermarket**."

For all Near Northside neighborhoods, visit the Greater North Michigan Avenue
Association's Web site at **www.gnmaa.com**, and click "**GNMAA Member listing**" for all services and "**Grocery**" for current places to find food.

– South –

South Loop: Visit the Greater South Loop Association at **www.greatersouth
loop.org** for up-to-date information about retail stores, grocery stores, and
services.

Getting around

Public Bus and Train Service

Chicago Transit Authority
www.transitchicago.com

Metra
Commuter train service
www.metrarail.com

Bike Routes/Trails

City of Chicago Department of Transportation
www.cityofchicago.org/Transportation/bikemap/keymap.html

Airports

Chicago/O'Hare International Airport
www.flychicago.com
  and click "**O'Hare**"

Midway International Airport
www.flychicago.com
  and click "**Midway**"

Intercity Trains

Amtrak
Union Station
225 South Canal Street
www.amtrak.com

Intercity Bus

Greyhound Stations
630 West Harrison Street
14 West 95th Street

CTA Transit Building
5800 North Cumberland Avenue
www.greyhound.com

Interstate Highways

I-94 (East/west from Milwaukee to South Bend, Indiana)
I-55 (South from Bloomington, Illinois)
I-57 (South from Kankakee, Illinois)
I-88 (East from DeKalb, Illinois)
I-80 (East/west from Davenport, Iowa, to South Bend, Indiana)
I-90 (East/west from Rockford, Illinois, to South Bend, Indiana)

Philadelphia, Pennsylvania

Philadelphia's nickname has long been the City of Brotherly Love. Now, the *National Geographic Traveler* has dubbed Philadelphia the "Next Great City"—and the new name could stick. The article goes on to say, "After decades of relative obscurity, Philadelphia, a classic American city, is ready to step back into the national limelight," and references hipsters and youngsters who are flocking here. Here are five reasons why this dynamic city would also make a remarkable place to retire.

1. **New York "lite"**

Introducing Old City, Rittenhouse Square, Washington Square West, Queen Village, and several other urban enclaves that have the flavor, energy, and diversity of New York neighborhoods like Greenwich Village, SoHo, etcetera. Philadelphia's are every bit as interesting, but with a cozier, smaller-scale feeling than the Big Apple's more famous enclaves.

2. **Second most populous**

Philadelphia's dynamic downtown has a lot to do with its substantial residential population. In 2000, the Brookings Institution reported that Center City Philadelphia had 78,349 residents, making it the second most populous downtown area in the United States behind New York's Lower Manhattan's 97,752. In 2005, the Center City Association estimates that nearly 90,000 people live in its core neighborhoods. This area is also a young population: 30 percent of residents are between twenty-five and thirty-four years old, and 79 percent have college degrees. Ruppies will enjoy the density and youthful vibrancy that Philadelphia provides.

3. **Pedestrian's dream city**
   In the late 1600s, William Penn, an English Quaker, had an ingenious vision for Philadelphia's original street plan. He laid the city between the Schuylkill and Delaware rivers with a north/south axis centered on a square, and four outlying squares joined by an extremely tight series of city blocks. Penn's three-hundred-year-old blueprint is the reason Philadelphia is one of the most pedestrian-friendly cities in America. As a result, Philly's neighborhoods resemble tiny European villages.

4. **What a rich history**
   Philadelphia was the largest and one of the most important cities in Colonial America. Today's residents walk the same streets as Ben Franklin and George Washington and bask in the splendor of colonial architecture. Some of the most revered structures from American history are here, including Independence Hall, originally completed in 1753 and home to the Second Continental Congress and the Liberty Bell, still with its famous crack. Edgar Allan Poe's house, the Betsy Ross House, and the awe-inspiring Christ Church are all in the area. Ancient row houses line old cobblestone streets throughout the city complete with mature, shady trees. Of all people, history buffs and historic preservation enthusiasts will love life in Philadelphia.

5. **Urban arts mecca**
   Philadelphia is one of America's sophisticated urban experiences. The Avenue of the Arts, Philly's signature north-south downtown street, is a concentration of theaters, fifty restaurants, numerous arts schools and colleges, and the city's most important music and performance venues. Benjamin Franklin Parkway is the city's version of the Champs Elysées, a gorgeous urban boulevard with striking statues, fountains, and anchored by the Philadelphia Museum of Art. Many of the other neighborhoods have their own arts districts with a range of galleries, fine cuisine, and specialty stores.

Target Retirement Districts and Neighborhoods

Center City proper is between the Schuylkill and Delaware rivers and bounded north/south by the Vine Street Expressway and South Street. The epicenter of the central business district is Penn Square where the city's main streets, Broad Street and Market converge at city hall, the structure that is topped by the famed statue of William Penn. The following are the primary retirement destination neighborhoods within the official center city.

Southwest

Neighborhoods in southwest Center City include posh Rittenhouse Square and Fitler Square.

Rittenhouse Square

Philadelphia's well-appointed hotels, charming boutiques, and finest restaurants are concentrated around this impeccably landscaped, tree-filled square. Luxury apartments and expensive high-rise condominiums are on the surrounding streets. Inside the square, locals and workers can enjoy the beautiful park with its public art, flower markets, and art shows.

Rittenhouse Square is the area between South Street (south), Market Street (north), Broad Street (east), and the Schuylkill River (west). For more information, visit the Center City Residents' Association Web site at **www .centercityresidents.org**.

Fitler Square

Southwest of Rittenhouse Square is Fitler Square, centered on a lovely half-acre park along Pine Street. The neighborhood has cobblestone streets, rows of single-family homes, quaint storefronts, and is only a few blocks from the new Schuylkill River Park. It's just a quick walk to biking and hiking trails, the dog run, and the tennis courts of Schuylkill, besides being close to all the amenities in Rittenhouse Square.

Fitler Square blends into the Rittenhouse Square neighborhood and is generally considered to be the area bounded by South Street (south), Spruce Street (north), 22nd Street (east), and the Schuylkill River (west). For more information and a business directory, visit the Fitler Square Improvement Association's Web site at **www.fitlersquare.org**.

Logan Square (Northwest)

Logan Square is the northwestern square in Penn's city plan. You can follow the roundabout past the Swann Memorial Fountain as you go to and from the Art Museum to Penn Square. Residents can enjoy walks along Benjamin Franklin Parkway, have close access to the popular park setting of Kelly Drive, enjoy the activity of Penn Square, and take in the elegance of nearby Rittenhouse Square.

Logan Square is bounded by Spring Garden Street (north), Broad Street (east), Market Street (south), and the Schuylkill River (west). For more information, visit the Logan Square Neighborhood Association Web site at **www.lsnaphilly.org**.

Old City (Northeast)

This neighborhood east of Chinatown and Franklin Square is home to Elfreth's Alley, the first continuously inhabited street in America. The area is known for its mix of new-old warehouses, vintage row houses, hip residents, and for its robust art scene. Old City's art galleries and boutiques, mostly along Second Street, are host to "First Friday," a celebration of the arts held on the first Friday of every month. The area also boasts several of Philadelphia's trendiest restaurants and outdoor cafés.

Old City is bounded by Callowhill Street (north), Chestnut and Walnut streets (south), the Delaware River (east), and 8th Street (west). For more information, visit the Old City Civic Association's Web site at **www.oldcity.org** and **www.oldcityarts.org**.

Southeast

Washington Square West and Society Hill make up the southeast Center City neighborhoods.

Washington Square West

"Wash West," west of Penn's southeastern square, is filled with coffee shops, bookstores, and nightclubs, and known for its substantial gay and lesbian population. Wash West has several notable business corridors such as America's oldest diamond district (ca. 1851) along Samson and 8th streets called Jeweler's Row. Pine Street is popular for its antiques, and the closeby Avenue of the Arts allows residents easy access to the theater, opera, and great shopping and dining opportunities.

Wash West is officially bounded by 8th Street (east), Market Street (north), Broad Street (Avenue of the Arts) (west), and South Street (south). For more information, visit the Washington Square West Civic Association at **www.washwestcivic.org**.

Society Hill

Contemporary condominiums, high-rise residential towers, and seventeenth-century colonial homes share cobblestone streets and tidy alleyways here. You can also find Independence National Park, the Liberty Bell, historic Washington Square, and the adjacent Penn's Landing restaurant and retail complex along the Delaware River. Just to the north is the Old City neighborhood, and the energy of South Street flanks Society Hill's southern boundary.

Society Hill's boundaries are Walnut Street (north), South Street (south), 6th Street (west), and the Delaware River (east). See the Society Hill Civic Associations' Web site at **www.societyhillcivic.com**.

Center City "Adjacent"

Center City's quality urban living opportunities don't stop at the Vine Street Expressway or at South Street. You can still live a good distance from Penn Square and enjoy a downtown lifestyle. The following neighborhoods are growing and redeveloping and are definitely worth considering.

Queen Village (Southeast)

Queen Village is one of the oldest neighborhoods in Philadelphia and easily one of the city's most desirable neighborhoods. Settled by Swedes in the late 1600s, before William Penn, the neighborhood was named for Queen Christina of Sweden. The Village features rows of Victorian-era homes, new and older row homes, grand old mid-rise buildings, parks, and packed side-walks. The 4th Street Fabric Row, a historic commercial district between South and Catherine streets, has long been the source for dressmakers, interior designers, and upholsters. Most notably, Queen Village is adjacent to and south of Society Hill and bordering South Street, one of Philadelphia's most fun shopping, entertainment, and restaurant corridors.

Queen Village is bounded by South 5th Street and East Passyunk Avenue (west), South Street (north), Delaware River (east), and Washington Avenue (south). For more information, see the Queen Village Neighbors Association at **www.qvna.org**. Also check South Street at **www.southstreet.com**.

Bella Vista (South Central)

Bella Vista, covering thirty blocks, combines the sensibility of South Philly with the splendor of Center City in a series of charming narrow streets, quaint homes, and businesses. It is pure Philly and home to the 9th Street Italian Street Market between Hall and Ellsworth. There are more than one hundred merchants offering breads, meats, fresh pasta, and a mix of other ethnic foods, and the famed Geno's Steaks, home of the Philly Cheese Steak Sandwich, is only a few blocks south.

Bella Vista is between South Street (north), Broad Street (west), South 5th and East Passyunk Avenue (east), and Washington Avenue (south). For restaurants, services, and other neighborhood information, see the Bella Vista United Civic Association at **www.bvuca.org**.

Southwest Center City

This area, sometimes called "SoSo" for South of South Street, is now considered an up-and-coming neighborhood. SoSo, about ten blocks south of Rittenhouse Square and anchored by Graduate Hospital on South Street, is on the rebound, with a particularly strong neighborhood association that's making good things happen here.

Southwest Center City's boundaries are South Street (north), Broad Street (east), the Schuylkill River (west), and Washington Avenue (south). For more information, visit the South of South Neighborhood Association's Web site at **www.southofsouth.org**.

Northern Liberties (Northeast)

As documented in the *New York Times*, Northern Liberties, a warehouse and row house district, has attracted artists from both Philadelphia and New York who are seeking lower rents and a higher quality of life. Northern Liberties (and "Fishtown" to the east) continues its reputation along the East Coast as the new up-and-coming neighborhood and a hotspot for the cool set.

Northern Liberties is generally north of Old City under I-676, between the Delaware River to 7th Street, and all the way to Girard Street on the north. For more, including shops, restaurants, real estate, and news, see **www.northernliberties.org**.

Downtown Philadelphia Essentials

Penn's Landing: Penn's Landing is on the western bank of the Delaware River adjacent to Society Hill. Residents from all over Philly visit this area for dinner and drinks in one of the many waterfront restaurants, summer concerts at the Festival Pier, and Jam on the River, a weekend of Creole and Cajun cooking and jazz. Don't forget ice skating, New Year's Eve, and the Fourth of July fireworks, and anticipate the city's first casino.

Chinatown: Northeast of Penn Square near the Philadelphia Convention

Dining al fresco along the recently revitalized West Chestnut Street corridor. (Photo courtesy of the Center City District, Philadelphia.)

Center, Philly residents can "visit" Asia as they pass under the Friendship Arch at 10th and Arch streets, enjoy authentic Chinese food, and browse through a variety of shops.

Mummer's Parade: In a New Year's Day tradition dating back to the 1700s, "Mummers" parade down Market Street toward city hall. Clowns begin the procession, followed by the crowd in fancy, colorful costumes, and then the string bands of glockenspiels and banjos. It's topped off with a "fancy brigade" contest, where brass bands play for marchers and dancers.

Geno's Steaks: Stop south of Bella Vista on 9th Street at Geno's Steaks for an original Philly Cheese Steak.

Playing Rocky: If you remember the original movie *Rocky*, you might not be able to resist running up the stairs of the Philadelphia Art Museum, throwing a few jabs into an invisible punching bag, and perhaps even a long yell, "*Adrian!*" It's a fun way to transition into a local Philadelphian.

General Statistics

Population: Center City: 78,349 (2000); City: 1,470,151 (2003); Metro: 5,772,947 (2003)

Terrain: Center City Philadelphia is generally flat and is situated between the Schuylkill River on the west and Delaware River on the east.

Climate Overview: cold winters/warm summers

Average January high/low temperature: 39/24F

Average July high/low temperature: 87/68F

Average annual total precipitation: 41 inches

Average annual snowfall: 21 inches

Number of cloudy days: 160

Cost of Living: Find out the current cost of living between Philadelphia and your community by visiting **www.homefair.com** and clicking **"Moving to a New State"** or **"Moving Locally,"** then follow the prompts.

Cost of Housing:

Zip code: 19103 (Rittenhouse Square, Logan Square, Fitler Square); price snapshot: $758,332; sq/ft: 1,903

Zip code: 19106 (Old City, Society Hill); price snapshot: $638,923; sq/ft: 1,861

Zip code: 19107 (Washington Square West, Chinatown); price snapshot: $421,690; sq/ft: 1,326

Zip code: 19123 (Northern Liberties); price snapshot: $325,737; sq/ft: 1,760

Zip code: 19146 (Southwest Center City and areas south); price snapshot: $226,017; sq/ft: 1,358

Zip code: 19147 (Queen Village, Bella Vista, and South Philadelphia); price snapshot: $376,753; sq/ft: 1,656

Real estate prices fluctuate. For up-to-date neighborhood housing cost information, input the zip codes above in the Homestore Web site (affiliated with Realtor.com) at **www.homestore.com/Cities**.

Rent Costs: If you want to rent, explore **www.rentnet.com** and also investigate the neighborhood Web sites for current rents and available properties.

Taxes

Property Tax: Varies widely by location. See the City Department of Revenue for specifics and updates: **www.phila.gov/revenue**.

Sales Tax: 7 percent. No sales tax for groceries and prescription drugs.

City Income Tax: 4.301 percent.

State Income Tax: 3.07 percent flat rate. No personal deductions.

Downtown Philadelphia Retirement Lifestyle Web Guide

Living

Find out more about urban residential real estate by visiting the Central Philadelphia Development Corporation's Web site at **www.centercityphila.org**. Then click "**Links**" for a listing of Realtor companies specializing in Center City neighborhoods and their Web site links.

City Hospitals

Graduate Hospital
1800 Lombard Street
www.graduatehospital.com

Hahnemann University Hospital
Broad and Vine streets
www.hahnemannhospital.com

Hospital of the University
  of Pennsylvania
3400 Spruce Street
www.pennhealth.com

Pennsylvania Hospital
800 Spruce Street
www.pennhealth.com/pahosp

Thomas Jefferson University Hospital
111 South 11th Street
www.jeffersonhospital.org

Health Clubs

An updated, comprehensive list of health clubs is available by visiting the Center City Development Corporation's Web site at **www.centercityphila.org** and clicking "**Living Here**," then "**Residential Resources**," and then "**Health and Fitness**."

Volunteering

United Way of
  Southeastern Pennsylvania
Seven Benjamin Franklin Parkway
www.uwsepa.org and click
  "**Volunteer**"

Southeastern Pennsylvania Red Cross
23rd and Chestnut streets
www.redcross-philly.org
  and click "**Volunteer Now**"

Educational opportunities

City Colleges and Universities

The Art Institute of Philadelphia
23rd and Chestnut Streets
www.aiph.artinstitutes.edu

Community College of Philadelphia
1700 Spring Garden Street
www.ccp.edu

Drexel University
3141 Chestnut Street
www.drexel.edu

Moore College of Art
20th Street and the Parkway
www.moore.edu

Pennsylvania Academy
 of the Fine Arts
1301 Cherry Street
www.pafa.org

Saint Joseph's University
5600 City Avenue
www.sju.edu

Thomas Jefferson University
 (medical related)
1020 Walnut Street
www.jefferson.edu

University of the Sciences
 in Philadelphia
600 South 43rd Street
www.usip.edu

La Salle University
1900 West Olney Avenue
www.lasalle.edu

Peirce College
1420 Pine Street
www.peirce.edu

Philadelphia University
School House Lane and
 Henry Avenue
www.philau.edu

Temple University
1801 North Broad Street
www.temple.edu

University of the Arts
320 South Broad Street
www.uarts.edu

University of Pennsylvania
3451 Walnut Street
www.upenn.edu

Libraries
Free Library of Philadelphia
 (main branch)
1901 Vine Street

Independence Branch
18 South 7th Street

City Institute Branch
1905 Locust Street

Southwark
7th and Carpenter streets
www.library.phila.gov

Entertainment

Restaurants, Bars, and Nightclubs

For a list of Center City's incredible array of restaurants, visit **www.center cityphila.org**, then click "**Shopping and Dining**," then "**Restaurants**" for a list of participating establishments.

For nightlife information click "**Going Out**," then "**Center City Nightlife**" for an up-to-date list of hot spots. Also check each neighborhood's Web site for additional current listings.

Professional Spectator Sports

Philadelphia Eagles (football)
Lincoln Financial Field,
 1020 Pattison Avenue
www.philadelphiaeagles.com

Philadelphia Phillies (baseball)
Citizens Bank Park,
 1001 Pattison Avenue
www.phillies.com

Philadelphia 76ers (basketball)
Wachovia Center,
 3601 South Broad Street
www.nba.com/sixers

Philadelphia Flyers (hockey)
Wachovia Center,
 3601 South Broad Street
www.philadelphiaflyers.com

Philadelphia Soul (football)
Wachovia Center,
 3601 South Broad Street
www.philadelphiasoul.com

College Sports

Drexel University
3141 Chestnut Street
Men's and women's basketball, crew, lacrosse, soccer, swimming and diving,
 tennis, men's golf, wrestling, women's field hockey, softball
www.drexeldragons.com

LaSalle University
1900 West Olney Avenue
Men's and women's basketball, cross-country, soccer, swimming and diving,

tennis, track and field, men's baseball, crew, football, golf, women's field hockey, lacrosse, volleyball
www.goexplorers.com

Philadelphia University
School House Lane and Henry Avenue
Men's and women's basketball, cross-country, soccer, men's baseball, golf, women's field hockey, lacrosse, softball, tennis, volleyball
www.philau.edu/athletics

Saint Joseph's University
5600 City Avenue
Men's and women's basketball, cross-country, lacrosse, rowing, track and field, soccer, tennis, men's baseball, golf, women's field hockey, softball
http://sjuhawks.cstv.com

Temple University
1801 North Broad Street
Men's and women's basketball, crew, cross-country, gymnastics, soccer, tennis, track and field, men's baseball, football, golf, women's fencing, field hockey, lacrosse, softball, volleyball
www.owlsports.com

University of Pennsylvania
3451 Walnut Street
Baseball, basketball, fencing, golf, lacrosse, rowing, soccer, squash, swimming, tennis, track and field, men's baseball, football, wrestling, women's gymnastics, softball
www.pennathletics.com

The Performing Arts

Opera Company of Philadelphia
Academy of Music,
　1420 Locust Street,
　Avenue of the Arts District
www.operaphilly.com

The Chamber Orchestra of Philadelphia
The Kimmel Center for the
　Performing Arts, 1520 Locust Street,
　Avenue of the Arts District
www.chamberorchestra.org

The Philadelphia Orchestra
The Kimmel Center for the
  Performing Arts, 1520 Locust Street,
  Avenue of the Arts District
www.philorch.org

Philadelphia Theatre Company
Plays & Players Theater,
  1714 Delancey Street,
  Rittenhouse Square
www.phillytheatreco.com

Society Hill Playhouse
507 South Eighth Street,
  Society Hill
www.societyhillplayhouse.com

For a large listing of theaters and productions, see the Theatre Alliance of Greater Philadelphia Web site at **www.theatrealliance.org**.

Major Museums

Academy of Natural Sciences
1900 Ben Franklin Parkway,
  Logan Square
www.acnatsci.org

Atwater Kent Museum
15 South 7th Street,
  Washington Square West
www.philadelphiahistory.org

Franklin Institute Science Museum
222 North 20th Street,
  Logan Square
www.fi.edu

Independence Hall and the Liberty Bell
313 Walnut Street, Old City
www.nps.gov/inde

Independence Seaport Museum
Penn's Landing at 211 South
  Christopher Columbus Boulevard,
  Society Hill
www.phillyseaport.org

Mummers Museum
1100 South 2nd Street,
  Queen Village
www.mummersmuseum.com

National Constitution Center
525 Arch Street, Independence
  Mall, Old City
www.constitutioncenter.org

Philadelphia Museum of Art
Benjamin Franklin Parkway
  and 26th Street
www.philamuseum.org

Rosenbach Museum and Library
2008 Delancey Place,
  Rittenhouse Square
www.rosenbach.org

Rodin Museum
Benjamin Franklin Parkway
  and 22nd Street, Logan Square
www.rodinmuseum.org

Special Events (Best Bets)

Equality Forum Fest
May. Gay/lesbian festival
www.equalityforum.com

First Friday
First Friday of the month arts walk
  in Old City
www.oldcityarts.org

International Dragon Boat Festival
October. Schuylkill River
www.philadragonboatfestival.com

Jam on the River
May. Music and food festival at
  Penn's Landing
www.jamontheriver.com

Mummers Parade
January 1 on Broad Street.
Most unbelievable parade ever
www.mummers.com

Odunde
June. African American
  heritage festival
www.odundeinc.org

Philadelphia Folk Festival
August. Folk music, dance, crafts
www.folkfest.org

Philadelphia Film Festival
March/April. Various venues
www.phillyfests.com

Welcome America Festival
July Fourth celebration
  in Center City
www.americasbirthday.com

St. Patrick's Day Parade
www.philadelphiastpatsparade.com

Movie Theaters

Ritz 5
  214 Walnut Street
Ritz at the Bourse
  400 Ranstead Street
Ritz East
  125 South 2nd Street
www.ritztheaters.com

Roxy Theater
2023 Sansom Street

United Artist Riverview Plaza 17
1400 South Columbus Boulevard
www.uatc.co

Favorite Downtown Parks

For more information on Philadelphia's city parks, visit **www.fairmount park.org**.

Fairmount Park
East Park and West Park along the
Schuylkill River

Independence National Historic Park
313 Walnut Street

JFK Plaza
Square created by Benjamin Franklin
Parkway, North 16th Street, North
15th Street, and John F. Kennedy
Boulevard

Logan Square
Convergence of Race Street, Benjamin
Franklin Parkway, Vine Street, and
19th Street

Rittenhouse Square
Square created by South 19th Street,
South 18th Street, Walnut Street,
and Rittenhouse Square

Schuylkill River Park
Riverpark and Dogwalk
25th and Delancey streets

Washington Square
Square created by South 6th Street,
Walnut Street, South Washington
Street, and West Washington Street

Shopping

Major Retail

Philadelphia, like all large cities, has enough stores to fill this entire book.
Center City Philadelphia provides an excellent way to browse available retail
stores. Visit **www.centercityphila.org** and click "**Residential Resources**" for
a comprehensive up-to-date listing. Also see each neighborhood's Web site for
additional details.

Groceries

Chef's Market (gourmet grocery)
231 South Street
www.chefsmkt.com

Essene Natural Foods
719 South 4th Street
www.essenemarket.com

Great Scot Rittenhouse Market
1733 Spruce Street

Superfresh
1001 South Street
5th and Pine streets
www.superfreshfood.com

Whole Foods
929 South Street
2001 Pennsylvania Avenue
www.wholefoods.com

South Square Thriftway
2221 South Street

Trader Joe's
2121 Market Street
www.traderjoes.com

City/Farmer's Markets

*Philadelphia 9th Street
  Italian Market*
9th Street from Wharton
  to Fitzwater streets
www.phillyitalianmarket.com

Fitler Square
23rd and Pine streets
www.fitlersquare.org

Reading Terminal Market
12th and Arch streets
www.readingterminalmarket.org

Rittenhouse Square
Walnut Street side
www.centercityphila.org

Getting around

Public Bus Service
Southeastern Pennsylvania Transportation Authority (SEPTA)
www.septa.org

City Bike Trails
www.septa.org

City Trains
Southeastern Pennsylvania Transportation Authority
Subway/trolley: **www.septa.org**
Regional rail: **www.septa.org**

Intercity Train

Amtrak
30th Street Station, 2955 Market Street
www.amtrak.com

Intercity Bus

Greyhound Terminal
1001 Filbert Street
www.greyhound.com

Airport

Philadelphia International Airport (PHL)
www.phl.org

Interstate Highways

I-95 (South/north from Wilmington, Delaware, to New York City, New York)
I-76 (West to Harrisburg, Pennsylvania)

San Francisco, California

San Francisco is the West Coast's dream city. Although much more laid-back and certainly more hilly, it has a lot in common with New York because of its large network of tight, dense, urban neighborhoods. The city by the Bay is compact, bounded by water on three sides and landlocked on one. Akin to Manhattan, San Francisco has one of the highest residential real estate prices in the country and is probably just a pipe dream for most people. But for those who can afford it, the following are five reasons retiring to San Francisco could be a dream come true.

1. **The city itself**

   San Francisco is filled with block after block of densely packed homes, restaurants, businesses, offices, and parks that line the tight streets. Its incredible architecture includes Victorian row homes, Spanish colonial revival structures, and cathedrals along urban corridors, such as trolley-intensive Market Street. It offers a beautiful waterfront, steep streets and hilly vistas, active sidewalks, and efficient public transportation. Most city connoisseurs who visit always find it tough to leave, and even tougher to come back down to earth when they arrive home.

2. **A vibe all its own**

   San Francisco is widely known as the most open-minded city, embracing human variety, cultural diversity, and alternative ideas and viewpoints. For example, the Castro District west of downtown is considered the gay capital of the world, while the Mission District's vibrant Hispanic community celebrates Latin culture in a variety of festivals and street fairs. And pinch yourself when walking through Chinatown to remind yourself that you're not in Beijing. San Francisco is a colorful, exciting city—its uniqueness is unparallelled.

3. **West Coast's best shopping**
San Francisco offers the best of both worlds: mom-and-pop specialty boutiques in every downtown neighborhood, along with mammoth department stores and multistory urban malls. Union Square is the third largest shopping area in the country and a consumer's paradise.

4. **Great restaurants**
San Francisco, like New York, has an array of restaurants waiting to be discovered. It's all there—from the extremely expensive and sophisticated to the smallest down-home diner—the choice is yours.

5. **Magnificent day trips**
Catch the ferry for a day of shopping in Sausalito, or take a drive to Napa or Sonoma Valley to explore the famous vineyards and sample wine at the wineries. Explore nearby Muir Woods and the towering redwoods, or take a ski trip to the Sierra Nevada Mountains and Lake Tahoe. You could hike under Yosemite National Park's waterfalls, or spend a day at the beach, or a weekend along Monterey Bay to play golf at Pebble Beach.

Target Retirement Districts and Neighborhoods

The entire northeast quadrant generally east of Van Ness Avenue is the most urban area. Target downtown neighborhoods include the core of downtown, South of Market (SoMa), North Beach and Telegraph Hill, Nob Hill, Russian Hill, and Civic Center/Hayes Valley.

Core of Downtown

The easternmost part features the tall skyscrapers of the **Financial District**, including the Transamerica Pyramid tower and many other corporate centers.

Within this area is the Embarcadero corridor, a street that flanks the piers and the historic Ferry Building. Moving west is the largest **Chinatown** in America, with its authentic food and unique shops. It's packed with tourists, and centered on Grant Avenue (beginning at Bush Street and under the arch). To the southwest along Post and Stockton streets is **Union Square**, one of the most impressive urban spaces in the world and arguably the best shopping on the West Coast. In the middle of the square, you'll find businesspeople having lunch, conventioneers watching street performers, and occasionally protest rallies may gather here. The grandeur of the historic St. Francis Hotel adds ambience and interest to an already fascinating area. The Theater District is just west of Union Square along Geary Street, where a variety of performances are held. The Tenderloin, the area west of Union Square between Mason and Polk streets, one of a few of the city's blighted areas in the midst of an otherwise posh neighborhood, transitions into the Civic Center District.

The core of downtown is a slender area generally between Market Street (south), Van Ness (west), and bounded by California, Stockton, and Broadway (north), and the San Francisco Bay (east). There's no downtown San Francisco Web site, but for more information, visit these local district sites: Union Square Business Improvement District at **www.unionsquarebid.com**, and Chinatown at **www.sanfranciscochinatown.com**.

Nob Hill and Russian Hill

Nob Hill, close to the adjacent Union Square District to the south, hosts many of San Francisco's fine restaurants and several luxury hotels. Cable cars, gingerbread-trimmed Victorian homes, and small, trendy boutiques can be seen in this exclusive residential area. Grace Cathedral with its stunning architecture and Huntington Park, the area's most beloved park, can also be found here.

Russian Hill, north of Nob Hill, is best known for Lombard Street, the "crookedest street in the world." The neighborhood is proud of its stairways that are manicured with gorgeous vegetation and well-maintained landscaping. At the center of the area, Hyde and Union are surrounded by expensive homes and apartments, many with great views of Fisherman's Wharf, San Francisco Bay, and the skyscrapers in the financial district.

Nob Hill is bounded north and south by Broadway and Bush streets, and east and west by Van Ness Avenue and Stockton Street. Russian Hill splits Nob Hill at Broadway and extends north to Bay Street, and is bounded on the west and east by Van Ness Avenue and Columbus and Mason streets. For more information, visit the Nob Hill Association's Web site at **www.nob hillassociation.org** and Russian Hill Neighbors at **www.rhn.org**.

South of Market (SoMa)

Once an industrial and warehouse area, South of Market Street is about twenty blocks between the Embarcadero and the Mission District and features the Moscone Convention Center, the Yerba Buena Gardens, the San Francisco Museum of Modern Art, and the California Academy of Sciences. Residents here can enjoy South Park, a small gem of trees and fountains between 2nd and 3rd streets, or the walk to a Giants baseball game at SBC Park, in the easternmost South Beach District. This is a trendy neighborhood with cafés, restaurants, and dance clubs. Since the area is enjoying the lion's share of the downtown residential development momentum, it offers choices for new high-rise condominiums and warehouse lofts.

South of Market is bounded by Market Street (north/south), Townsend (south), 12th Street (west), and by Embarcadero (east). Currently, there is no active Web site for SoMa.

North Beach and Telegraph Hill

North Beach, the center of the 1960s "Beat Generation" and San Francisco's version of Little Italy, is a great place to shop, stop for lunch or dinner, or hit the clubs. Columbus Avenue, the neighborhood's main commercial corridor, is lined with interesting stores and cafés, most concentrating on Italian cuisine. One of the city's notable urban spaces is Washington Square, a park that is bordered by the ancient Romanesque Church of Saints Peter and Paul and is the setting for festivals and special events, including the Oyster Festival. Farther east North Beach blends into Telegraph Hill, which is centered on the slopes of a hill of the same name that's topped by Coit Tower—the observation tower frequented by tourists. Residents in this quiet neighborhood can easily walk to Columbus Avenue, the Financial District, and the piers along the Embarcadero corridor.

North Beach is the area generally bounded between Broadway (south), the Embarcadero (east), North Point Street (north), and Columbus Street (west). For more information, visit San Francisco's Historic North Beach Web site at **www.sfnorthbeach.org**. Also see Telegraph Hill Dwellers at **www.thd.org**.

Civic Center/Hayes Valley

The Civic Center District houses government and culture. City Hall's golden dome resembles a state capitol and is the most prominent and classic structure here. The War Memorial Opera House, Davies Symphony Hall, and the Asian Art Museum are also important district anchors. Open urban parks and formal lawns combined with the surrounding historic structures resemble cities in Europe. The Haynes Valley neighborhood, just west across Franklin Street, has become one of the trendiest shopping spots in the city. Design studios, art stores and galleries, cool restaurants, and mom-and-pop specialty stores make this neighborhood a local treasure.

Civic Center is the general area between California Street (north), Polk (east), Market (south), and Franklin Street (west). Hayes Valley is bounded by Market Street (south), Franklin Street (east), Webster (west), and Fulton Street (north). For more information, visit the Hayes Valley Neighborhood Association's Web site at **www.hayesvalleysf.org**.

Downtown San Francisco Essentials

Ferry trips: Take a ferry and enjoy a day of shopping and dining in quaint Sausalito and other destinations in Marin County.

Street cars: MUNI metro's historic electric streetcars run frequently along Market and other major streets and provide a fun and functional ride to most parts of the city.

Strengthening muscles: Walking up and down the hills of the city will strengthen your calves and leg muscles.

Earthquake insurance: Since the city is near the San Andreas Fault, occasionally tremors can be expected, but this hasn't stopped locals from enjoying San Francisco's one-of-a-kind urban lifestyle.

Celebrating the Chinese New Year: Make your way to Chinatown for a fabulous, extravagant parade on the Chinese New Year (date varies according to the Chinese calendar).

General Statistics

Population: Downtown: 43,531 (2000); City: 744,230 (2003) Metro: 4,157,377 (2003)

Terrain: Downtown San Francisco is surrounded by views of San Francisco Bay and has a variety of topographies. It's flat near the Bay with steep hills and valleys not far inland.

Climate Overview: mild winters/cool summers

Average January high/low temperature: 56/46F

Average July high/low temperature: 66/54F

Average annual total precipitation: 21 inches

Average annual snowfall: <.01 inches

Number of cloudy days: 105

Cost of Living: Find out the current cost of living between San Francisco and your community by visiting **www.homefair.com** and clicking **"Moving to a New State"** or **"Moving Locally,"** then follow the prompts.

Cost of Housing:

Zip code: 94102 (Hayes Valley, Civic Center); price snapshot: $818,461; sq/ft: 3,152

Zip code: 94103 (West half of SoMa); price snapshot: $774,086; sq/ft: 1,783

Zip code: 94105 (Financial District); price snapshot: $718,520; sq/ft: 998

Zip code: 94109 (Nob Hill, Russian Hill); price snapshot: $1,144,202; sq/ft: 3,452

Zip code: 94111 (Financial District/Embarcadero); price snapshot: $824,914; sq/ft: 1,508

Zip code: 94133 (North Beach, Telegraph Hill); price snapshot: $1,366,113; sq/ft: 2,406

Real Estate prices fluctuate. For up-to-date neighborhood housing cost information, input the zip codes above in the Homestore Web site (affiliated with Realtor.com) at **www.homestore.com/Cities**.

Rent Costs: If you want to rent, explore **www.rentnet.com** and also investigate the neighborhood Web sites for current rents and available properties.

Taxes

Property Tax: 1.1400 percent, applied to the net assessed property value as determined by the county assessor. Stay current with property tax assessments by visiting **www.sfgov.org/site/assessor_index.asp**.

Sales Tax: 8.25 percent. Food and prescription drugs are exempted.

State Income Tax: 1.0 percent to 9.3 percent. (Six income tax brackets. Single: low $6,319 to high $41,477 and over, with additional 1 percent over $1,000,000. Filing jointly: Joint returns taxes are twice the tax imposed on half the income.)

Downtown San Francisco Retirement Lifestyle Web Guide

Living

San Francisco has no downtown organization Web site. Contact a local Realtor by browsing the San Francisco Association of Realtors at **www.sfrealtors.com**.

City Hospitals

California Pacific Medical Center
California Campus
  3700 California Street
Davies Campus
  Castro Street and Duboce Avenue
Pacific Campus
  2333 Buchanan Street
East Campus
  3698 California Street
www.cpmc.org

Kaiser Permanente Medical Center
Geary Campus
  2425 Geary Boulevard
French Campus
  4131 Geary Boulevard
www.kaiserpermanente.org

Laguna Honda Hospital
375 Laguna Honda Boulevard
www.dph.sf.ca.us/chn/
   LagunaHondaHosp

St. Francis Memorial Hospital
900 Hyde Street
www.saintfrancismemorial.org

St. Luke's Hospital
3555 Caesar Chavez Street
www.stlukes-sf.org

St. Mary's Medical Center
450 Stanyan Street
www.stmarysmedicalcenter.org

San Francisco General Hospital
1001 Potrero Avenue
www.dph.sf.ca.us/chn/SFGH

University of California,
  San Francisco
Medical Center
  (Moffitt and Long Hospital)
505 Parnassus Avenue
www.ucsfmedicalcenter.org

University of California,
  San Francisco
Mount Zion Medical Center
1600 Divisadero Street
www.ucsfmedicalcenter.org

Health Clubs

San Francisco has the most downtown sports and fitness clubs—more than any city featured in this book. Here are several of the best bets:

24 Hour Fitness
100 California Street,
   Financial District
303 2nd Street in SoMa
1200 Van Ness Avenue, between
   Civic Center and Nob Hill
1645 Bryant Street,
   Mission District bordering SoMa
www.24hourfitness.com

Gold's Gym—San Francisco
1001 Brannan Street, SoMa
www.goldsgym.com

Crunch Fitness
61 New Montgomery Street
   in the Financial District
1000 Van Ness Avenue in the
   Civic Center/Tenderloin District
www.crunch.com

Pinnacle Fitness
1 Post Street in the
   Financial District
345 Spear Street in South
   Beach/SoMa
www.pinnaclefitness.com

Club One Fitness Club
Union Square, 535 Mason Street
Federal Fitness at the Civic Center,
   450 Golden Gate Avenue
2 Embarcadero Center,
   Financial District
Citicorp Center, 1 Sansome Street
   950 California Street in Nob Hill
Yerba Buena in SoMa
www.clubone.com

San Francisco Bay Club
150 Greenwich Street, Telegraph
   Hill/Embarcadero
www.sfbayclub.com

San Francisco Tennis Club
645 5th Street in SoMa
www.sftennis.com

Volunteering

The Volunteer Center
www.thevolunteercenter.net

American Red Cross Bay Area Chapter
www.bayarea-redcross.org
   and click "**Volunteer**"

Educational opportunities

City Colleges and Universities

Academy of Art College
79 New Montgomery Street
   in SoMa
www.academyart.edu

California Culinary Academy
625 Polk Street in the
   Civic Center District
www.baychef.com

Alliant International University
1 Beach Street, Fisherman's Wharf
www.alliant.edu

City College of San Francisco
Downtown Campus
   88 4th Street
Alemany Campus
   750 Eddy Street
Chinatown Campus
   940 Filbert Street
Mission Campus
   50 Phelan Avenue
www.ccsf.org

Golden Gate University
536 Mission Street,
   SoMa/Financial District
www.ggu.edu

University of California Hastings
  College of the Law
200 McAllister Street,
  Civic Center/Tenderloin District
www.uchastings.edu

Heald College
350 Mission Street,
  SoMa/Financial District
www.heald.edu

San Francisco Law School
20 Haight Street,
  Civic Center/Mission District
www.sfls.edu

San Francisco State University
1600 Holloway Avenue,
  Stonestown neighborhood
www.sfsu.edu

University of California,
  San Francisco (medical)
505 Parnassus Avenue
www.ucsf.edu

University of San Francisco
2130 Fulton Street, Haight-
  Ashbury/Long Mountain area
www.usfca.edu

Libraries
San Francisco Public Library
100 Larkin Street at Grove Street

Chinatown Branch
1135 Powell Street

Mission Bay Branch
4th and Berry streets

North Beach Library
2000 Mason Street
http://sfpl.lib.ca.us

Entertainment

Restaurants, Bars, and Nightclubs
Going out in downtown San Francisco is a matter of walking down the street and choosing from innumerable dining and nightlife establishments. San Francisco Gate (San Francisco Chronicle online) is the best place to browse: **www.sfgate.com**, then click "**Entertainment**" and/or "**Food and Dining**" for hundreds of fun places. Also explore the neighborhood Web sites for current local lists.

Professional Spectator Sports

San Francisco 49ers (football)
Monster Park, 602 Jamestown
   Avenue, far southeast
www.sf49ers.com

Oakland Athletics (baseball)
Take BART to McAfee Coliseum
   in Oakland
www.oaklandathletics.com

San Francisco Giants (baseball)
AT&T Park, 24 Willie Mays Plaza
   in South Beach/SoMa
www.sfgiants.com

Golden State Warriors (basketball)
Take BART to McAfee Coliseum
   in Oakland
www.nba.com/warriors

College Sports

San Francisco State University Gator Athletics
1600 Holloway Avenue, Stonestown neighborhood in far southwest
Men's and women's basketball, cross-country, soccer, men's baseball,
   wrestling, women's softball, indoor and outdoor track and field
http://athletics.sfsu.edu

University of San Francisco Dons Athletics
West of downtown in the Haight-Ashbury/Lone Mountain area
Men's and women's basketball, cross-country, golf, soccer, rifle, tennis,
   men's baseball, women's track and volleyball
http://usfdons.cstv.com

The Performing Arts

San Francisco Ballet
War Memorial Opera House,
   301 Van Ness Avenue,
Civic Center District
www.sfballet.org

San Francisco Opera
War Memorial Opera House,
   301 Van Ness Avenue,
Civic Center District
www.sfopera.com

San Francisco Symphony
Davies Symphony Hall,
   201 Van Ness Avenue,
Civic Center District
www.sfsymphony.org

Palace of Fine Arts Theater
3601 Lyon Street, Marina District
www.palaceoffinearts.org

For theater companies' daily performance listings, show times, and venue locations, see the Theatre Bay Area's Web site at **www.theatrebayarea.org**.

Major Museums

Asian Art Museum of San Francisco
200 Larkin Street,
   Civic Center District
www.asianart.org

California Academy of Sciences
California Natural History Museum,
   Morrison Planetarium,
   and Steinhart Aquarium
875 Howard Street, SoMa
www.calacademy.org

Cable Car Museum
1201 Mason Street, Nob Hill
www.cablecarmuseum.com

Contemporary Jewish Museum
121 Steuart Street,
   Financial District
www.jmsf.org

Fine Arts Museum of San Francisco
In Golden Gate Park and the
   Legion of Honor in Lincoln Park
www.thinker.org

Mexican Museum
Mission and 3rd streets
www.mexicanmuseum.org

San Francisco Museum
   of Modern Art
151 3rd Street, SoMa
www.sfmoma.org

San Francisco Performing Arts
   Library and Museum
401 Van Ness Avenue,
   Civic Center District
www.sfpalm.org

Yerba Buena Center for the Arts
701 Mission Street, SoMa
www.ybca.org

Wells Fargo History Museum
420 Montgomery Street,
   Financial District
www.wellsfargohistory.com

Special Events (Best Bets)

It's possible to go to a festival or special event every day in San Francisco. The following are some of the standouts.

Carnaval San Francisco Festival and Parade
May. Pre-Lent Mardi Gras–inspired Latin American music and arts festival

and parade and California's largest multicultural celebration. Held in the Mission District just southwest of downtown.
www.carnavalsf.com

Chinese New Year Festival and Parade
February. Elaborate floats, costumes, fanfare, and fireworks in Chinatown
www.chineseparade.com

Fourth of July Waterfront Festival
July 4. San Francisco's Fourth of July party with food, music, and fireworks in Fisherman's Wharf
www.pier39.com

Ghirardelli Square Chocolate Festival
September. Celebration of fine chocolate in Fisherman's Wharf
www.ghirardellisq.com

How Weird Street Faire
May. A celebration of weirdness in SoMa along Howard (How-weird) Street
www.howweird.org

KaBoom!
May. Fireworks and concerts on Pier 31
www.kfog.com

Litquake
October. Authors and poets speak at various venues around town
www.litquake.org

LGBT Pride Parade and Festival
June. "Biggest gay pride parade in the world"
www.sfpride.org

North Beach Jazz Festival
July. Local jazz talent performs in neighborhood celebrations
www.nbjazzfest.com

Oktoberfest by the Bay
October. German heritage, food, and beer celebration at the Fort Mason
    Center, Festival Pavilion, in the Marina District, northwest of downtown
www.oktoberfestbythebay.com

Oyster and Beer Festival
April. Oyster and beer in North Beach's Washington Square
www.oreillysoysterfestival.com

Russian Festival
February. Celebration of Russian arts, music, and food held at the Russian
    Center
www.russiancentersf.com

Saint Stupid's Day Parade
April 1. It's a San Francisco–only kind of April Fool's Day parade held in
    the Financial District
www.saintstupid.com

San Francisco Blues Festival
September. Billed as the oldest blues festival in America, and held at Fort
    Mason's Great Meadow in the Marina District, northwest of downtown
www.sfblues.com

San Francisco International Beer Festival
April. Enormous beer festival held at Fort Mason's Festival Pavilion in the
    Marina District, northwest of downtown
www.sfbeerfest.com

San Francisco Independent Film Festival
February. San Francisco's premier indie film festival, various venues
www.sfindie.com

San Francisco International Film Festival
April/May. Various venues throughout San Francisco
www.sffs.org

San Francisco Jazz Festival
October/November. Local, national, and international performances held
at various locations
www.sfjazz.org

Summerfest Festival
July. Choreographers' dance festival. Check Web site for locations
www.summerfestdance.org

Movie Theaters

Landmarks Embarcadero Cinema
1 Embarcadero Center
at Battery Street
www.landmarktheatres.com

Lumiere Theater
1572 California Street at Polk,
western Nob Hill area
www.landmarktheatres.com

Loews Theatre at Metreon
101 4th Street

Opera Plaza Cinema
601 Van Ness Avenue,
Civic Center neighborhood
www.landmarktheatres.com

Favorite Downtown Parks

For more information on San Francisco's city parks, visit the City and
County of San Francisco's Recreation and Parks Web site at **www.sfgov.org**,
then click "**City Agencies**" and then "**Recreation and Parks**." Also see the
San Francisco Neighborhood Parks Council Web site at **www.sfneighbor
hoodparks.org**.

Civic Center Plaza
Bounded by Polk, McAllister, Larkin, and Grove streets

Coit Tower/ Pioneer Park at Coit Tower
1 Telegraph Hill Boulevard in the Telegraph Hill neighborhood

Helen Wills Park and Playground
Corner of Larkin Street and Broadway in the Russian Hill neighborhood
www.sfneighborhoodparks.org/parkhistories/helenwills.html

Huntington Park
Corner of California and Taylor streets in Nob Hill
http://nobhillassociation.org/HuntingtonPark.asp

Justin Herman Plaza
1 Market Street in the Embarcadero Corridor, Financial District

St. Mary's Square
California Street between Grant and Kearny streets in Chinatown

San Francisco Maritime National Historical Park
499 Jefferson Street in Fisherman's Wharf
www.nps.gov/safr

Union Square Park
333 Post Street (Powell, Geary, Stockton, and Post)
http://unionsquarepark.us

Washington Square
Columbus Avenue and Union Street in North Beach/Telegraph Hill

Yerba Buena Gardens
Mission between 3rd and 4th streets in SoMa
www.yerbabuenagardens.com

Shopping

Major Retail

If you retire in dynamic downtown San Francisco, be assured that you will have the widest variety for everyday and specialty shopping. The primary shopping areas are:

Union Square and Market Street
This is the primary shopping district for locals and tourists and includes giant anchor stores, such as Saks Fifth Avenue, Macy's, and Neiman Marcus among others. The Westfield San Francisco Shopping Centre, a huge intown

mall, is only three blocks from Union Square on Market Street at Powell Street. See **www.unionsquareshop.com**.

North Beach
Boutiques and specialty stores abound along Columbus Avenue. See the North Beach Web site at **www.sfnorthbeach.org**.

Financial District/the Embarcadero
Embarcadero Center is the major shopping anchor along Sacramento Avenue. See **www.embarcaderocenter.com** for more information.

Hayes Valley
This is the arty and colorful shopping experience near the downtown area. See the Hayes Valley Neighborhood Association's Web site at **www.hayes valleysf.org**.

A fantastic shopping resource for all of San Francisco's districts can be found at **www.sfbayshop.com**, which includes a current listing for every district. Also check out the neighborhood Web sites for more local shopping opportunities.

Grocery Stores

San Francisco has scores of small corner stores and carry-outs. The following list provides best-bet full-service grocery stores that serve multiple neighborhoods.

Safeway
298 King Street, SoMa
350 Bay Street in North Beach
www.safeway.com

Whole Foods Market
1765 California Street
399 4th Street in SoMa
www.wholefoodsmarket.com

Trader Joe's
555 9th Street, SoMa
www.traderjoes.com

Rainbow Grocery
1745 Folsom Street, SoMa/Mission
 District
www.rainbowgrocery.org

City/Farmer's Markets

The Cannery Farmer's Market
  (Del Monte Square)
2801 Leavenworth Street,
  Fisherman's Wharf
www.delmontesquare.com

Crocker Galleria Farmer's Market
50 Post Street, Financial District
www.shopatgalleria.com/
  events.htm

Ferry Building Marketplace
1 Ferry Building, Financial District
www.ferrybuildingmarket
  place.com

Heart of the City Farmer's Market
1182 Market Street,
  United Nations Plaza,
  Civic Center District

Getting around

City Transit

San Francisco Municipal Railway (MUNI)
Operates a surface light rail train network, streetcars (including "metros" and
  historic streetcars), electric trolleys and rubber wheeled electric buses, cable
  cars, and proposing a central subway from Union Square south to the Caltrain Terminal.
www.sfmuni.com

City Bike Trails

For a comprehensive list and map of San Francisco's biking and walking
  trails, see the City and County of San Francisco's bicycle program site at
  www.bicycle.sfgov.org.

Interbay-Community Trains

Bay Area Rapid Transit (BART)
Subway, surface, and aerial trains serving the Bay Area from San Francisco
  International Airport, to Oakland, Berkeley, Richmond, Dublin, and
  Fremont. Subway stations in downtown along Market Street.
www.bart.gov

Intercity Trains

Amtrak
Bus connections from the
  Caltrain Station to
  Oakland's Amtrak Terminal
www.amtrak.com

Caltrain
Daily regular service to San Jose
700 4th Street Station
www.caltrain.com

Ferries

Alameda Oakland Ferry
From the Ferry Building or Pier 39,
  serving Alameda and Oakland
www.eastbayferry.com

Baylink Ferry
From the Ferry Building
  or Pier 41 to Vallejo
www.baylinkferry.com

Blue and Gold Fleet
Serves San Francisco's Pier 39 to
  Tiburon and Sausalito
www.blueandgoldfleet.com

Golden Gate Ferry
Service from San Francisco Ferry
  Terminal to Larkspur in central
  Marin County and Sausalito in
  southern Marin County
www.goldengateferry.org

Alameda Harbor Bay Ferry
Ferry Terminal to Alameda
  (Oakland)
www.harborbayferry.com

Intercity Bus

Greyhound Terminal
Transit Terminal, 1st and Mission streets
www.greyhound.com

Airports

San Francisco International Airport (SFO)
www.flysfo.com

Oakland International Airport (OAK)
www.flyoakland.com

Interstate Highways

I-80 (Across the San Francisco Bay to Oakland, California)
I-280 (South to San Jose, California)
U.S. 101 (Across the Golden Gate Bridge north to Marin County)

9

Seattle, Washington

Seattle has attracted newcomers from around the world and added thousands of residential homes in recent years. Downtown Seattle is an emergent and ever-vibrant system of urban neighborhoods and a popular destination for Ruppies. And even with the absence of local trains, this northwestern city provides a big-city lifestyle, lively sidewalks, retail stores, and a high quality of life. In fact, it tops the list of American cities for downtown population growth since 1970, increasing its downtown population by 85 percent. Here are five reasons to consider Seattle as your retirement home.

1. **A "cool" address**

    Although Seattle was considered "cooler" in the early 1990s when the grunge rock scene emerged and everyone was watching *Frasier*, it will always be a sought-after city. Today, Seattle is the hub of the world's high-tech industry, including Microsoft, Boeing, and Nintendo. Corporations have the option of filling their job pool from the city's 40,000 University of Washington students. The city continues to draw newcomers to the area for its mild climate, beautiful scenery, and innovative music scene.

2. **Verticality**

    Because Seattle's center city is constrained by water and steep hills, development has built up rather than out. Neighborhoods such as north downtown's Belltown have seen a boom of mid- and high-rise condominium buildings. Other areas, such as the Denny Triangle, are poised for higher-density residential and commercial growth, attracting more full-time residents, shops, and walkers.

3. **Seattle Center**
   Seattle Center, on the northern side of downtown, is the city's "festival central," hosting a wide array of cultural and arts festivals. One of Seattle's big events is Bumbershoot, a music and arts festival. The vicinity is also home to several museums, including the Science Fiction Museum and Hall of Fame, the Seattle Children's Museum, and the Pacific Science Center.

4. **Pike Place Market**
   Shop for fresh produce, seafood, or arts and crafts. Watch street performers near the Seattle waterfront, or have a bite to eat—the market is a lot of fun, and there's a nearby grassy park that's great for relaxing or conservation.

5. **Elliott Bay and Mount Rainier**
   If you live in downtown Seattle, you're likely to have gorgeous views of Elliott Bay. On clear days you can enjoy the breathtaking sunsets, watch the cruise ships, and catch a glimpse of Mount Rainier in the distant southern sky. Seattle is called the Emerald City and offers a natural environment that's hard to beat with lush evergreen hills that surround the area.

Target Retirement Districts and Neighborhoods

There are many superior downtown districts and neighborhood choices, from high-rise living to hilly garden neighborhoods.

Central Business District

This vibrant area includes the Retail Core and West Edge. The Retail Core is lined with stores and several large shopping centers, including Pacific Place and Westlake Center. The area also contains many of Seattle's tallest skyscrapers and office towers.

West Edge houses Pike Place Market, where fresh produce and seafood is sold. It's also filled with the city's most notable seafood restaurants, bars, taverns, and shops, and residences that link the Pioneer Square and Belltown neighborhoods. South of the Pike Place Market is the Seattle Aquarium, ferry and cruise ship terminals, parks, and scenic pedestrian walkways.

The downtown core of Seattle is generally bounded by Lenora Street (northwest), 6th Avenue and Olive Way (north), Columbia (south), Elliott Bay (west), and I-5 (east). For more information, visit the Downtown Seattle Association Web site at **www.downtownseattle.org**.

Belltown

Belltown comprises the northern downtown waterfront and is the primary core city residential neighborhood. Modern mid- and high-rise condominiums offer expansive views of the waterfront and Mount Rainier. Belltown is also a popular nightspot, featuring jazz clubs, trendy bars, and restaurants. Commercial corridors here are lined with specialty shops and art galleries. Another Belltown plus is the opening of Olympic Sculpture Park, an eight-acre waterfront outdoor art gallery, which will feature permanent and temporary sculptures as well as musical performances on the green.

Belltown is bound by the Puget Sound (southwest), 5th Avenue (east and northeast), Lenora Street (south and southeast), and Denny Way (north). For more information, visit the Belltown Business Association's Web site at **www.belltown.org**.

Denny Triangle

Denny Triangle, on the north and east of Belltown, is tomorrow's exciting area. It has already lured the Cornish College of the Arts there. Currently there are new high-rise office construction, plans for residential and "mixed-use" developments, and a new flagship grocery store. The neighborhood is embracing tall buildings and high density, advertising itself as "Where the Future Meets Tomorrow," and could become one of the most sought-after urban neighborhoods in Seattle.

Denny Triangle is bounded by Denny Way (north), the jagged south edge of Pike, 7th, and Olive Way, and by I-5 and 5th Street (west/east).

For more information, visit the Denny Triangle Marketing Committee at **www.dennytriangle.org**.

Pioneer Square

Historic Pioneer Square, the city's oldest downtown district, features red brick and stone buildings, old street lamps, and tight, hilly streets. Tourists and locals are lured to the restaurants and art galleries and romantic little Pioneer Square Park with its historic iron pergola, a giant totem pole, and busts of Chief Seattle (Sealth). Sports fans frequent Quest Field (Seattle Seahawks) and Safeco Field (Seattle Mariners), which are located on its southern boundary.

The International District, formerly known as Chinatown, is adjacent and east of Pioneer Square. In addition to Chinese residents, other Asian cultures, including Vietnamese, Japanese, Malaysian, Filipino, and Cambodian immigrants, now call this area home. The neighborhood includes shops and Asian restaurants, such as the Uwajimaya Market, a two-level Asian-infused megastore.

Pioneer Square is between Columbia Street (north), south along South Royal Brougham Way, and Puget Sound and 4th Avenue (west/east). For more information, visit the Pioneer Square Community Association at **www.pioneersquare.org**. For additional information on the International District's shopping, grocery stores, entertainment, arts, and more, visit the Chinatown International District Business Improvement Area at **www.inter nationaldistrict.org**.

South Downtown

Just south of Safeco Field and south of the Pioneer Square neighborhood is "SODO," short for South Downtown. This area, a manufacturing, freight, and rail hub, has new retail stores, galleries, and restaurants moving in (can housing be far behind?). There are even plans for changing 5th Avenue's name to "Urban Art Corridor" and infusing public art along the street. See the SODO Business Association's Web site for more information on this intriguing area: **www.sodobusinessassociation.org**.

Also see the South Downtown Foundation for information on improvements here, in Pioneer Square, and in the International District: **www.southdowntown.org**.

Up the Hills

A short distance from downtown are two glorious (and still very much urban) neighborhoods to consider: Capitol Hill and Queen Anne.

Capitol Hill (Including Pike/Pine and First Hill)

This area, one of Seattle's most popular neighborhoods, is known for its multiethnic community, large gay population, and lively street life. You'll find nightclubs, great restaurants, cool coffee shops, and fancy boutiques here.

Capitol Hill is separated from downtown by two adjoining sister neighborhoods: First Hill and Pike/Pine. First Hill, the first residential neighborhood in Seattle, is a lovely enclave of old homes and lush gardens. It hosts the Swedish Medical Center and Seattle University. Just east of I-5 along Pike Street is the Pike/Pine neighborhood, with its edgy clubs, attention-grabbing shops, and pedestrian-friendly streets. Seattle Community College is located here, keeping the area perpetually young, but the best aspect of these magnificent middle neighborhoods is their easy access to downtown.

Capitol Hill runs from Olive Street to far north inner-city Seattle toward Volunteer Park. Pike/Pine is generally west of Broadway and east of I-5 to Olive Street, and First Hill is south of Union Street down to Jackson Street. For more information, visit the Capitol Hill Neighbors Web site at **www.capitolhillneighbors.com**.

Queen Anne

Queen Anne is north of Denny Way and the Belltown and Denny Triangle neighborhoods. The Seattle Center Space Needle, Pacific Science Theater, Experience Music Project Museum, and the KeyArena (where the Sonics NBA team plays) are at the foot of the hill. Follow Queen Anne Avenue north up the hill and you'll find boutiques, coffee shops, and quaint streets. Beautiful community parks, the proximity to downtown, and dramatic views of the skyline, Elliott Bay, and Lake Union all make this collection of inner-city homes among Seattle's most sought-after.

Although Queen Anne has no official neighborhood Web site, you can learn more about its history by visiting the Queen Anne Historical Society's Web site at **www.qahistory.org**.

Downtown Seattle Essentials

Coffee: Besides being home to the world's first Starbucks coffee shop, downtown Seattle has long been known for its coffee. You can find coffee shops everywhere: Starbucks, Seattle's Best Coffee, and even a number of mom-and-pop varieties.

Ferry trips: The ferries offer trips to Victoria, British Columbia, or to Bainbridge Island, just across the sound. Enjoy a spectacular day trip while taking in the skyline views, looking for whales, or exploring maritime towns.

The Underground: Did you know that Seattle's original main streets are now located underground? In the late 1800s the city solved its sewage problems by raising the streets and the building entrances, creating "Underground Seattle" deep below the existing streets of Pioneer Square.

General Statistics

Population: Downtown core: 21,745 (2000); City: 571,480 (2003); Metro: 3,141,777 (2003)

Terrain: Downtown Seattle is northeast of Elliott Bay and east of Puget Sound. It is generally flat near the bay, but becomes hilly inland.

Climate Overview: mild winters/cool summers

Average January high/low temperature: 45/36F

Average July high/low temperature: 74/56F

Average annual total precipitation: 36 inches

Average annual snowfall: 7 inches

Number of cloudy days: 200

Cost of Living: Find out the current cost of living between Seattle and your community by visiting **www.homefair.com** and clicking **"Moving to a New State"** or **"Moving Locally,"** then follow the prompts.

Cost of Housing:

Zip code: 98101 (North Central Business District and southwest Capitol Hill); price snapshot: $354,493; sq/ft: 934

Zip code: 98102 (North sections of Capitol Hill); price snapshot: $481,762; sq/ft: 1,581

Zip code: 98104 (Southern downtown core, Pioneer Square, International District, First Hill); price snapshot: $558,196; sq/ft: 1,220

Zip code: 98109 (Queen Anne—east); price snapshot: $472,110; sq/ft: 1,475

Zip code: 98121 (Belltown, Denny Triangle); price snapshot: $463,458; sq/ft: 957

Zip code: 98122 (Eastern and southern Capitol Hill and near east Seattle); price snapshot: $818,461; sq/ft: 3,152

Real estate prices fluctuate. For up-to-date neighborhood housing cost information, input the zip codes above in the Homestore Web site (affiliated with Realtor.com) at **www.homestore.com/Cities**.

Rent Costs: If you want to rent, explore **www.rentnet.com** and also investigate the neighborhood Web sites for current rents and available properties.

Taxes

Property Tax: Keep current with property tax assessments at the King County Department of Assessments at **www.metrokc.gov/Assessor**.

Sales Tax: 7.25 percent. Food and prescription drugs exempted.

State Income Tax: No state income tax.

Downtown Seattle Retirement Lifestyle Web Guide

Living

Seattle's downtown Web site and most of the city's local neighborhoods do not concentrate on real estate, so contact a local Realtor who specializes in downtown Seattle neighborhoods at the Seattle-King County Association of Realtors: **www.nwrealtor.com**. For local Capitol Hill properties see **www.capitolhillneighbors.com** and click "**Local Real Estate**."

City Hospitals

*Fred Hutchinson Cancer
   Research Center*
1100 Fairview Avenue North
www.fhcrc.org

Harborview Medical Center
325 9th Avenue in First Hill
www.uwmedicine.org

Swedish Medical Center
747 Broadway in First Hill
www.swedish.org

UW Medical Center (Harborview)
325 9th Avenue, First Hill
www.uwmedicine.org

Virginia Mason Hospital
1100 9th Avenue, First Hill
www.virginiamason.org

Health Clubs

24 Hour Fitness
1827 Yale Avenue in Denny Triangle
www.24hourfitness.com

All Star Fitness
509 Olive Way in the Retail Core
700 5th Avenue,
   Retail Core/Pioneer Square
www.allstarfitness.com

Gold's Gym
401 Broadway in Capitol Hill
825 Pike Street in the Retail Core
www.goldsgym.com

Headquarters Health & Fitness
217 Pine Street in the Retail Core
www.hq-fitness.com

Pure Fitness
808 2nd Avenue in the Retail Core
www.purefitnessclubs.com

Rain Fitness
159 Western Avenue West in
   Belltown/Queen Anne
www.rainfitness.com

Seattle Athletic Club, downtown
2020 Western Avenue, West Edge
www.sacdt.com

Seattle Fitness
83 South King Street,
   Pioneer Square/SODO
www.seattlefitness.com

Washington Athletic Club
1325 6th Avenue in the Retail Core
www.wac.net

Zum
2235 5th Avenue,
   Belltown/Denny Triangle
www.clubzum.com

Volunteering

United Way of King County
www.uwkc.org and click
   "**Volunteer**," then "**Select Our
   Volunteer Listings**"

Southeastern Washington Red Cross
www.seattleredcross.org and click
   "**Volunteer**"

Educational opportunities

Colleges and Universities

Antioch University Seattle
2326 6th Avenue in Denny Triangle
www.antiochsea.edu

Cornish College of the Arts
1000 Lenora Street
   in Denny Triangle
www.cornish.edu

University of Washington
1705 NE Pacific Street,
   University District
www.washington.edu

Seattle University
901 12th Avenue
900 Broadway in First Hill
www.seattleu.edu

Seattle Pacific University
3307 3rd Avenue West,
   Queen Anne
www.spu.edu

Seattle Central Community College
1701 Broadway in Capitol Hill
www.seattlecolleges.com

Libraries
Seattle Public Library
1000 4th Avenue in the Retail Core
www.spl.org

Entertainment

Restaurants, Clubs, Bars, and Nightclubs
The Downtown Seattle Association provides an excellent way to browse each
downtown neighborhood's restaurants. Visit **www.downtownseattle.com** and
click "**For Visitors and Residents**," then click "**Dining**" for a comprehensive
list. For nightlife, also check each neighborhood's Web site for current listings.

Professional Spectator Sports

Seattle Mariners (baseball)
Safeco Field, 1250 First Avenue
  South in SODO
seattle.mariners.mlb.com

Seattle Seahawks (football)
Qwest Field, 800 Occidental
  Avenue in SODO
www.seahawks.com

Seattle Sounders (soccer)
Qwest Field, 800 Occidental
  Avenue in SODO
www.seattlesounders.net

Seattle SuperSonics (basketball)
KeyArena, 305 Harrison Street in
  lower Queen Anne
www.nba.com/sonics

Seattle Storm (women's basketball)
KeyArena, 305 Harrison Street in
  lower Queen Anne
www.wnba.com/storm

Seattle Thunderbirds (hockey)
KeyArena, 305 Harrison Street in
  lower Queen Anne
www.seattle-thunderbirds.com

College Sports

University of Washington Huskie Athletics
25th Avenue NE, University of Washington campus
Men's and women's basketball, crew, cross-country, golf, soccer, tennis,
  track, men's basketball, football, women's gymnastics, volleyball
www.gohuskies.com

Seattle University Redhawks
Campus facilities in First Hill neighborhood
Men's and women's basketball, cross-country, soccer, swimming, track and
  field, women's softball and volleyball
www.seattleredhawks.com

Seattle Pacific University Falcons
Men's and women's basketball, cross-country, gymnastics, soccer, track and
  field, women's gymnastics, volleyball
www.spu.edu/depts/athletics

The Performing Arts

For theater performance companies, visit **www.downtownseattle.com** and click "**For Visitors and Residents**," then "**Attractions**" for a comprehensive up-to-date listing.

Pacific Northwest Ballet
Marion Oliver McCaw Hall, 321 Mercer Street in lower Queen Anne
www.pnb.org

Seattle Symphony
Benaroya Hall, 200 University Street in the Retail Core
www.seattlesymphony.org

Seattle Opera
Marion Oliver McCaw Hall, 321 Mercer Street in lower Queen Anne
www.seattleopera.org

Major Museums

Experience Music Project
Seattle Center Campus at
   325 5th Avenue North in
   lower Queen Anne
www.emplive.com

Olympic Sculpture Park
Elliott Bay, Western Avenue,
   and Broad Street
www.iamsamcampaign.org

Pacific Science Center
200 Second Avenue North Seattle
   Center, in lower Queen Anne
www.pacsci.org

Seattle Aquarium
1483 Alaskan Way
www.seattleaquarium.org

Seattle Children's Museum
Seattle Center, 305 Harrison Street
   in lower Queen Anne
www.thechildrensmuseum.org

Science Fiction Museum
   and Hall of Fame
Seattle Center Campus at 325 5th
   Avenue North in Queen Anne
www.sfhomeworld.org

Seattle Art Museum
100 University Street in West Edge
www.seattleartmuseum.org

The Wing Luke Asian Museum
407 7th Avenue South
   in the International District
www.wingluke.org

Special Events (Best Bets)

Bastille Day
July. Seattle's celebration of the French Revolution held at the Seattle Center
www.seattle-bastille.org

Bite of Seattle
July. The Northwest's largest food festival held at the Seattle Center
www.biteofseattle.com

Bumbershoot, the Seattle Arts Festival
Labor Day weekend. One of America's biggest arts festivals. Held at the
   Seattle Center
www.bumbershoot.com

Capitol Hill Block Party
July. Music festival featuring dozens of live band performances and held at
   East Pine Street and Broadway in Capitol Hill
www.capitolhillblockparty.com

Chinatown International District Summer Festival
July in Hing Hay Park. Largest Pan-Asian street fair in the Pacific Northwest
www.internationaldistrict.org/events.asp

Earshot Jazz Festival
October/November. Various venues
www.earshot.org

Festál Cultural Festivals
The Seattle Center is the home to the majority of the city's year-round
   cultural festivals including Bastille Day, Brazil Fest, Turk Fest, Festival
   Sundiata, Asian Pacific American Heritage, and many more. See the Center's Web site for a complete list: **www.seattlecenter.com/events/festivals**

Fiestas Patrias
September. A celebration of Mexican Independence, Seattle Center
www.seattlecenter.com

SEAFAIR
July/August. Seattle's premier summer celebration on the water, with community events, boat, and air shows
www.seafair.com

Seattle International Film Festival (SIFF)
May/June. It claims to be the largest film festival in the United States. Various
venues around Seattle
www.seattlefilm.com

Seattle Pride March
June. Huge gay pride parade in Capitol Hill
www.seattlepride.org

Summer Nights at the Pier
Summerlong concert series held at the South Union Lake Pier, east of
Capitol Hill
www.summernights.org

Movie Theaters

(The Historic) Seattle Cinerama Theater
2100 4th Avenue
www.cinerama.com

Pacific Place Cinema (multiplex)
600 Pine Street

Meridian 16 Cinemas
1501 Seventh Avenue at Pike Street

(The Historic) Paramount Theater
911 Pine Street
www.theparamount.com

Favorite Downtown Parks

For more information on these and more city parks, visit **www.seattle
.gov/parks**.

Denny Park
100 Dexter Avenue North, Denny
   Triangle/lower Queen Anne.
   Small neighborhood green space
   and Seattle's first park

Freeway Park
700 Seneca Street in the Retail Core.
   Urban park with benches and
   landscaping

Kinnear Park
899 West Olympic Place. Fourteen
   acres of woods and skyline
   views in lower Queen Anne

Kobe Terrace Park
South Main Street and 6th Avenue
   South in the International District

Myrtle Edwards Park
3130 Alaskan Way on Elliott Bay
   in lower Queen Anne, with
   pedestrian trails and a great view
   of the bay

Occidental Square
Occidental Avenue South and
   South Main Street in historic
   Pioneer Square

Victor Steinbrueck Park
2001 Western Avenue. Green,
   grassy space north of Pike Market
   on the waterfront

Waterfront Park
1301 Alaskan Way between Pier 57
   and Pier 59 on the waterfront

Shopping

Major Retail

The Downtown Seattle Association provides a comprehensive listing of over 1,800 downtown retailers (including grocery stores and major shopping centers) sorted by neighborhood. Visit **www.downtownseattle.com** and click **"For Visitors and Residents,"** then **"Shopping"** for an up-to-date listing. Also see each neighborhood Web site for additional current retail listings.

City/Farmer's Markets

Pike Place Market
Pike Place and 1st Avenue
www.pikeplacemarket.org

Seattle Neighborhood Farmer's
   Markets
Capitol Hill on Broadway
www.seattlefarmersmarkets.org

Getting around

Public Bus Service
King County Metro
Free downtown bus service
http://transit.metrokc.gov

City Bike Trails
Seattle has one of the most extensive urban trail systems in any major American city. See the Seattle Department of Transportation's Web site for more information at **www.seattle.gov/transportation/bikeprogram.htm**.

City Trains
Local: Seattle Center Monorail
Limited service between the Space Needle and Westlake Center (tourists, and not locals, use the monorail)
www.seattlemonorail.com

Intercity Trains
Amtrak
303 South Jackson Street
www.amtrak.com

Ferry
Washington State Ferries
Service to Vashon and Bainbridge Islands, Bremerton, and Sidney (Victoria), British Columbia, at Pier 54
www.wsdot.wa.gov/ferries

Intercity Bus
Greyhound Terminal
811 Stewart Street
www.greyhound.com

Airport

Seattle-Tacoma International Airport (SEA)
www.seatac.org

Interstate Highways

I-5 (South/north from Tacoma, Washington, to Bremerton, Washington)
I-90 (East to Spokane, Washington)

Distinctively Different Downtowns

Distinctively different downtowns are unique and unforgettable places. They have especially unusual cultural idiosyncrasies and distinguishing geographic features, and are places where citizens love their city. When locals enthusiastically celebrate and promote their city's special qualities, their enthusiasm becomes infectious, word spreads, and the cities then become great places to retire.

In this section, discover America's best distinctively different downtowns: Asheville, North Carolina; Austin, Texas; Madison, Wisconsin; and Providence, Rhode Island.

Asheville, North Carolina

Ruppies who prefer culture and the arts ordinarily choose to live in big cities. However, another alternative far from Manhattan is Asheville, North Carolina, a very special, small city set in the middle of the vast Blue Ridge Mountains.

Appalachian Mountain towns and sophistication don't normally coincide, but downtown Asheville is a diamond in the rough—an urbane island in the mountain wilds. The city has a wealthy flair, due in large part to the many historic structures constructed outside of downtown—especially the largest private residence in America, George Vanderbilt's Biltmore Estate, which opened on Christmas Eve in 1895. The Grove Park Inn, circa 1913, is another lavish structure. It's built of hand-cut boulders resembling a European Tudor castle, and is perched on a hill overlooking the downtown and the mountains. Asheville's 1920s opulent art deco city hall features vintage marble and terracotta materials, while the county building is a neo-classical revival masterpiece. Asheville's architecture and preservation efforts are only a part of the city's otherwise eccentric personality. The following are five more good reasons to retire there.

1. Wonderful bizarre atmosphere

There is a curious counterculture spirit here as a significant number of residents gleefully live life out of the mainstream. Asheville has gained a lot of attention for its distinctive population of outgoing and expressive individuals. Downtown is a people-watching area: Individuality is embedded and celebrated in the local culture.

Although the historic Biltmore House and the area's beautiful scenery are usually featured in advertising campaigns, the most intriguing aspect of Asheville is its everyday people. For example, a young man with multiple piercings on his face and covered with tattoos might be dancing to a pan flute with someone who looks like Grandma Moses. Or perhaps hippies may be reading poetry to a crowd in one of several city parks. Or even protestors may be carrying signs while belly dancers try to get an audience of sidewalk onlookers. The weekend drum circle party is certainly an interesting event, where people of all persuasions, ages, and income levels bang on their drums in Pritchard Park. There's no other city like Asheville.

2. A mini city

Asheville, with only 70,000 people, seems so much bigger. Downtown's narrow streets are crammed with restaurants, coffee shops, and boutiques similar to a Lower Manhattan neighborhood. A short distance away, however, the streets will suddenly open up into urban parks and stately grand plazas with monuments and fountains. At the same time, the sidewalks are abuzz with activity, giving this tiny downtown's ten or so square blocks its big-city ambiance.

3. Performing arts paradise

Asheville's music scene rivals cities ten times its size. Its wide-ranging performing arts include local contemporary dance, Shakespeare in the Park, the Asheville Symphony Orchestra, and an opera company, but its local street artists are just as important to the quality of life. Little bluegrass or folk bands perform near the Civic Center, while women with banjos and violins may play for dancers. Or a saxophone player may serenade churchgoers with gospel hymns at the end of Sunday services.

4. Artisans abound

Asheville is known for its creative spirit and people: perhaps because of its inspiring mountain setting, or maybe because of the city's reputation for embracing expression. Whatever the reason, it has become a major draw for a variety of artists, and downtown Asheville acts like a big art gallery. Many artists display their paintings in storefronts while other works including ceramics will be shown in galleries.

5. **Might as well have mountains**

At an elevation of 2,300 feet and cradled by peaks reaching up to 6,000 feet, mountain vistas only add to the city's appeal. Locals and visitors drive the Blue Ridge Parkway to Mount Mitchell (6,684 feet), the highest point east of the Mississippi. Ski slopes surround the city, as do fly-fishing streams, and mountain hiking and nature trails. During the winter and in early spring you can see the snow-covered Smoky Mountain peaks glisten in the sun. Consequently, it makes sense when Asheville's official tourism Web site says that "Altitude affects attitude."

Target Retirement Districts and Neighborhoods

Asheville's downtown core sits on a hill east of the French Broad River, west of a ridge, bounded by I-240 on the north, and another hill slopes down to Biltmore Village, which is a small urban enclave to the south.

The Downtown Core

There are about fifteen coffee shops, fifty restaurants, and an array of art galleries and specialty stores within downtown Asheville. What's appealing about the core city is that there are several distinct districts and building anchors covering every section of downtown.

The Battery Hill District, northwest of downtown, is anchored by the Grove Arcade, which was built in 1929. This original public market has been meticulously restored and now is a vibrant food and crafts center. Rows of outdoor cafes also add to the energetic atmosphere on Battery Park and Page avenues. Wall Street, just to the south, is an extremely narrow one-way street. South of here there are delightful impromptu shows at Pritchard Park. East and north is the Lexington Park District, very much a small SoHo, with antique stores, restaurants, and a row of art galleries. North/south oriented Broadway Avenue is speckled with bars, galleries, and restaurants, especially the Eagle/Market Street area. Just east is Pack Place, an education, art, and science center. It's framed by the Asheville Art Museum and the Vance Monument, a 125-foot-tall obelisk commemorating Zebulon B. Vance. There's also a fountain and a long reflecting pool here. A few blocks past is the city hall and county building. Walking north on Market is the Asheville Community Theatre and a memorial to one of the most celebrated novelists in American literature, Thomas Wolfe. Downtown Asheville may be tiny, but it packs a wallop.

Although this area has enjoyed a renaissance in recent years, its small size provides very limited opportunities for residential living. The most notable housing development is a seven-story mid-rise condominium in the Battery Park area. There are, however, several commercial buildings that have been converted to apartments and condominiums, such as the above-storefront apartments in the old Hotel Oxford. Ruppies should have a much wider choice of living opportunities in the near future, as a major infill construction boom is bound to occur. Because of the small space and limited development, finding an inexpensive condominium is less likely than other cities listed in this section. The trick for the success of Asheville's future will be how to provide more housing in downtown at a wider price range—an increased supply will eventually decrease the cost. For more information, visit the Asheville Downtown Association Web site at **www.ashevilledowntown.org**.

Historic Montford

Because of the limited availability of housing, a good alternative is Montford, a lush, hilly area within easy walking distance to the middle of downtown and just north of I-240. Its mix of Victorian and bungalow-style single-family homes make it a natural area for many bed and breakfasts. Montford also offers historic apartment buildings for those who don't want to take care of a yard.

Montford is bounded by I-26 (west), I-240 (south), Broadway (east), and the intersection of I-26 and Broadway (north). For more information, see the Montford Resource Center's Web site at **www.montford.org**.

River District

Although nearly a mile from the western edge of downtown, the developing River District deserves consideration. It was originally an old industrial warehouse district along the railroad tracks of the French Broad River. Buildings that were once tanneries, lumber yards, and ice storage facilities are now home to artists' studios and feature oils, watercolors, pottery, jewelry, woodworking, photography, and most other media. Area artists hold a "Studio Stroll" to encourage the public to walk from one studio to the next. The River District has just begun to redevelop into a functioning urban district. It wouldn't be out of the question to expect hundreds of new residents to be living here in the upcoming years. Although it's quite a walk to downtown, this area will be a viable alternative for creative Ruppies.

The River District is generally bounded by I-240 and Lymon Street (north/south), French Broad River (west), and Clingman Avenue (east). For more information, see the River District Artists' Web site at **www.river districtartists.com**.

Downtown Asheville Essentials

Expressive behavior: If you move to downtown Asheville, learn to become expressive in your own way.

Outdoor movies in Pritchard Park: Pritchard Park is movie central during the spring and fall. Silent films are usually shown with accompanying live music.

Learning a craft: You'll have many opportunities to make pottery, paint, and dance, or learn any other craft that interests you.

Philosophical diversity: Asheville is a center for New Age philosophies, holistic medicines, and Eastern religions.

The urban trail: It's a 1.8-mile walk through downtown and a celebration of architecture and local flavor. The trail will take you past familiar restaurants, shops, and parks.

Your personal set of drums: Get your drums out and beat the streets at the weekly drum circle. It's a throwback to the peace protest days of the Vietnam War, but it remains stylish here.

General Statistics

Population: Downtown: 13,580 (mostly includes the Montford neighborhood) (2000); City: 70,400 (2003); Metro: 381,789 (2003)

Terrain: Downtown Asheville is hilly and surrounded by views of the nearby Appalachian Mountains.

Climate Overview: warm summers/cool winters

Average January high/low temperature: 47/28F

Average July high/low temperature: 82/60F

Average annual total precipitation: 38 inches

Average annual snowfall: 16 inches

Number of cloudy days: 150

Cost of Living: Find out the current cost of living between Asheville and your community by visiting **www.homefair.com** and clicking **"Moving to a New State"** or **"Moving Locally,"** then follow the prompts.

Cost of Housing:

Zip code: 28801 (Montford represents the majority of the available housing stock); price snapshot: $305,475; sq/ft: 1,733

Real estate prices fluctuate. For up-to-date neighborhood housing cost information, input the zip code above in the Homestore Web site (affiliated with Realtor.com) at **www.homestore.com/Cities.**

Rent Costs: If you want to rent, explore **www.rentnet.com** and also investigate the neighborhood Web sites for current rents and available properties.

Taxes

Property Tax: 53 cents per $100 of assessed valuation. See the Buncombe County Tax Office's Web site at **www.buncombecounty.org/governing/depts/Tax/propTaxCollection.htm.**

Sales Tax: 7.0 percent (Food not subject to state taxes but subject to local sales taxes; prescription drugs exempt.)

State Income Tax: 6.0 percent to 8.25 percent (Four income tax brackets. Single: low $12,750 to high $120,000 and over; personal exemption: $3,300; Married: $21,250 to $200,000 and over; personal exemption: $6,600. Child exemption: $3,300.) North Carolina also has an individual personal property tax.

Downtown Asheville Retirement Lifestyle Web Guide

Living

There are currently no comprehensive real estate sites that exclusively feature urban living opportunities in downtown Asheville. Visit the Asheville Board of Realtors' site at **www.abr-nc.com** to find professionals who specialize in the downtown Asheville market.

City Hospitals

Mission St. Joseph Hospitals
509 Biltmore Avenue
www.missionhospitals.org

Veteran's Administration Medical Center
1100 Tunnel Road
www.va.gov

Health Clubs

Asheville YMCA
30 Woodfin Street
www.ymcawnc.org

Volunteering

Volunteer Asheville
50 South French Broad Avenue
www.volunteerasheville.com or
  www.unitedwayabc.org

American Red Cross:
  Asheville-Mountain Area Chapter
100 Edgewood Road
www.ashevillemountainredcross.org

Educational opportunities

City Colleges and Universities

University of North Carolina Asheville
1 University Heights
www.unca.edu

Asheville-Buncombe Technical College
340 Victoria Road
www.abtech.edu

Library
Pack Memorial Library
67 Haywood Street, downtown
www.buncombecounty.org/governing/depts/Library/locations_Pack.htm

Entertainment

Restaurants, Bars, and Nightclubs
Visit **www.ashevilledowntown.org** and click "**Visit Downtown**," then "**Where to Eat**" or "**Live Music, Music, Music**" for a listing of restaurants and interesting things to do.

College Sports
University of North Carolina at Asheville
Men's and women's basketball, soccer, track and field, tennis, cross-country, men's baseball, women's volleyball
www.uncabulldogs.com

The Performing Arts

Asheville Bravo Concerts
Thomas Wolfe Auditorium,
 87 Haywood Street
www.ashevillebravoconcerts.org

Asheville Contemporary
 Dance Theatre
Bebe Theatre, 20 Commerce Street
www.acdt.org

Asheville Lyric Opera
Diana Wortham Theatre at
 Pack Place Arts Center,
 2 South Pack Square
www.ashevillelyric.org

Asheville Symphony Orchestra
Thomas Wolfe Auditorium,
 87 Haywood Street
www.ashevillesymphony.org

North Carolina Stage
33 Haywood Street
www.ncstage.org

Asheville Community Theatre
35 East Walnut Street
www.ashevilletheatre.org

Montford Park Players
Shakespeare in Montford Park at
 the Hazel Robinson Amphitheatre
www.montfordparkplayers.org

Major Museums

Pack Place Education, Arts, & Science Center
Includes: The Health Adventure, Asheville Art Museum, Colburn Earth Science Museum, and the Diana Wortham Theatre
2 South Pack Square
www.packplace.org

Y.M.I. Cultural Center
39 South Market Street
www.ymicc.org

Thomas Wolfe Memorial
52 North Market Street
www.wolfememorial.com

Special Events (Best Bets)

Bele Chere
In late July, 400,000 people cram into downtown Asheville to enjoy an average of one hundred bands playing a variety of bluegrass, country, rock, and rhythm and blues—there's arts and crafts, too
www.belecherefestival.com

Mountain Dance and Folk Festival featuring "Shindig on the Green"
August. Diana Wortham Theatre hosts banjo pickers, dulcimer sweepers, mountain fiddlers, and dancers. Thousands gather on the plaza with their blankets and lawn chairs and then dance to Southern Appalachian music
www.folkheritage.org

Center City Art Walk
Thirty downtown galleries keep their doors open for art walks during various times of the year
www.ashevilledowntowngalleries.org

River District Artists Studio Stroll
Stroll through the artists' studios in the River District several times a year
www.riverdistrictartists.com

Southern Highland Craft Guild
October. More than two hundred craftspeople converge on the Asheville Civic Center
www.southernhighlandguild.org

Asheville Percussive Dance Festival
May. Includes clogging, tapping, flatfoot, flamenco, Irish, West African, and
other "sounds" in dance in an annual spring festival in downtown
www.percussivedance.org

Friday After 5 Series
Summer music concerts on the City/County Plaza
www.ashevilledowntown.org

Goombay
August. African and Caribbean cultural fest on Eagle and Market streets
in downtown
www.ymicc.org/goombay.html

Drum Circle
Not really a festival but just as much fun. The best people-watching experience happens every Friday night in Pritchard Park. Bring your drum and
dress creatively—don't worry, you'll blend right in

Movie Theater
Fine Arts Theatre (showing first-run and independent films)
36 Biltmore Avenue
www.fineartstheatre.com

Favorite Downtown Parks
Pritchard Park
Home to street performers, drum circles, and all kinds of interesting impromptu
entertainment. Triangular park Patton Avenue/Haywood and College

Pack Square
The heart of the city with stunning reflecting pool and the Vance Monument

City/County Plaza
The premier open space in downtown anchored by the city hall and the
county building

Food Lion SkatePark
Watch kids on skateboards and Rollerblades or join in yourself at the corner of Flint and Cherry streets north of I-240
www.foodlionskatepark.com

Shopping

Visit **www.ashevilledowntown.org** and click "**Visit Downtown**," then "**Shopping**" for recommendations on great places to shop. In addition, Asheville Mall is just east on Tunnel Road. Asheville is so small it's not a big hassle to go to an outlying mall—it's only a short drive but you do need a car. Major chain stores of all kinds surround the mall. 3 South Tunnel Road **www.asheville-mall.com**.

Groceries
Greenlife Grocery
A full-service natural foods store. Features tailgate markets on Wednesdays and Sundays.
70 Merrimon Avenue just north of the I-240 connector
www.greenlifegrocery.com

City/Farmer's Markets
Grove Arcade
1 Page Avenue
www.grovearcade.com

Mountain Fresh Market
Features organic foods
1 Page Avenue in the Grove Arcade

Grove Corner Market
Features home delivery
1 Page Avenue in the Grove Arcade

Getting around

Public Bus Service
Asheville Transit System
www.ci.asheville.nc.us/transit.htm

Bike Routes/Trails/Greenways

City of Asheville Parks

www.ci.asheville.nc.us/parks/greenways.htm

Downtown Greyhound Terminal

2 Tunnel Road

www.greyhound.com

Airport

Asheville Regional Airport (AVL)

www.flyavl.com

Interstate Highways

I-40 (East/west from Knoxville, Tennessee, to Winston-Salem, North Carolina)

I-26 (South/north from Greenville, South Carolina, to Johnson City, Tennessee)

Austin, Texas

esidents talk it up in Austin, thankful that they are lucky enough to live in such a great place. Over the years, Austin has lured urban developers who are building an increasingly dense, livable, and fun city. Here's why downtown Austin is a distinctively different city.

1. It's weird

In the vast majority of cities, leaders responsible for creating catch-phrases and marketing their area's amenities are mostly conservative and will use general adjectives that could describe any other city. But not Austin. For example, the Austin Downtown Alliance uses "weird," "hippie," "chic," "intellectual," and "fashionable" in their promotional brochures and Web site. And the one used most for Austin is *weird*. In fact, the phrase "Keep Austin Weird," which began innocently by a local Austinite, has become the entire city's catchphrase, fueled by bumper stickers, T-shirts, and a popular Web site (**www.keepaustinweird.com**). "What are you doing?" the webmaster asks, imploring everyone to do *something* to add to the city's weirdness. The "Idea City" is a trendsetter, and now many other cities are copying this weird idea.

To stay weird, a city must already be weird, which begs the question, why is Austin so weird in the first place? No one is sure, but it seems to be a combination of how people look, the way they dress, and what they do—in an infinite variety of ways and as distinct as each personality. Local examples that are featured on the Keep Austin Weird Web site include: the Lizardman, who received plastic surgery and tattooed his body to morph into a human lizard; the Texas Rollergirls, a roller derby competition where skaters dress up in the most unusual costumes; and a "foot sculpture," a sculpture of a foot cut in half.

The bottom line is that Austin is not what most people expect in a conservative state like Texas. What's incredible is that the city leaders seem to embrace anything and everything that is not normal. Austin is the perfect place for Ruppies to express themselves with few restraints and without inhibition. Not everyone here is weird, of course, but they have at least thought about ways that they could be.

2. The University of Texas

The largest university in America, located in downtown Austin, injects a permanent youthful outlook and spirit in the community—and this is an environment that the mature crowd needs to stay young. The University of Texas offers a vast array of continued learning experiences, including cultural museums and libraries, and of course, yelling for victory at Longhorns football games and other sporting events. Imagine living in a neighborhood with 50,000 students. It's this kind of an activity base that will keep Austin vital for years to come.

3. 6th Street

Seven blocks of 6th Street, between I-35 and Congress Avenue, have the most intense activity and energy of the entire city. Austin is called "The Live Music Capital of America," and this is one of the country's premier music corridors. It's similar to New Orleans' Bourbon Street and Memphis' Beale Street, but 6th Street can't be pinned down to one musical genre. It's eclectic: country, hip-hop, metal, punk, rock, and jazz fuse into a music lover's street of dreams. Ruppies will have a ball on 6th Street, and revel in the idea that being mature does not always mean behaving maturely.

4. The "it" factor

Every American city wants a vibrant downtown, but Austin is in a different and enviable situation. People want to move there, and they want to experience its unique urban lifestyle themselves. Austin seems to "get it" when it comes to enhancing the city's vitality. The current population increase has forced the city to talk about, prepare for, and embrace quality urban growth. In fact, a new downtown Austin plan calls for 25,000 residents by 2010! They can expect lots of new neighbors, and all kinds of new stores in the foreseeable future.

5. **Hill Country**

Unlike all the other large cities in Texas, the Texas Hill Country is visible from the downtown high-rises. Suddenly, the normally flat landscape begins rolling near Austin, creating a mini mountain range where residents can go to enjoy a nature drive, a swim or boat ride on Lake Travis, horseback riding, hiking on hilly trails, or camping.

Target Retirement Districts and Neighborhoods

Downtown Austin is a compact area that acts more like one big neighborhood but with tiny, distinct districts and enclaves. The majority of residential areas are located in the southern sections near Town Lake, on Austin's waterfront. Districts are very close and connected, and residential housing is popping up in and around all of downtown.

For more information on all of Austin's neighborhoods, please see the Downtown Austin Neighborhood Alliance's Web site at **www.downtown austin.org** and the Austin Downtown Association's Web site: **www.down townaustin.com**.

Downtown Core

The center of downtown is around Congress Avenue, known as the "Congress District," and is the heart of the city. It's a beautiful street with the State Capitol framing the northern view. The area is also one of Austin's primary cultural centers, and includes the Austin Museum of Art, the Paramount and State Theaters, the Mexic-Arte Museum, and the ArtHouse at the Jones Center. Continuing south, the Congress Avenue Bridge crosses Town Lake, and during the warm weather 1.5 million Mexican free-tail bats make their home here.

It's an exciting time to live downtown. Urban residences are being planned and constructed around the existing shops and lively streets. There are also proposals for new high-rise towers that will combine retail stores, offices, and residential homes.

East 6th Street District

Ruppies will quickly become acquainted with this street's nightclubs, restaurants, shops, and most importantly, its people-watching opportunities. To the south, Brush Square, one of Austin's premier urban parks, provides an outdoor music area, and many of the city's festivals are centered here. Existing housing and new construction can be found on the surrounding blocks, especially south toward the convention center, where new condos and apartments are located.

The 6th Street District begins east from the intersection with Congress Avenue and extends seven blocks to I-35. For more information, see the 6th Street Web site at **www.6street.com**.

The Warehouse District

The district houses many of Austin's avant-garde restaurants and sophisticated nightclubs and is considered the "chic" entertainment section of downtown.

The district is bounded by Congress Avenue (east), 6th Street (north), Guadalupe (east), and Third (south). For more information, see the Warehouse District's page on the 6th Street Web site at **www.6street.com/6s_pg_ware house.htm**.

2nd Street District

This is a small area, only two blocks wide, but it packs a big punch. The new 2nd Street District, with its flashy retail stores, is a model for downtown development. Residents who retire here have immediate access to the amenities of the Town Lake waterfront, including its heavily used hike and bike trail.

This district centers around 2nd Street between Town Lake and Cesar Chavez Street (south), the Austin Convention Center (east), and San Antonio Street (west). For more information, see the 2nd Street District Web site at **www.2ndstreetdistrict.com**.

Market District

The famous Whole Foods Grocery Store is located on the corner of Lamar and 6th streets, and the area to the east comprises the new Market District. This flagship store is a behemoth showcase of prepared and fresh food, local musicians, and a community gathering place for thousands of downtown residents. Since new city homes will be built around it, this district will become one of Austin's fastest-growing neighborhoods. For more information, see **www.downtownaustin.com**.

Downtown Austin Essentials

Leslie for mayor: If you move to downtown Austin you'll come to know a locally famous celebrity named Leslie. Although homeless, Leslie runs for mayor every chance he gets. He dresses in short skirts, halter tops, and lives in a big box covered with campaign slogans. Leslie also transports his home on a trailer behind his bicycle, and businesses let him camp out on their sidewalks during the elections. He's never won, but he has never come in last either.

Keeping Austin weird: It's the city's catchphrase—do your best to contribute.

Whole Foods: Whole Foods is the coveted urban grocery store in cities around the country, but the flagship store and headquarters is in downtown Austin. Even if you decide to shop in the suburbs, you will probably still fall in love with this place.

Austin bats: Walking on the hike and bike trail, you'll want to stop at the Congress Avenue Bridge to watch one of Austin's best free shows—1.5 million bats swarming around their nightly bug dinner.

Dressing casually: Austin means hip, stylishly dressing down. You'll quickly figure out your own version of what casual means as a new resident.

A trip to the hills: A horseback ride on a Texas hill country ranch could accompany your new downtown hobbies.

General Statistics

Population: Downtown core: 3,855 (2000) City: 681,804 (2003); Metro: 1,377,633 (2003)

Terrain: Downtown Austin is situated on Town Lake (Colorado River) with rolling terrain adjacent and east of the heart of the Texas Hill Country.

Climate Overview: mild winters/very hot summers

Average January high/low temperature: 60/40F

Average July high/low temperature: 95/74F

Average annual total precipitation: 32 inches

Average annual snowfall: 1 inch

Number of cloudy days: 136

Cost of Living: Find out the current cost of living between Austin and your community by visiting **www.homefair.com** and clicking **"Moving to a New State,"** or **"Moving Locally,"** then follow the prompts.

Cost of Housing:

Zip code: 78701 (Downtown Austin)

Price snapshot: $222,385; sq/ft: N/A

Real estate prices fluctuate. For up-to-date neighborhood housing cost information, input the zip code above in the Homestore Web site (affiliated with Realtor.com) at **www.homestore.com/Cities**.

Rent Costs: If you want to rent, explore **www.rentnet.com** and also investigate the neighborhood Web sites for current rents and available properties.

Taxes

Property Tax: $2,743 per $100,000 (depending on tax district). For the latest assessments, see the Travis County Tax Office's Web site at **www.travis countytax.org**.

Sales Tax: 8.25 percent. Food and prescription drugs exempt.

State Income Tax: No state income tax.

Downtown Austin Retirement Lifestyle Web Guide

Living

Visit the Downtown Austin Alliance Web site for an extensive listing of current housing opportunities in downtown at **www.downtownaustin.com/living**. Also try the Austin Board of Realtors at **www.abor.com**.

City Hospitals
Brackenridge Hospital
601 East 15th Street
www.seton.net and click on "**Our Locations**," then "**Central**"

Health Clubs
Visit **www.downtownaustin.com/directory** and click "**Living**," then "**Services**" and then "**Fitness and Exercise**" for the latest listing of health clubs in downtown Austin.

Volunteering

United Way Capital Area
2000 East Martin Luther King Jr. Boulevard
www.unitedwaycapitalarea.org/volunteer

Educational opportunities

City Colleges and Universities
University of Texas
Martin Luther King Jr. Boulevard and Red River Street
www.utexas.edu

Library
John Henry Faulk Central Library
800 Guadalupe Street
www.ci.austin.tx.us/library/faulk_central.htm

Entertainment

Restaurants, Bars, and Nightclubs
Visit **www.downtownaustin.com** and click "**Having Fun**" for restaurants or clubs, for live music, art, and an up-to-date listing of coffee shops, nightclubs, and bars in downtown Austin.

Professional Spectator Sports

Austin Ice Bats (hockey)
Chaparral Ice Arena
14200 IH-35 North
www.icebats.com

Austin Wranglers (arena football)
Frank Erwin Center
1701 Red River Street
www.austinwranglers.com

Austin Toros (basketball)
Austin Convention Center
500 East Cesar Chavez Street
www.nba.com/dleague/austin

Round Rock Express (baseball)
The Dell Diamond
3400 East Palm Valley Boulevard,
  Round Rock, Texas
www.roundrockexpress.com

College Sports

University of Texas
Men's and women's basketball, cross-country, golf, swimming, diving, track and field, men's football, baseball, and women's rowing, soccer, softball, tennis, and volleyball
www.texassports.com

The Performing Arts

Austin Lyric Opera
901 Barton Springs Road
www.austinlyricopera.org

Paramount Theatre
713 Congress Avenue
www.austintheatre.org

The Austin Symphony
Bass Concert Hall
23rd Street and
  Robert Dedman Drive
www.austinsymphony.org

State Theatre Company
719 Congress Avenue
www.austintheatre.org

Ballet Austin
501 West 3rd Street
www.balletaustin.org

Texas Folklife Resources
1317 South Congress Avenue
www.texasfolklife.org

Major Museums

ArtHouse at the Jones Center
700 Congress Avenue
www.arthousetexas.org

Austin Children's Museum
201 Colorado Street
www.austinkids.org

Austin Museum of Art
823 Congress Avenue
www.amoa.org

Blanton Museum of Art
Martin Luther King Jr. Boulevard
  at Congress Avenue
www.blantonmuseum.org

*Bob Bullock Texas State History
  Museum*
1800 North Congress Avenue
www.thestoryoftexas.com

Center for American History
Sid Richardson Hall,
  1 University Station
www.cah.utexas.edu

French Legation Museum
802 San Marcos Street
www.frenchlegationmuseum.org

George Washington Carver Museum
1165 Angelina Street
www.ci.austin.tx.us/carver

Harry Ransom Center
21st and Guadalupe streets
www.hrc.utexas.edu

*Lyndon B. Johnson Library
  and Museum*
2313 Red River Street
www.lbjlib.utexas.edu

Mexic-Arte Museum
419 Congress Avenue
www.mexic-artemuseum.org

O. Henry House and Museum
409 East 5th Street
**www.ci.austin.tx.us/parks/
  ohenry.htm**

*Texas Memorial Museum of Science
  and History*
2400 Trinity Street
www.utexas.edu/tmm

Special Events (Best Bets)

Austin Chamber Music Festival
July. Various venues
**www.austinchambermusic.org/ht
ml/festival.htm**

Austin City Limits Festival
September. Dozens of bands play
    for over three days of fun
Zilker Park, 2100 Barton Springs
    Road
www.aclfest.com

Austin Film Festival
October. Various venues
www.austinfilmfestival.com

Austin Fine Arts Festival
April. Republic Square Park, 5th
    and Guadalupe streets
www.austinfineartsfestival.org

Austin International Poetry Festival
April. Two hundred poets from
    around the world. Various venues
www.aipf.org

Carnival Brasileiro
Huge Brazilian samba party
February. Palmer Events Center,
    900 Barton Springs Road
www.sambaparty.com

Cinco de Mayo
May. Various venues
www.austin-cincodemayo.com

*Fourth of July Fireworks and
    Symphony*
July Fourth at Town Lake
**www.austinsymphony.org/sea-
son/july**

Republic of Texas Biker Rally
June. "Largest motorcycle enthusiast
    festival in Texas"
Travis County Exposition Center,
    7311 Decker Lane
www.rotrally.com

Spamarama
Often on April Fool's Day featuring
    SPAM Ball, SPAM Cook-off, SPA-
    MALYPICS and SPAM Jam. Vari-
ous venues
www.spamarama.com

South by Southwest
March. Austin's signature music and
    film festival
Austin Convention Center, 500 East
    Cesar Chavez Street
www.sxsw.com

Star of Texas Fair and Rodeo
March. Livestock shows, barbecue,
    and more
Travis County Exposition Center
7311 Decker Lane
www.staroftexas.org

Summerfest
August. African American cultural
   festival
Givens Recreation Center
3811 East 12th Street
www.austinsummerfest.org

Texas Book Festival
November. Capitol Building at 11th
   Street and Congress Avenue
www.texasbookfestival.org

Zilker Kite Festival
March. Kites and more kites
Zilker Park, 2100 Barton Springs
   Road
www.zilkerkitefestival.com

Movie Theaters

Alamo Drafthouse Cinema
409 Colorado Street
www.drafthouse.com

Dobie Theater
2025 Guadalupe Street in the
   Dobie Mall
www.landmarktheatres.com

Downtown Parks

Brush Square
Featuring the O. Henry Museum,
   noontime concerts, giant chess
420 East 5th Street
**www.ci.austin.tx.us/parks/
   ohenry.htm**

Republic Square
Movies in the park, farmer's market
422 Guadalupe Street
**www.ci.austin.tx.us/parks/republic
   square.htm**

Symphony Square
1101 Red River Street
**www.austinsymphony.org/
   symphony/square**

Town Lake Park
Red River hike and bike trails
50 miles of riverside trails
**www.ci.austin.tx.us/parks/
   trails.htm**

Wooldridge Square
Historic urban square
900 Guadalupe Street
**www.austinparks.org/
   Downtown/history.html**

Shopping

Visit the Downtown Austin Alliance Web site for an extensive listing of current retail opportunities in downtown Austin at **www.downtownaustin.com/directory/Retail**.

Groceries
Whole Foods
525 North Lamar Boulevard
www.wholefoodsmarket.com

City/Farmer's Markets
Austin Farmer's Market
Republic Square Park,
4th and Guadalupe streets
www.austinfarmersmarket.org

Plaza Saltillo Farmer's Market
412 Comal Street
www.austinfarmersmarket.org

Getting around

Public Bus Service
Capital Metro
www.capmetro.org

Bike Routes/Trails
www.ci.austin.tx.us/parks/traildirectory.htm

Airport
Austin-Bergstrom International Airport (AUS)
www.ci.austin.tx.us/austinairport

Intercity Bus
Greyhound Terminal
916 East Koenig Lane
www.greyhound.com

Interstate Highways
I-35 (South/north from San Antonio, Texas, to Waco, Texas)

12

Madison, Wisconsin

Madison, a small city of around 250,000 people, is eighty miles west of Milwaukee, and only a two-hour drive to Chicago. Even though it's small, Madison offers an unusual downtown lifestyle because it's one-of-a-kind. Perhaps that's the best way to describe its personality. Here are five reasons why downtown Madison is one of the best distinctively different retirement downtowns.

1. Isthmus and the lakes

Madison has a one-of-a-kind geography because its downtown is located on a narrow strip of land between Lake Mendota on the north and Lake Monona on the south. At its widest point, Madison's downtown isthmus is less than ten city blocks. It is even narrower around the State Capitol, a historic domed building perched on a hill that has clear views of both lakes. Madison is a dense, compact, vibrant city. Downtown residents can walk or bike along the city's beaches while enjoying the views. There are urban parks, including open spaces, boat marinas, and bike trails along the lakes. Madison's physical setting is ideal for both city buffs and outdoor enthusiasts.

2. No freeways

It's possible to hop on a freeway on the fringes of the city and drive to Chicago or Milwaukee, but downtown Madison is one of the few cities without an on-ramp to a controlled-access highway. This has allowed Madison to keep more of its historic downtown neighborhoods.

3. **The University of Wisconsin**

   The Madison campus, on the shores of Lake Mendota, has an enrollment of more than 40,000. It's a great place to take continuing education classes or walks to the locally famous activity center, the Memorial Union. The university's two museums, the Chazen Museum of Art and the Wisconsin Historical Museum, are on the downtown side of the campus. Sports fans can take in a Badgers home football game here. The symbiotic relationship between the university and downtown Madison, although not without its problems, is one of the strongest in America, an influence that's certain to keep downtown retirees and empty nesters young.

4. **State Street**

   Only pedestrians, bikes, and buses are allowed on State Street. This half-mile street links the University of Wisconsin campus to the State Capitol building, and is crammed with gourmet and ethnic restaurants, eateries for students on a budget, art galleries, museums, outdoor cafés, bars, and nightclubs, and over two hundred specialty stores.

5. **Dream town**

   Madison has received numerous accolades by surveys and quality of life studies. Name the magazine—*Entrepreneur, Money, Men's Health, Ladies Home Journal, Forbes, US News and World Report*—and the list goes on; Madison is either at the top of or is named the best of something. Madison's titles (to mention a very few) include: "Best Schools in the Nation," "America's Safest Cities," "America's Best Places to Live and Work," "Best Bike Towns in the County," "Most 'Child-Friendly' Cities," "Best City for Women," "Best Places in America to Start and Grow a Company," "America's Best City for Business and Careers," "Top Walking City," and more. It even won the "American Dream Town" competition. It's no surprise that it's also a best downtown for Ruppies.

Target Retirement Districts and Neighborhoods

Madison's downtown is narrow and tight, with an intricate patchwork of urban neighborhoods and dozens of tiny historic districts joining together from one end of the isthmus to the other.

Capitol Neighborhoods

These districts are centered on Capitol Square and feature the State Capitol Building. The area is generally bordered by the University of Wisconsin on the west and by Blair Street on the east. These are small community-oriented districts that work together to ensure that the high quality of life is sustained. The historic Bassett neighborhood is between Main Street and Bassett Street in the southwestern corner of the isthmus, and has recently enjoyed substantial growth and new residential development. High-quality adult living complexes, masterfully designed condominiums, and bold lofts enhance the character of the existing neighborhood.

The Mifflin West neighborhood encompasses the area northwest of the State Capitol and includes the lively State Street corridor, Overture Hall, the Madison Museum of Contemporary Art, and the Capitol Theater. State/Langdon, an adjacent neighborhood, includes the west blocks of State Street and the Langdon Street corridor near Lake Mendota, and is a residential area with many university students and locals.

The Mansion Hill district borders Lake Mendota just east of Mifflin West and northwest of the Capitol and contains large German Romanesque–style sandstone homes from the 1850s, including the old governor's mansion.

First Settlement, a lovely old neighborhood southeast of the Capitol, has become very popular in recent years and is a vital, high-quality area of the city. For more information, see Capitol Neighborhoods Inc.'s Web site at **www.capitolneighborhoods.org**.

Old Market Place

This area, sometimes referred to as the near-northeast side, is a stone's throw from the Capitol, and begins at the eastern border of the Capitol Neighborhoods near the James Madison Park waterfront. It's a stately historic district once home to architect Frank Lloyd Wright, who made his "Prairie style" house design famous. For more information, see the Old Market Place Neighborhood Association's Web site at **http://danenet.wicip.org/ompna**.

Marquette

East of Blair Street and south along East Washington Street all the way to the eastern end of the isthmus is Marquette, one of Madison's most diverse areas—both in terms of architecture and people. In fact, the local neighborhood association's motto is "Where Everyone Is Welcome." Marquette has two historic bungalow districts near a long stretch of Lake Monona, which is known for its parks, special events, and festivals. Yahara Place Park hosts the mid-July Marquette Waterfront Festival with a variety of musical acts, food, and other activities. August's Orton Park Festival is a citywide celebration of life in Marquette and on the isthmus. This neighborhood has a big personality. For more information, see the Marquette Neighborhood Association's Web site at **www.marquette-neighborhood.org**.

Tenney-Lapham

East of Old Market Place and north of Marquette (across East Washington Avenue), Tenney-Lapham is centered around the East Johnson Street business corridor. It's a four-block strip where locals can shop in a small-town urban atmosphere. Tenney-Lapham, like the other sections of the isthmus, has a wide variety of architectural housing styles: stucco-covered historic Craftsman, Lloyd Wright's Prairie House, bungalows, and Queen Anne homes. Tenney Park and the Yahara River corridor are local favorites for relaxing, walking, ice skating, and boating. For more information, see the Tenney-Lapham Neighborhood Association's Web site at **http://danenet .danenet.org/tlna**.

Keep in mind that these are all small neighborhoods and even smaller districts, tightly knitted together as a long isthmus quilt of great places to live.

Downtown Madison Essentials

State Street strolling: You will enjoy watching people as you stroll up and down State Street: shoppers, street performers, and even "Zombies" who come out during their "March of the Dead" walk. Madison's State Street will be your connection to the soul of the city.

Jumping around: Even if you're not a football fan, you must go at least once to Camp Randall Stadium for a Wisconsin Badgers football game. At the start of the fourth quarter, most of the 80,000 fans jump in unison—up and down, again and again. The Badgers hop to a weird, frenetic song that was popular during the early 1990s by the House of Pain called, appropriately, "Jump Around."

Mad city: It's short for Madison, but locals will tell you it's because many people think that the city is "mad" in the crazy sense. Madison (like Austin) is home to liberal-leaning thinkers and experimental politics.

Discover the others: Lakes Mendota and Menona are not the only lakes in Madison. Nearby Lake Wingra is to the west of the isthmus and south of the University of Wisconsin; Lake Waubesa is south of U.S. Highway 18; and Lake Kegonsa is a few miles south of Waubesa near Pleasant Springs. See what's going on at the other lakes on a day trip getaway.

Capitol Square: Besides the waterfronts, make sure you walk around Capitol Square. It's the center of the city and the home of the Dane County Market, one of the most successful outdoor farmer's markets in the country. Capitol Square also hosts the Wisconsin Book Festival, a Taste of Wisconsin, and other specifically Madison special events.

A bike: After all, this is not the "Best Bike City" in the country for nothing.

General Statistics

Population: Downtown: 26,715 (2000); City: 220,332 (2003); Metro: 526,742 (2003)

Terrain: Madison's isthmus contains rolling hills that meet the flat beaches and shores of Lakes Mendota and Monona.

Climate Overview: cold winters/mild summers

Average January high/low temperature: 26/8F

Average July high/low temperature: 79/55F

Average annual total precipitation: 32 inches

Average annual snowfall: 43 inches

Number of cloudy days: 180

Cost of Living: Find out the current cost of living between Madison and your community by visiting **www.homefair.com** and clicking **"Moving to a New State"** or **"Moving Locally,"** then follow the prompts.

Cost of Housing:

Zip code: 53703 (Downtown Madison); price snapshot: $324,983; sq/ft: 1,388

Real estate prices fluctuate. For up-to-date neighborhood housing cost information, input the zip codes above in the Homestore Web site (affiliated with Realtor.com) at **www.homestore.com/Cities**.

Rent Costs: If you want to rent, explore **www.rentnet.com** and also investigate the neighborhood Web sites for current rents and available properties.

Taxes

Property Tax: $2,346 per $100,000 of assessed value. See the Dane County Treasurer's Office for changes at **www.countyofdane.com/treasure/**.

Sales Tax: 5.5 percent. Groceries and prescription drugs are exempt.

State Income Tax: 4.6 percent to 6.75 percent. (Four income tax brackets. Single: low $8,840 to high $132,580 and over. Married: $11,780 to $176,770. Exemptions: Single: $700; married: $1,400; child: $400; over 65: $250.)

Downtown Madison Retirement Lifestyle Web Guide

Living

There are no Web sites that cater exclusively to the thriving downtown Madison real estate market. The best place to go to find a Realtor in Madison will take a bit of clicking. Start with the Wisconsin Realtor's Association at **www.wra.org**, then click on "**Find a Realtor**," then "**South**

Central" then "**Madison**." The best bet is to visit **www.realtor.com** and input downtown's 53703 zip code to explore current residential listings. Also check Downtown Madison Inc.'s Web site for its annual Downtown Living Tour at **www.downtownmadison.org**.

City Hospitals

Meriter Health Services
202 South Park Street
www.meriter.com

St. Mary's Hospital Medical Center
707 South Mills Street
www.stmarysmadison.com

University of Wisconsin Hospital and
  Clinics
600 Highland Avenue
www.uwhealth.org

Health Clubs

Capital Fitness
302 East Washington Avenue
www.capitalfitness.net

Capital Fitness Women's Facility
44 East Mifflin Street
www.capitalfitness.net

Monkey Bar Gym
600 Williamson Street, # K2
www.monkeybargym.com

Volunteering

Volunteer Your Time (United Way of Dane County)
www.volunteeryourtime.org

Educational opportunities

City Colleges and Universities

University of Wisconsin
716 Langdon Street
www.wisc.edu

Edgewood College
1000 Edgewood College Drive
www.edgewood.edu

Madison Area Technical College
Downtown Education Center,
  211 North Carroll Street
http://matcmadison.edu

Library
Madison Public Library
201 West Mifflin Street
www.madisonpubliclibrary.org

Entertainment

Restaurants, Bars, and Nightclubs
For the latest listing of restaurants and nightclubs, visit Downtown Madison Inc.'s Web site at **www.downtownmadison.org** and find the downtown map and guide with a hundred bars and restaurants.

College Sports
The University of Wisconsin
Men's and women's basketball, golf, soccer, track and field, tennis, rowing, swimming, cross-country, men's hockey, baseball, football, wrestling, women's field hockey, softball
www.uwbadgers.com

The Performing Arts
Madison Opera
Overture Center for the Arts,
  Overature Hall
201 State Street
www.madisonopera.org

Madison Repertory Theatre
Overture Center for the Arts,
  The Playhouse
201 State Street
www.madisonrep.org

Madison Symphony Orchestra
Overture Center for the Arts,
  Overature Hall
201 State Street
www.madisonsymphony.org

Wisconsin Chamber Orchestra
Overture Center for the Arts,
  Capitol Theater
201 State Street
www.wcoconcerts.org

Major Museums

Chazen Museum of Art
800 University Avenue, University
  of Wisconsin
http://chazen.wisc.edu

Madison Children's Museum
100 State Street
**www.madisonchildrens
  museum.com**

*Madison Museum
  of Contemporary Art*
227 West Washington Avenue
www.mmoca.org

Wisconsin Veterans Museum
30 West Mifflin Street
http://museum.dva.state.wi.us

Wisconsin Historical Museum
816 State Street
**www.wisconsinhistory.org/
  museum**

Special Events (Best Bets)

Art Fair on the Square
July. Capitol Square
www.mmoca.org/events/artfair

Great Taste of the Midwest Beer Festival
August. Sample beer from one hundred breweries in Olin-Turville Park
www.mhtg.org

Jazz at Five
Jazz concerts on Wednesdays
  in August and September
  on State Street
www.jazzat5.org

Kites on Ice
February. Winter kite flying festival.
  Changes location over years
www.madisonfestivals.com

Mad-City Marathon
May. Race through Madison
www.madisonfestivals.com

*Madison Museum of Contemporary
  Art Gallery Night*
Semiannual gallery walk
www.mmoca.org

Taste of Madison Festival
September—Labor Day weekend.
  Sample local restaurants, listen
  to live music in downtown
www.madisonfestivals.com/taste

The Wisconsin Book Festival
October. Various downtown venues
www.wisconsinbookfestival.org

Wisconsin Film Festival
Midspring. Festival featuring
   independent film and experimental documentaries
www.wifilmfest.org

Movie Theater
Orpheum Theater
Historic movie house showing art and documentary films
216 State Street
www.orpheumtheatre.net

Favorite Downtown Parks
Bridges Golf Course
Championship eighteen-hole golf course bordering downtown Madison
2702 Shopko Drive
www.golfthebridges.com

Brittingham Park
Monona lakeside fishing, bike paths
401 Brittingham Place
www.ci.madison.wi.us/parks/major/BrittPark.html

James Madison Park
Beaches along Lake Mendota, canoeing, open spaces
614 East Gorham Street
www.ci.madison.wi.us/parks/major/jmPark.html

Olbrich Park
Sixty-one-acre Lake Mendota waterfront park
3527 Atwood Avenue
www.ci.madison.wi.us/parks/major/olbrich.html

Tenney Park
Lake Mendota waterfront park with beaches
1414 East Johnson Street
www.ci.madison.wi.us/parks/major/tenney.html

University of Wisconsin Arboretum
1,260 acres of ecological restoration, trails, visitor's center
1207 Seminole Highway
http://uwarboretum.org

Shopping

For the latest listing of retail establishments, visit Downtown Madison Inc.'s
Web site at **www.downtownmadison.org** and find the downtown map and
guide with over two-hundred unique shops.

Groceries

Capitol Centre Foods
111 North Broom Street
www.capcentrefoods.com

Copps Food Centers-East
2502 Shopko Drive

Copps Food Centers-West
1312 South Park Street
www.copps.com

Mifflin Street Community Co-Op
32 North Bassett Street
www.mifflincoop.com

Williamson Street Grocery Co-Op
1221 Williamson Street
www.willystreet.coop

City/Farmer's Markets

Dane County Farmer's Market on the Square
Lining the grounds of the State Capitol
www.madfarmmkt.org

Getting around

Public Bus Service

Madison Metro Transit System
www.mymetrobus.com

Bike Routes/Trails

City of Madison
www.ci.madison.wi.us/transp/bicycle.html

Intercity Bus

Greyhound Terminal
2 South Bedford Street
www.greyhound.com

Intercity Trains

Amtrak
Station at 800 Langdon Street
University of Wisconsin Memorial Union
www.amtrak.com

Airport

Dane County Regional Airport (MSN)
www.co.dane.wi.us/airport

Interstate Highways

Highways do not extend into downtown Madison.
I-90 (East/west from Chicago, Illinois, to La Crosse, Wisconsin)
I-94 (East to Milwaukee, Wisconsin)

Providence, Rhode Island

Providence is another city that's been showered with accolades, primarily because of its downtown renaissance. In fact, renaissance and Providence are often used together in book titles, magazine and newspaper articles, and various thesis and dissertation titles. This is a wonderful place: a small and ever-improving urban environment, with narrow streets, wide plazas, and historic preservation. Providence is indeed distinctively different, and one of America's few "European cities."

Providence's new birth didn't happen overnight. During most of the 1900s, it was a highly industrial little city in the shadow of Boston, and known mostly as the capital of tiny Rhode Island. It was not the kind of place most people would want to visit—much less live. The state of Providence's economy and failing downtown was a call-to-action for local leaders. Conditions here were going to get much better, or the city would fall the way of other rust belt cities and simply die. With a lot of money, elbow grease, and hope for a brighter tomorrow, the city is becoming one of America's showcase downtowns. Here are a five more reasons why you should give it serious consideration.

1. Historic splendor

Few other places in America can claim that their 400th birthday is on the horizon. The Providence Preservation Society, established in 1956, is one of the oldest historic preservation organizations in the country and continues to work with community activists and local leaders to keep the flavor and colonial character of this beautiful city alive. Providence suffered as other cities did during the "urban renewal" movement of the 1950s and 1960s, but locals here helped save many irreplaceable colonial-period houses and mercantile buildings.

When you walk through downtown and the surrounding neighborhoods, it's like a walk back in time, and similar in some respects to the special qualities found in Savannah, Georgia; Charleston, South Carolina; and in nearby central Boston. Just consider the following three examples of hundreds of interesting old buildings that continue to tell their stories: the Providence Athenaeum, America's fourth-oldest library, founded in 1753; the First Baptist Church, established in 1838; and the 1792 cobblestone-paved Benefit Street's Nightingale-Brown House, of Brown University fame. Historic sculptures embellish Providence's preserved ambiance, including the Ambrose Burnside Monument (1887) at Kennedy Plaza, the Bajnotti Fountain (1899) at Brown University, and the Roger Williams Memorial on Prospect Terrace. Today, all of downtown Providence is listed on the National Register of Historic Places.

2. Manageability

Have you ever heard of a city that decided to move a river? Providence did. Downtown's two underground canals, once covered by pavement, were exposed and repositioned as the rivers they were meant to be. Now, the city has a riverfront with gondolas floating under pedestrian bridges and a river celebration called WaterFire, where a series of bonfires blaze above the surface of the water and the event is celebrated with music. In a similar way, I-195, a freeway spur through the downtown, is also being moved. Since the freeway opens up over forty prime acres of downtown real estate, a new riverfront development is emerging, featuring new construction and the preservation, recovery, and rehabilitation of historic river mills. Even the railroad tracks that once separated neighborhoods have been moved to create a more livable city.

3. City of artists

The Rhode Island School of Design (RISD), one of the country's most exclusive art and design colleges, is in the East Side neighborhood of downtown Providence. It's one reason why Providence acts as an unjuried art gallery where people are encouraged to create, express, and sell their art. In the 1990s, an Arts and Entertainment District was established as a tax-incentive program for artists. All they had to do was live in the middle of the Downcity District, create art, and sell it within the defined area—and their sales would be exempt from taxes. Although the idea never fully reached its potential, it is still a model for ambitious and creative thinking.

4. Great downtown colleges
Downtown Providence has Ivy League's Brown University, and Johnson and Wales. In addition, the University of Rhode Island has a Providence campus, and there's also Providence College, Rock Island College, and the Providence branch of the Community College of Rhode Island. Ruppies will enjoy the varied higher-education offerings in Providence.

5. Boston and Cape Cod
You can take a short train ride or drive to nearby Boston and enjoy the myriad cultural offerings and entertainment venues. Or perhaps a nature outing to Narragansett Bay or a jaunt to Newport, or you could take the ferry and explore Cape Cod or Martha's Vineyard.

Target Retirement Districts and Neighborhoods

Although the downtown area has small enclaves with emerging residential and retail districts, there are long-established residential neighborhoods surrounding the city center. Here are the major areas.

Downcity

Downcity, an arts district in the very middle of the downtown area, is setting an example for revitalization for the rest of the city. There's new interest in the district's late nineteenth-century mercantile buildings and warehouses. Condominiums and apartments are now creating a residential neighborhood to the arts and culture theme of Downcity's entertainment district. Residential and retail activity is beginning to refocus on Westminster Street, once the city's retail Main Street.

Financial District

The historic Financial District, the business core of downtown Providence, is northeast of Downcity. This district was once the city's retail hub and home to the historic Providence Arcade (1828), the nation's first indoor shopping "mall." The area is also home to the taller buildings that make up the city's skyline. Slightly behind Downcity in its revitalization, this district is bound to catch up with proposed condominium towers, loft conversions around Kennedy Plaza, and new student apartments.

Downcity is bounded by Fountain, Empire, Weybosset, and Dorrance streets. The Financial District lies within this area between Kennedy Plaza, Memorial Boulevard, and Pine and Dorrance streets, but the prime area of focus is on Westminster and Weybosset streets. For Downcity and the Financial District, visit the Downtown Improvement District's Web site at **www.providencedowntown.com** and the Providence Downtown Merchants Association Web site: **www.downtownprovidence.org**.

College Hill (Near East Side or "East Side")

A vintage New England neighborhood surrounds Brown University and the Rhode Island School of Design. Stately churches and Federal and colonial mansions front streets with nineteenth-century street poles and readily fit the image of an Ivy League neighborhood. Although adorable restaurants and coffee shops cater to locals and students, this is also the city's major bed and breakfast area. The east side is the "soft" side of downtown.

The general boundaries of College Hill are Main Street (west) extending to Arlington Avenue and Governor Street (east), to John Street (south) and to Olney Street (north). For more information, see the College Hill Neighborhood Association's Web site at **www.savecollegehill.com**.

Federal Hill

Also called "Little Italy," this area is one of Providence's most charming and walkable neighborhoods. Specialty shops, including authentic Italian food stores and Italian restaurants, have long established followings. Visitors are greeted to this fun enclave by an arch spanning Atwells Avenue, with a pinecone (an Italian symbol of abundance) hanging from the center. Multi-family buildings predominate and the area is being revitalized with newcomers who love the old world charm but want the close proximity of Downcity, which is only a short walk to the east.

Greater Federal Hill is generally bounded by I-95 (east), Westminster Street (south), and the Huntington Expressway (west/north). For information on Federal Hill, see the West Broadway Neighborhood Association's Web site at **www.wbna.org**.

Downtown Providence Essentials

WaterFire: Like New Orleans' annual Mardi Gras, WaterFire is Providence's signature festival that takes place all summer. It features bonfires that blaze above the surface of the three downtown rivers, where "firetenders" pass flames around "burning" water vessels. The festival is enjoyed by thousands who listen to the music and soak up the medieval atmosphere. WaterFire, like Mardi Gras, is spreading. Columbus, Ohio, has its own version, and other cities will probably also copy Providence's originality.

Urban ice skating: Downcity's illuminated ice rink features the Providence skyline as a backdrop (much like Manhattan's Rockefeller Plaza) and is a triumph of city planning and design. You will enjoy spending a winter's evening skating with hundreds of others here under the stars.

Gallery nights: You can attend Gallery Night, an art-filled night touring thirty galleries, historic sites, and museums. Get on the "Art Bus," from 5:00 to 9:00 p.m., and enjoy all of the neighborhood galleries.

Gondola rides: From May to October, you can spend a romantic forty-minute ride through the "Venice" of New England on an authentic Venetian gondola.

Studying architecture: "Is that building Federal, Greek Revival, Italianate, or colonial?" When you live in a city as architecturally significant as Providence, it's fun to learn "what is what" and the time periods for each style.

Becoming an Italian: Once you cross under the bronzed pinecone on Atwells Avenue, regardless of your ethnic makeup, you "become" an Italian. Sip an espresso while enjoying the outdoors at one of many cafés, then shop for pasta and just the right herbs for your tomato sauce that you'll cook tomorrow. Don't miss the Federal Hill Stroll, where you'll find great people-watching to go along with the one-of-a-kind shopping experience.

General Statistics

Population: Downtown core: 9,342 (2000); City: 178,126 (2003); Metro: 1,623,172 (2003)

Terrain: Greater downtown Providence is generally flat (along the riverfront) with gently rolling hills.

Climate Overview: cold winters/mild summers

Average January high/low temperature: 37/20F

Average July high/low temperature: 77/57F

Average annual total precipitation: 45 inches

Average annual snowfall: 36 inches

Number of cloudy days: 165

Cost of Living: Find out the current cost of living between Providence and your community by visiting **www.homefair.com** and clicking "**Moving to a New State**" or "**Moving Locally**," then follow the prompts.

Cost of Housing:

Zip code: 02903 (Downcity, Financial District, Federal Hill); price snapshot: $408,566; sq/ft: 1,597

Zip code: 02906 (College Hill and the Greater East Side neighborhoods); price snapshot: $466,629; sq/ft: 2,181

Real estate prices fluctuate. For up-to-date neighborhood housing cost information, input the zip codes above in the Homestore Web site (affiliated with Realtor.com) at **www.homestore.com/Cities**.

Rent Costs: If you want to rent, explore **www.rentnet.com** and also investigate the neighborhood Web sites for current rents and available properties.

Taxes

Property Tax: Typical rate of $2,965 per $100,000 of assessed value. Visit the City of Providence at **www.providenceri.com/government** and click "**Tax Assessor**" for the latest assessments and rates.

Sales Tax: 7 percent. Groceries, clothing, newspapers, and prescription drugs are exempt.

State Income Tax: 25 percent of federal income tax liability.

Downtown Providence Retirement Lifestyle Web Guide

Living

There are currently no comprehensive real estate sites that exclusively feature urban living opportunities in downtown Providence. The best bet is to visit **www.realtor.com** and input downtown Providence's 02903 and 02906 zip codes to explore current residential listings. A good place to make contacts to find out more about the area is through the Greater Providence Board of Realtors at **www.gpbor.com**.

City Hospitals

Rhode Island Hospital
593 Eddy Street
www.lifespan.org

Roger Williams Medical Center
825 Chalkstone Avenue
www.rwmc.com

Health Clubs

InTown Providence Family YMCA
164 Broad Street
www.ymcagreaterprovidence.org

Volunteering

Volunteer Center of Rhode Island
www.volunteersolutions.org

Educational opportunities

City Colleges and Universities

Brown University
45 Prospect Street
www.brown.edu

Rhode Island College
600 Mount Pleasant Avenue
www.ric.edu

Community College of Rhode Island
   (Providence "Liston" campus)
1 Hilton Street
www.ccri.edu

Rhode Island School of Design
2 College Street
www.risd.edu

Johnson and Wales University
   (Downcity campus)
111 Dorrance Street
www.jwu.edu

University of Rhode Island
   (Feinstein Providence campus)
80 Washington Street
www.uri.edu

Providence College
549 River Avenue
www.providence.edu

Library

Providence Public Library
150 Empire Street
www.provlib.org

Entertainment

Restaurants, Bars, and Nightclubs

Downtown Providence Improvement District provides a fantastic Web resource for the latest listing of restaurants and nightclubs: **www.providence downtown.com**.

Professional Spectator Sports
Providence Bruins (hockey)
Dunkin' Donuts Center
1 LaSalle Square
www.providencebruins.com

College Sports
Brown University (Ivy League)
Men's and women's crew, basketball, soccer, golf, ice hockey, lacrosse, soccer, squash, swimming and diving, track and field, tennis, cross-country, water polo, gymnastics, skiing, wrestling, men's baseball, women's equestrian, softball, volleyball
www.brownbears.com

The Performing Arts
Perishable Theatre
95 Empire Street
www.perishable.org

Providence Black Repertory Company
276 Westminster Street
www.blackrep.org

Trinity Repertory Company
Lederer Theater Center,
   201 Washington Street
www.trinityrep.com

Rhode Island Philharmonic Orchestra
VMA Arts and Cultural Center
Corner of Park and
   Avenue of the Arts streets
www.ri-philharmonic.org

Opera Providence
VMA Arts and Cultural Center
Corner of Park and
   Avenue of the Arts streets
www.operaprovidence.org

Major Museums
Culinary Archives and Museum
Johnson and Wales University
315 Harborside Boulevard
www.culinary.org

Museum of Natural History and
   Cormack Planetarium
Roger Williams Park, 1000 Elmwood Avenue
www.osfn.org/museum

The Providence Athenaeum
251 Benefit Street
www.providenceathenaeum.org

Providence Children's Museum
100 South Street
www.childrenmuseum.org

Rhode Island School of Design Museum
224 Benefit Street
www.risd.edu/museum.cfm

Russian Submarine/
  USS Saratoga Museum
Collier Point Park
www.saratogamuseum.org

Special Events (Best Bets)

Bright Night Festival
New Year's Eve Celebration,
  downtown Providence
www.brightnight.org

Gallery Night Providence
Third Thursday of every month
  from March to November,
  downtown Providence
www.gallerynight.info

Providence Craft Show
October. Rhode Island
  Convention Center
www.providencecraftshow.com

Providence French Film Festival
February and March.
  Cable Car Cinema
204 South Main Street
www.provfrenchfilm.com

Providence Latin American
  Film Festival
April. Various venues
www.murphyandmurphy.com/plff

WaterFire
Summer months festival along
  Providence's three rivers
www.waterfire.org

Movie Theaters

Cable Car Cinema
204 South Main Street
www.cablecarcinema.com

Providence Place Cinemas 16
10 Providence Street
www.providenceplace.com

Avon Cinema
260 Thayer Street in the East Side
www.avoncinema.com

Feinstein IMAX Theater
9 Providence Street
www.imax.com/providence

Favorite Downtown Parks

Bank of America Skating Center
2 Kennedy Plaza—Providence's
 version of New York's
 Rockefeller Plaza
www.providenceskating.com

Collier Point Park
Allens Avenue

Roger Williams Park Zoo
 (near downtown)
1000 Elmwood Avenue
www.rogerwilliamsparkzoo.org

Providence River Walk
Water Place Park to James Street
 in Fox Point

Shopping

Major Retail

Providence Place Mall
1 Providence Place at Kennedy Plaza
www.providenceplace.com

Also visit Downtown Providence Improvement District's Web site at **www.down townprovidence.com**, then click "**Downtown Directory**" for a map of every shopping opportunity in downtown Providence.

Groceries

Visit Downtown Providence Improvement District's Web site at **www.down townprovidence.com**, then click "**Downtown Directory**" for a map of every grocery store in downtown Providence.

City/Farmer's Markets

Monday Market
Mondays in season
Bank of America City Center
 at Kennedy Plaza
www.farmfreshri.com

Broad Street Farmer's Market
807 Broad Street

Downcity Farmer's Market
Parade Street and Hope High
 School on Hope Street

Governor Dyer Cooperative Market
Between Promenade and
 Valley streets

Getting around

Public Bus Service
Rhode Island Public Transportation Authority
www.ripta.com

Airports
T. F. Green Airport (PVD)
www.pvdairport.com

Intercity Trains
Amtrak and Massachusetts Bay Transportation Authority (to Boston)
Providence Railroad Station
100 Gaspee Street
www.amtrak.com or www.mbta.com

Intercity Bus
Bonanza Bus and Greyhound Lines
Kennedy Plaza
http://bonanzabus.com or www.greyhound.com

Interstate Highways
I-95 (South/north from New Haven, Connecticut, to Boston, Massachusetts)
I-195 (East to Fall River, Massachusetts)

Sunbelt Downtowns

Sunbelt downtowns are perfect for the millions of Northerners who wish to escape cold, snowy winters and retire to a warmer climate. These Southern cities provide mild, tolerably short (or no) winters and long, hot summers. Because of their sunny location, these regions are also the country's growth areas, and as a result, their downtown residential populations are growing at an equally fast pace. In this section, find out more about the best sunbelt downtowns: Atlanta, Georgia; Charlotte, North Carolina; Memphis, Tennessee; and Miami, Florida.

14 Atlanta, Georgia

Atlanta, Georgia, is the unofficial capital of the southeastern United States and by far Georgia's largest metropolitan area. Passengers can take nonstop flights to destinations around the world from the Hartsfield-Jackson International Airport. The airport is the world's busiest, and Atlanta's skyline is one of the tallest, brightest, and most impressive in the country. Here are five reasons why Atlanta is getting a lot of attention from Ruppies.

1. It's transforming fast

"Wow!" is the only word for what is happening in Atlanta. Over the past ten years Atlanta has encountered a construction boom: in-town residential homes, town homes, apartments, mid-rise condominiums, and tall twenty-, thirty-, or seventy-story towers. Atlanta has just taken off.

People are fed up with commuting to the suburbs. Clogged freeways and rush hour traffic has become an unwanted daily event. Even the fourteen-lane freeways still clog up as easily as when they were half their width. Ironically, city planners who were against spending more money to build wider ones can now, at least in part, thank Atlanta's urban growth on their failure to move traffic efficiently.

With all of the Atlanta urban living buzz, there is a downside: The sidewalk-level activity that is usually found in big cities is just not there yet. Many of the new buildings are not "street-friendly"—they're big on prominent parking garages but short on street appeal. It's not uncommon to be in the skyscraper section of Midtown (with the tallest buildings in the southeast United States) and feel all alone on the sidewalk.

But this is all changing. Many permanent residents are converging on the city and it's just a matter of time before the new Atlanta emerges.

2. A variety of choices

Other than Miami, no other city in the southeasten United States is building more in-town homes than Atlanta, and there are choices here. Multimillion dollar luxury penthouses and starter studio lofts are not far from each other, bringing all kinds of people with varied incomes into one place. As always, it's a size trade-off: The square footage of living space will be much less than a suburban Atlanta home.

3. Three "downtowns" in one

Downtown Atlanta is one of three major urban activity centers that is "ITP"—local jargon for "Inside the Perimeter" freeway loop, a bypass that surrounds the city. The area is the most southern activity center and home to the Georgia State Capitol, city hall, and other government buildings associated with old downtowns. Buckhead's "downtown" skyline alone is bigger and taller than many major cities. Midtown, the midpoint activity center, is home to Piedmont Park, and is surrounded by mega-skyscrapers. Buckhead and Midtown are, for all practical purposes, also downtowns, offering retirees and empty nesters distinct choices for Atlanta-style city living.

4. Diversity

Atlanta continues to draw a large influx of African Americans, and it's also home to big numbers of Hispanics, Asians, and gays. There's an incredibly diverse blend of citizens in this city.

5. Retail, retail—RETAIL

Atlanta has a lot of stores that most suburbanites take for granted. Buckhead's long-standing favorite Lennox Mall and sister Dunwoody Mall have over four hundred stores and there are hundreds more in the nearby corridors. Midtown's Atlantic Station has a multiplex movie theater, department stores, grocery store, and other retail establishments normally found in traditional malls. Although downtown lost many retail strongholds, six million people, especially local employees, still visit Underground Atlanta every year—the original downtown that was covered by a street viaduct in the 1920s.

The entire area is linked by MARTA (Metro Atlanta Rapid Transit Authority) trains and buses providing easy access to shopping.

Target Retirement Districts and Neighborhoods

Atlanta is exploding with city dwellers within its three major areas, but downtown, Midtown, and Buckhead also have several distinct neighborhoods of their own.

Downtown Core

The downtown center is aptly named "Five Points" because Marietta Street, Decatur Street, Edgewood Avenue, and Peachtree Street (north and south legs) converge at one point. Woodruff Park, an open city square (and haven for panhandlers), which features a dog run, is considered the middle of downtown. This is a busy place because the main MARTA rail hub, Underground Atlanta's shopping, and Georgia State University are all here.

Five Points and downtown have suffered in the last few decades. While it will always be a government anchor, many businesses and headquarters have moved north to the Midtown area or to the suburbs for a variety of reasons. The area, however, is enjoying new popularity as a residential neighborhood with new condominiums and lofts. Although still a haven for panhandlers, new neighbors and an active Business Improvement District are working hard to improve the downtown's reputation.

Fairlie-Poplar

This adjacent district, often associated with Five Points, is a neighborhood with tightly constructed historic buildings, pedestrian-friendly brick sidewalks, and the city's Manhattan-looking enclave—all located on about twenty square blocks. The area has become popular with urban history and architecture buffs who now live here. Neighbors have close access to concerts, planned activities, festivals, and other fun things to do in Centennial Olympic Park, which is adjacent and northwest of the neighborhood. The district also borders the Philips Arena (Atlanta Hawks), and the Georgia Dome, which is home to the Atlanta Falcons, concerts, and special events.

Fairlie-Poplar is generally bounded by Techwood Drive, Wall Street, Peachtree Street, and Carnegie Way. For more information, see the Fairlie Poplar Web page at **www.fairliepoplar.org**. Also visit the Atlanta Downtown Neighborhood Association's Web site at **www.atlantadna.org**.

Centennial Hill/Centennial Place

The area north of Fairlie-Poplar is gaining an impressive number of permanent residents with new residential condos, town homes, and proposed skyscrapers. Named for its southwestern anchor Centennial Olympic Park, the Centennial neighborhoods are home to Coca-Cola's world headquarters and the new Georgia Aquarium. Residents here can also take advantage of the Georgia Institute of Technology, bordering the area on the north, with its huge bookstore, coffee shops, and restaurants. Because of all the urban redevelopment that's occurring, there are many living choices for Ruppies here.

Centennial Hill/Place is generally between International Boulevard, Marietta Street, I-75, and Peachtree Street. For more information, see the Central Atlanta Progress Web site at **www.centralatlantaprogress.org**.

Marietta Street Artery — (locally spelled ARTery)

Old warehouse and industrial buildings are the backdrop for new residential and business opportunities here. "ARTery" is appropriate, because this strip hosts the Atlanta Contemporary Arts Center, art galleries, and even a photography district with a concentration of professional photographers.

The district begins at Centennial Park to the King Plow/Railroad Historic District about three miles north. Marietta Street runs along the western border of Centennial Hill (these neighborhoods bleed together) and flanks the western border of the Georgia Tech campus. See the Marietta Street Artery Neighborhood's Web site at **www.artery.org** for more information.

SoNo

Formerly Bedford Pine, the SoNo neighborhood (short for South of North Avenue) has lagged behind other areas in redevelopment interest. This section should connect the downtown area to Midtown, but the unflattering urban design of the 1960s and 1970s never provided for a smooth, continuous urban transition. Watch for SoNo to explode with new housing in the next few years.

SoNo is a large area between I-75, North Avenue, Parkway Drive, and Ralph McGill Boulevard. See **www.centralatlantaprogress.org** for more information.

Castleberry Hill

Here's a fascinating warehouse district with old railroad buildings, galleries, and new specialty shops. Castleberry, historically Atlanta's meat-packing district with its associated old processing structures, is fast becoming one of Atlanta's preeminent loft districts.

Castleberry Hill is bounded by I-20, Mitchell Street SW, Spring Street SW, and McDaniel Street southwest of Five Points and due south of the landmark Georgia Dome Arena and east of Clark Atlanta University. Visit the Castleberry Hill Historic District's Web site for more information at **www.castleberryhill.org**.

Sweet Auburn

The historically black business district on Auburn Avenue is still an African American commercial stronghold today. Notably, this neighborhood was Martin Luther King Jr.'s childhood home. The Sweet Auburn Curb Market, Atlanta's fresh city market, is also here and specializes in soul food such as chitlins and hog jowl. For the first time in decades, significant new residential development opportunities are beginning to emerge in this area.

Sweet Auburn is between Piedmont Avenue, DeKalb Avenue, Randolph Street, and Freedom Parkway. See the latest on the Friends of Sweet Auburn's Web site at **www.sweetauburn.com**.

Midtown

Midtown, which begins at Ponce de Leon Avenue, has huge skyscrapers, including the Bank of America Plaza, Sun Trust Plaza, and One Atlantic Center. The residential neighborhoods here are extremely varied. Some are edgy urban landscapes and others are built on green rolling hills with leafy open spaces. This area has had a head start on redevelopment efforts, especially compared to the neighborhoods to the south, and has also been the preferred location for most urbanites since the 1980s—and it continues to grow.

The heart of Midtown

The middle of Midtown is flanked by Atlanta's beloved Piedmont Park, the city's version of New York's Central Park. The park has almost two hundred acres and is surrounded by residential towers and with great skyline views. Juniper, Piedmont, and Peachtree streets bisect this area while impressive residential housing can be found throughout the neighborhood. Midtown has some of Atlanta's best restaurants, is the historic heart of the city's gay community, and boasts the Fox Theatre, located on Peachtree and Ponce de Leon Avenue. The huge Atlantic Station lifestyle development, with 5,000 apartments and condominiums planned, is surrounded by retail establishments, restaurants, and office space and is across the new 17th Street bridge. Midtown delivers a broad range of housing opportunities for Ruppies.

The heart of urban Midtown is north of Ponce de Leon and south of 14th Street. For more information on Midtown, see the Midtown Neighbor's Association at **www.midtownatlanta.org** and the Atlantic Station Web site at **www.atlanticstation.com**.

Virginia-Highland

This gorgeous "first suburb" east of Piedmont Park has curvy, hilly streets, stately single-family homes, and huge yards. It's known for the small, quaint, and popular commercial district at the intersection of Virginia and Highland where restaurants, boutiques, bars, and coffee shops thrive. This area is more like an urban suburb for potential retirees and empty nesters who want to be close and yet far away at the same time.

Virginia-Highland is the area bounded by Monroe Drive (west), Briarcliff (east), Elizabeth Street (south), and University Avenue (north). For more information, see the Virginia-Highland Civic Association's Web site at **www.vahi.org**.

Ansley Park

This area, similar to Virginia-Highland, is a charming urban neighborhood with a decidedly suburban feel—it even has a golf course. Among mature trees and small parks on hilly lanes, residents can walk to the Atlanta Symphony Hall, or catch MARTA for a day of shopping.

Ansley Park is north of 15th Street and bordered by Peachtree Street (west), Piedmont Avenue (east), and the Ansley Golf Club (north). For more information, see the Ansley Park Civic Association's Web site at **www.ansleypark.org**.

Buckhead

Buckhead is an affluent northern district filled with mansions and much of Atlanta's highest-end housing, and has premier retail shopping centers. This area not only has exclusive residential enclaves with golf courses but it also has an emerging and exciting city skyline. There are twenty-five- to seventy-story residential condominium skyscrapers and many of Atlanta's most popular nightclubs, hotels, and major indoor malls. It's a vivacious, linear urban center.

Buckhead begins north of Peachtree Creek (just south of Lindbergh Drive) where Peachtree Street winds north and bleeds northward along Peachtree Road toward the I-285 beltway. See Buckhead Incorporated for more information at **www.buckhead.net**.

Downtown Atlanta Essentials

A MARTA pass and a car: Take advantage of the long-established MARTA rail and bus lines that go through the city's three "downtowns." Just remember, residents really love their cars here.

Hot dogs: Atlanta is famous for its special Varsity Inn hot dogs, a 1950s-style drive-in restaurant featuring these processed sausages. You might want to try the local delicacy with chili and onions this time, or perhaps with a side of delicious, greasy onion rings.

A walk around Piedmont park: It's a wide-open expanse of land featuring a large pond, grassy knolls, paved pedestrian and bike paths, park benches, and skyscraper views that peek over the trees. If you're a city lover, Piedmont Park will make your spirit soar while you get your daily exercise.

The Sweet Auburn Curb Market: You'll love the soul food at this historic market on the near east side of downtown. Shoppers can browse the stalls for the freshest fish, steaks, just-cut flowers, and even specialty African dresswear.

Coca-Cola and CNN: Atlanta is the world headquarters of many companies including Coca-Cola, which began here and continues operations from downtown. Ted Turner's Cable News Network's headquarters is down the street.

Hip-hop music: Atlanta is the capital of hip-hop, which includes rap and/or rhythm and blues. You can come to enjoy this style of music, and marvel at the platinum-selling local artists who are known and respected throughout the world.

General Statistics

Population: Downtown 24,931 (2000); City: 419,122 (2003); Metro: 4,610,032 (2003)

Terrain: In-town Atlanta's topography is slightly hilly.

Climate Overview: cool winters/hot summers

Average January high/low temperature: 52/33F

Average July high/low temperature: 89/70F

Average annual total precipitation: 51 inches

Average annual snowfall: 2 inches

Number of cloudy days: 149

Cost of Living: Find out the current cost of living between Atlanta and your community by visiting **www.homefair.com** and clicking **"Moving to a New State"** or **"Moving Locally,"** then follow the prompts.

Cost of Housing:

Zip code: 30303 (Five Points, Fairlie-Poplar, Castleberry Hill, and the southern Centennial neighborhoods); price snapshot: $203,251; sq/ft: N/A

Zip code: 30305 (Southern urban Buckhead); price snapshot: $457,158; sq/ft: N/A

Zip code: 30306 (Virginia-Highland); price snapshot: $417,472; sq/ft: 3,255

Zip code: 30308 (Southern Midtown, SoNo); price snapshot: $238,398; sq/ft: N/A

Zip code: 30309 (Northern Midtown, Ansley Park); price snapshot: $335,068; sq/ft: N/A

Zip code: 30319 (Midtown East); price snapshot: $416,011; sq/ft: N/A

Zip code: 30326 (central urban Buckhead); price snapshot: $446,722; sq/ft: N/A

Real estate prices fluctuate. For up-to-date neighborhood housing cost information, input the zip codes above in the Homestore Web site (affiliated with Realtor.com) at **www.homestore.com/Cities**.

Rent Costs: If you want to rent, explore **www.rentnet.com** and also investigate the neighborhood Web sites for current rents and available properties.

Taxes

Property Taxes: 40 percent of the property's value times the local millage rate, minus all applicable homestead exemptions (for example: $17.86 per $1,000 of fair market value). See the Fulton County Board of Assessors Web site for changes at **www.fultonassessor.org**.

Sales Tax: 8 percent state, local sales, and use taxes. Food is not subject to state taxes but subject to local sales taxes; prescription drugs are exempt.

State Income Tax: 1.0 percent to 6.0 percent. (Six tax brackets. Single: low $6,750 to high $7,000 and over; personal exemption: $2,700. Married filing jointly personal exemption: $5,400; married filing separately: use same rates but use income brackets $500 to $5,000; child exemption: $3,000.)

Downtown Atlanta Retirement Lifestyle Web Guide

Living

A good place to begin to find out more about the area is by viewing the latest real estate options for downtown Atlanta on the Atlanta Downtown Neighborhood Association's Web page at **www.atlantadna.org/adnamap.htm**. For other areas, try the Atlanta Board of Realtors' Web site at **www.abr.org**.

City Hospitals

Atlanta Medical Center
303 Parkway Drive NE
www.atlantamedcenter.com

Emory Crawford Long Hospital
550 Peachtree Street NE
www.emoryhealthcare.org

Grady Health System
80 Jesse Hill Jr. Drive SE
www.gradyhealthsystem.org

Northside Hospital
1000 Johnson Ferry Road
www.northside.com

Piedmont Hospital
1968 Peachtree Road NW
www.piedmonthospital.org

Health Clubs
Downtown:

Atlanta YMCA
555 Luckie Street NW
www.ymcaatlanta.org

Peachtree Center Athletic Club and Spa
227 Courtland Street NE
www.peachtreeac.com

Gold's Gym
215 Peachtree Street
www.goldsgym.com

Midtown: Visit the Midtown Business Community Web site at **www.midtown businesscommunity.com**, then click "**Services**"
Buckhead: See **www.buckhead.net** and click "**Fitness**"

Volunteering

United Way of Atlanta, volunteer services
www.volunteersolutions.org

Educational opportunities

City Colleges and Universities

Georgia State University
33 Gilmer Street
www.gsu.edu

Morehouse College
830 Westview Drive SW
www.morehouse.edu

Georgia Institute of Technology
  (Georgia Tech)
225 North Avenue
www.gatech.edu

Spelman College
350 Spelman Lane SW
www.spelman.edu

Clark Atlanta University
223 James P. Brawley Drive SW
www.cau.edu

Library

Atlanta-Fulton County Public Library System
1 Margaret Mitchell Square (and numerous in-town locations)
www.af.public.lib.ga.us

ENTERTAINMENT

Restaurants, Bars, and Nightclubs

For an up-to-date listing of nightlife and dining in urban Atlanta, visit:
Downtown Atlanta Neighborhood Association: **www.atlantadna.org/links.htm**
Midtown Business Community: **www.midtownbusinesscommunity.com**
Buckhead Incorporated: **www.buckhead.net**

Professional Spectator Sports

Atlanta Braves (baseball)
Turner Field, 755 Hank Aaron
    Drive SW
www.atlantabraves.com

Atlanta Falcons (football)
Georgia Dome,
    1 Georgia Dome Drive
www.atlantafalcons.com

Atlanta Hawks (basketball)
Philips Arena, 1 Philips Drive
www.nba.com/hawks

Atlanta Thrashers (hockey)
Philips Arena, 1 Philips Drive
www.atlantathrashers.com

Georgia Force (football)
Philips Arena, 1 Philips Drive
www.georgiaforce.com

College Sports

Georgia Tech
Men's and women's basketball, track and field, swimming and diving,
    tennis, cross-country, men's football, baseball, golf, tennis, women's soft-
    ball, and volleyball
www.gatech.edu/sports

The Performing Arts

Atlanta Symphony Orchestra
Woodruff Arts Center,
  Atlanta Symphony Hall
1280 Peachtree Street NE
www.atlantasymphony.org or
  www.woodruffcenter.org.

Atlanta Coalition of Performing Arts
Lists numerous theater productions
www.atlantaperforms.com

Atlanta Opera
Boisfeuillet Jones
  Atlanta Civic Center
Piedmont Avenue and
  Ralph McGill Boulevard
www.atlantaopera.org

Major Museums

*Atlanta Cyclorama and Civil War
  Museum*
800 Cherokee Avenue SE

Atlanta History Center
130 West Paces Ferry Road NW
www.atlhist.org

CNN Center Studio Tour
190 Marietta Street NW
www.cnn.com/StudioTour

Georgia Aquarium
225 Baker Street
www.georgiaaquarium.org

High Museum of Art
1280 Peachtree Street NE
www.high.org

Jimmy Carter Library and Museum
441 Freedom Parkway
www.jimmycarterlibrary.org

Margaret Mitchell House and Museum
990 Peachtree Street
www.gwtw.org

*Martin Luther King Jr. Park,
  National Historic Site*
450 Auburn Avenue NE
www.nps.gov/malu

Museum of Design Atlanta
285 Peachtree Center Avenue
www.museumofdesign.org

*The William Breman
  Jewish Heritage Museum*
1440 Spring Street at 18th Street
www.thebreman.org

World of Coca-Cola
55 Martin Luther King Jr. Drive
  at Central Avenue
www.woccatlanta.com

Special Events (Best Bets)

Atlanta Dogwood Festival
April. Music, arts and crafts in a celebration of Atlanta's favorite tree, held in
   Piedmont Park
www.dogwood.org

Atlanta Jazz Festival
Memorial Day in Piedmont Park
www.atlantafestivals.com

Atlanta Pride Festival
June. Southeast's largest gay pride festival in Piedmont Park
www.atlantapride.org

Downtown Neighborhood Festival
May in downtown, usually in Fairlie-Poplar. Showcasing downtown living
www.atlantadna.org/festival

Music Midtown
June, often in the SoNo neighborhood. Various stages. Top artist music festival
www.musicmidtown.com

Shake at the Lake
Various times of year. Shakespeare in the park at Lake Clara Meer in
   Piedmont Park
www.gashakespeare.org

Summerfest
June. Artist market in the middle of the neighborhood
www.vahi.org

Sweet Auburn Spring Fest
Spring. Celebration of African American achievements and the neighborhood
   preservation of Auburn Street businesses
www.sweetauburn.com

Movie Theaters

AMC Phipps Plaza 14
3500 Peachtree Road NE

Atlantic Station Stadium 16
17th Street west of I-75
www.atlanticstation.com

Midtown Art Cinema
931 Monroe Drive
**www.landmarktheatres.com/
   market/Atlanta/MidtownArt
   Cinema.htm**

Favorite In-town Parks

Centennial Olympic Park
Marietta Street NW and Centennial Olympic Park Drive NW
www.centennialpark.com

Hurt Park
25 Courtland Street NE at Edgewood Avenue, Georgia State campus

Piedmont Park
Piedmont Avenue and 10th Street
www.piedmontpark.org

Woodruff Park
Auburn Avenue NE and Peachtree Street NE
www.centralatlantaprogress.org/woodruffpark.asp

SHOPPING

Major Retail

Downtown:
Underground Atlanta
50 Upper Alabama Street
www.underground-atlanta.com

Midtown:
Atlantic Station
17th Street west of I-75
www.atlanticstation.com

Buckhead:
Lennox Square Mall
3393 Peachtree Road
www.lenoxsquare.com

Phipps Plaza
3500 Peachtree Road
www.phippsplaza.com

For an up-to-date listing of shops in urban Atlanta, visit Downtown Atlanta
   Neighborhood Association: **www.atlantadna.org/links.htm**
Midtown Business Community: **www.midtownbusinesscommunity.com**
Buckhead Incorporated: **www.buckhead.net**

Groceries
See the Downtown Atlanta Neighbors Association's "Grocery Map" at **www**
.atlantadna.org/groceries

Midtown and Buckhead:
Many major grocery stores, such as Kroger and Publix

City/Farmer's Markets

Sweet Auburn Curb Market
209 Edgewood Avenue SE
www.sweetauburn.com

DeKalb Farmer's Market
3000 East Ponce de Leon Avenue

Getting around

Atlanta Transit
*Metropolitan Atlanta Rapid Transit
   Authority (MARTA)*

Train and Bus Service
www.itsmarta.org

Airport
*Hartsfield-Jackson Atlanta
   International Airport (ATL)*
www.atlanta-airport.com

Intercity Train
Amtrak
1688 Peachtree Street NW
www.amtrak.com

Intercity Bus
Downtown Greyhound Terminal,
   2 Tunnel Road
232 Forsyth Street
www.greyhound.com

Interstate Highways
I-20 (East/west from Birmingham,
   Alabama, to Augusta, Georgia)
I-75 (South/north from Macon,
   Georgia, to Chattanooga,
   Tennessee)
I-85 (South/north from
   Montgomery, Alabama, to
   Greenville, South Carolina)

Charlotte, North Carolina

harlotte is getting bigger and better. Workers are drawn to the city's economic and employment powerhouse. It's the home of Bank of America, Wachovia Bank, and other companies' world headquarters. Corporations are even investing in and financing new in-town housing for thousands of their employees. This in turn brings new services and more people, and stimulates the economy. Charlotte is building a dense collection of urban neighborhoods perfect for Ruppies. Here are the five reasons this is a wonderful place to retire.

1. It's gone vertical

It makes sense that Charlotte calls its downtown "Uptown," because unlike many other cities, Charlotte is unafraid of height. Retirees and empty nesters who want to live in tall buildings with fabulous views can now consider Uptown's excellent vertical living environment. It's become a Southern marvel, with the sixty-story plus Bank of America Corporate Center, the forty-seven-story Hearst Tower, two upcoming fifty-story residential towers, and a rousing influx of existing and proposed midrise residential buildings. If you like sky-high structures, you'll love Charlotte today and even more tomorrow.

2. New and gleaming

There are lovely, old historic districts in and around Uptown, but the brand-new look (and feeling) of the city is a powerful reminder of Charlotte's optimism and growth-oriented philosophy. Ruppies who decide to move here will find it a very progressive place. There's no telling what will be built here next, but whatever it is, it's going to be awesome.

3. Full-service urban neighborhoods

The city is aggressively and continuously encouraging developers to fill in any housing gaps with impressive "mixed-use" structures, mid-rise condos, apartments, and skyscrapers. Gateway Village on West Trade Street, for example, is a large-scale residential, commercial, transportation, education, and retail center. It's a prototype of future places where residents will be able to live, work, play, and shop, all in the same general area. In addition, Uptown residents already have two full-service grocery stores.

4. Colleges abound in Uptown

Charlotte's major university, the University of North Carolina–Charlotte is located ten miles northeast of Uptown, but the main campus of the Central Piedmont Community College is located east of I-277, easily within walking distance or just a short bus ride. Johnson and Wales University's modern building is located in the Gateway Center area of West Trade Street, where residents can take a cooking class or learn a new trade. Even the suburban UNCC campus is planning a large building to house its Architecture and Business School in the First Ward neighborhood. This is a great urban college town for the mature population.

5. The trolleys and trains

Charlotte's vintage electric trolley adds character to what would otherwise be an ordinary industrial corridor. According to the Charlotte Trolley Institute, property values along the trolley corridor have increased 89 percent since the first cars began serving the city in 1998. In the next few years, a light-rail train network will join the trolley, in addition to the Charlotte Area Transit buses and Amtrak at a $200 million multimodal station. The city is increasing its transit corridors into higher-density areas where it's easy to get around without a car. Add urban residential development with these trains and this area is clearly a model American city.

Target Retirement Districts and Neighborhoods

Uptown (really Charlotte's downtown) is the area inside the inner freeway loop where there are varied alternatives for residential living. Other superb urban neighborhoods include the Historic South Side and Dilworth, which flank the Uptown area on its southern boundary.

Uptown Core

Charlotte's Uptown neighborhoods are separated into four sections called wards. Although each ward is considered its own distinct district, they are separated by Trade and Tryon streets. The wards are small and easy to navigate, and residents can easily walk from neighborhood to neighborhood, which often means simply crossing the street.

The Second Ward of Uptown Charlotte features the new Ratcliffe condominiums (center). Wachovia Cultural Campus is directly across the street, home to the Mint Museums, the Bechtler Museum, the Afro American Cultural Center, a 1,200-seat theater for North Carolina Dance Theater, and the Wake University Babcock School of Business. It's connected to the thirty-eight-story "Wachovia 3" office tower with first-floor dining and retail, a public library branch, and a police substation.

Fourth Ward

The Fourth Ward, arguably Uptown's most upscale, is a lovely historic district with old Victorian homes, turn-of-the-century office buildings, hospital buildings from the late 1800s now turned into condos, old churches with tall steeples, and existing modern high-rise condominiums. Gateway Village on West Trade Street is a development that set the example for Uptown in the early 2000s, with its mix of apartments, shops, hotels, and offices. Residents here enjoy great shopping, including many specialty and chain stores, coffee shops, and full-service grocery stores. New residential skyscrapers are being built alongside the Ward's preserved historic structures, quickly making this area a major center for residential development.

The Fourth Ward is located between North Tryon and West Trade streets and bounded by I-77 and I-277. For more information, see the Friends of Fourth Ward Web site at **www.fofw.com**.

First Ward

A mixed-income neighborhood was first constructed here in the mid-1990s. Development is now continuing northwestward in a new section called First Ward Urban Village. Hundreds more homes will join a new campus of the University of North Carolina–Charlotte and a new children's museum will also be built. Near the Tryon Street Corridor in the center of Uptown, residents can frequent the public library, the Levine Museum of the New South, the Mint Museum of Craft and Design, and the Old Carolina Theater. Locals here can also walk to the Central Piedmont Community College located directly across I-277 and enjoy a game at the new home of the Charlotte Bobcats' NBA basketball arena. The First Ward continuously welcomes new condominium and apartment complexes that bring newcomers into the neighborhood.

First Ward is the wedge of the Uptown pie between the freeway loop and North Tryon and East Trade streets. For more information, see the Charlotte Center City Partners' Web site at **www.charlottecentercity.org**.

Third Ward

This area is a mix of old skyscrapers, quaint historic plazas, and a series of small residential and commercial neighborhoods. The Third Ward has big plans for redevelopment providing new opportunities for Ruppies to find exciting places to live. For instance, the Third Ward is in the middle of converting several office buildings into residential housing. There are also plans for a new office, commercial, and residential complex, including a forty-story skyscraper and other smaller buildings that will host hundreds of condominiums, a movie theater, museums, Wake Forest University's Business School, and a park. The Charlotte Johnson and Wales campus on West Trade Street is adjacent to the much anticipated Gateway Multimodal Station, a hub for city buses, trains, trolleys, and Charlotte's Amtrak Station. A new park is planned on what is currently a huge surface parking lot, to serve the thousands of anticipated new residents. In addition, the Brevard Court and Latta Arcade on South Tryon Street is a great place to eat lunch, shop, and people watch. Football fans will also enjoy walking to the Carolina Panthers Stadium.

The Third Ward is bounded by South Tryon Street and West Trade Street and Interstates 77 and 277. For more information, see the Charlotte Center City Partners' Web site at **www.charlottecentercity.org**.

Second Ward

This area includes the Charlotte Convention Center, the Federal Reserve Bank, and the future NASCAR Hall of Fame. A large section of the Second Ward is devoted to local government, including the Charlotte-Mecklenburg government campus, taking up several blocks along South Davidson and South McDowell streets. Although housing is now relatively scarce here, the Second Ward is the area's future residential neighborhood. There are plans for new high-rise condominium towers, entertainment districts with restaurants and bars, and even a bowling alley.

The Second Ward is bounded by South Tryon Street and East Trade Street and the I-277 freeway loop. For more information, see the Charlotte Center City Partners' Web site at **www.charlottecentercity.org**.

The Historic South End

The area just south of I-277, a former center for cotton milling and textile manufacturing, has now transformed into a historic residential loft district. The Historic South End centers on South Boulevard, one of Charlotte's art corridors, and features several galleries, restaurants, and design shops. The South End is also home to many architectural firms, design showrooms, and interior designers, where old mill buildings now provide office and retail space. The area is probably best-known locally as the beginning of Charlotte's historic trolley line.

The Historic South End is the area between South Tryon Street and South Boulevard all the way down to Remount Road and Ideal Way. For more information, visit the Historic South End's Web site at **www.historicsouthend.com**.

Dilworth

Dilworth, a historic district, originally called the Eighth Ward, blends with the Historic South End and is east of South Boulevard. In the late 1800s, Dilworth was a first suburb that was linked by a streetcar from Latta Park, a popular city park just north of East Boulevard. Dilworth offers large yards and lush vegetation and is only a short distance from the excitement and bustle of Uptown. For more information, visit the Dilworth Community's Web site at **www.idilworth.org**.

Uptown Charlotte Essentials

The New South: Charlotte is in the "New South," a term used to contrast the "Old South" of the antebellum and slavery periods, and embraces change rather than clings to old traditions. It's more urban than agrarian, and progressive, not repressive.

Queen City history: Charlotte, the Queen City of the South, was named by Scotch-Irish settlers after Charlotte, the wife of England's King George III from Mecklenburg, Germany (Charlotte is in Mecklenburg County).

Trolley traversing: You will enjoy taking the trolley, learning about the past, and understanding how trains are important to Charlotte's future. A must-do is the Trolley A-Go-Go-Crawl, an arts-viewing event featuring local South End and Uptown art galleries.

A cat of two kinds: It's "required" that you morph into two kinds of ferocious felines here: Bobcats and Panthers. As a resident, you'll have fun cheering at pro basketball and football games in your new neighborhood.

"Mixed uses": It's a Charlotte phenomenon—a tall building full of homes, shops, offices, and entertainment, and this has only just begun here. Get acquainted with the term "mixed use" as in "mixed-use development."

Appreciating the grocery stores: Most cities are still waiting for their full-service downtown grocery store. As a Ruppie here, you can take your pick of two and enjoy walking, not waiting and wishing.

General Statistics

Population: Downtown core: 6,327; (2000); City: 594,359 (2003); Metro: 1,437,427 (2003)

Terrain: Center City Charlotte is generally flat to slightly rolling.

Climate Overview: cool winters/hot summers

Average January high/low temperature: 51/31F

Average July high/low temperature: 89/69F

Average annual total precipitation: 42 inches

Average annual snowfall: 6 inches

Number of cloudy days: 150

Cost of Living: Find out the current cost of living between Charlotte and your community by visiting **www.homefair.com** and clicking **"Moving to a New State"** or **"Moving Locally,"** then follow the prompts.

Cost of Housing:

Zip code: 28202 (Covers all of downtown)

Price snapshot: $313,996; sq/ft: 1,262

Zip code: 28203 (Covers the Historic South End, Dilworth, and beyond)

Price snapshot: $324,581; sq/ft: 1,694

Real estate prices fluctuate. For up-to-date neighborhood housing cost information, input the zip codes above in the Homestore Web site (affiliated with Realtor.com) at **www.homestore.com/Cities**.

Rent Costs: If you want to rent, explore **www.rentnet.com** and also investigate the neighborhood Web sites for current rents and available properties.

Taxes

Property Taxes: $1.2568 per $100 of fair market value in 2005. See the Mecklenburg County Web site for updates at **www.charmeck.org/Departments/ Home.htm** and click "Property Assessment & Land Records Management."

Sales Tax: 7.5 percent. Groceries are not subject to state taxes but subject to 2.0 percent local sales taxes; prescription drugs are exempt.

State Income Tax: 6.0 percent to 8.25 percent. (Single: low $12,750 to high $120,000 and over; personal exemption: $3,300. Married: $21,250 to $200,000; personal exemption: $6,600. Child exemption: $3,300.) North Carolina also has an individual personal property tax.

Uptown Charlotte Retirement Lifestyle Web Guide

Living

The best place to start looking for your urban home in Charlotte is at the Charlotte Center City Partners' Web site: **www.charlottecentercity.org**, then click "**Center City Housing**." You'll find new development project maps for each Uptown ward, and a list of Uptown Realtors who specialize in urban living.

City Hospitals

Carolinas Medical Center
1000 Blythe Boulevard
www.carolinas.org

Presbyterian Hospital
200 Hawthorne Lane
www.presbyterian.org

Mercy Hospital
2001 Vail Avenue
www.carolinas.org

Health Clubs

For an up-to-date listing of Uptown Charlotte health and fitness centers, visit **www.charlottecentercity.org**, then click "**Things to Do**," then "**Athletic Clubs**."

Volunteering

United Way of Central Carolinas
301 South Brevard Street
www.uwcentralcarolinas.org/volunteer

Educational opportunities

City Colleges and Universities

Central Piedmont Community College
1201 Elizabeth Avenue
www1.cpcc.edu

Johnson and Wales University
801 West Trade Street
www.jwu.edu/charlotte

Johnson C. Smith University
100 Beatties Ford Road
www.jcsu.edu

University of North Carolina at Charlotte
9201 University City Boulevard
  (Uptown campus at 220 North
  Tryon Street)
www.uncc.edu

Queens University of Charlotte
1900 Selwyn Avenue
www.queens.edu

Library

Public Library of Charlotte and Mecklenburg County
310 North Tryon Street
www.plcmc.org

Entertainment

Restaurants, Bars, and Nightclubs

For an up-to-date listing of restaurants and nightclubs visit **www.charlotte
centercity.org**, then click "**Things to Do**," then "**Dining**" or "**Nightlife**."

Professional Spectator Sports

Carolina Panthers (football)
Bank of America Stadium
800 South Mint Street
www.panthers.com

Charlotte Sting (women's basketball)
Charlotte Bobcats Arena
333 East Trade Street
www.wnba.com/sting

Charlotte Bobcats (basketball)
Charlotte Bobcats Arena
333 East Trade Street
www.nba.com/bobcats

Charlotte Checkers Hockey (hockey)
Charlotte Bobcats Arena
333 East Trade Street
www.gocheckers.com

College Sports

University of North Carolina at Charlotte
Men and women's basketball, cross-country, soccer, tennis, track and field,
    men's baseball, golf, women's softball, volleyball
http://Charlotte49ers.com

The Performing Arts

For an up-to-date listing of plays and other theater events, visit **www.charlotte
centercity.org**, then click "**Things to Do**," then "**Arts and Entertainment**."

Charlotte Symphony Orchestra
201 South College Street
www.charlottesymphony.org

Opera Carolina
Blumenthal Performing Arts Center
130 North Tryon Street
www.operacarolina.org

Major Museums

The Charlotte History Museum
3500 Shamrock Drive
www.charlottemuseum.org

The Levine Museum of the New South
200 East 7th Street
www.museumofthenewsouth.org

Discovery Place
301 North Tryon Street
www.discoveryplace.org

The Mint Museum of Art
2370 Randolph Road
www.mintmuseum.org

Mint Museum of Craft + Design
220 North Tryon Street
www.mintmuseum.org

Special Events (Best Bets)

Artoberfest
October celebration of art in the
　NoDa neighborhood north of
　downtown
www.noda.org

Center City After Five
Monthly concerts at Wachovia
　Center at 301 South Tryon Street
www.charlottecentercity.org

Charlotte Shout
September in Uptown.
　Three-week-long festival of
　every genre of the arts
www.charlotteshout.com

CityFest Live
May. Gigantic live music festival
　in Uptown
www.cityfestlive.com

Festival in the Park
September. Arts, crafts, entertainment
Freedom Park, Dilworth
　neighborhood
**http://festival.lfchosting.com/
　festival**

Fourth Ward Fall Festival
www.charlottecentercity.org

The Fourth Ward Frolic
April/May. A celebration of art,
　history, and music
www.charlottecentercity.org

Gallery Crawls
Uptown and Historic South End
　neighborhoods, various times of
　year in various Uptown galleries
www.charlottecentercity.org or
　www.historicsouthend.com

Movie Theaters

EpiCentre
(Upcoming) Trade and College streets

Favorite Downtown Parks

9th Street Park
417 West 9th Street

Frazier Park
1201 West 4th Street Extension

First Ward Park
301 North McDowell Street

Third Ward Park
1001 West 4th Street

Fourth Ward Park
301 North Poplar Street

Shopping

For an up-to-date listing of retail stores, visit **www.charlottecentercity.org**, then click "**Shopping**."

Groceries
Harris Teeter
325 West 6th Street
www.harristeeter.com

Reid's Fine Foods
225 East 6th Street
www.reids.com

City/Farmer's Markets
Center City Green Market (seasonal)
7th Street between College and Brevard streets

Getting around

Public Transit
Charlotte Transit System (CATS)
City bus, streetcars, upcoming light rail
www.charmeck.org/Departments/CATS
Charlotte trolley: **www.charlottetrolley.org**

Intercity Rail
Amtrak
1914 North Tryon Street
www.amtrak.com

Bike Routes/Trails/Greenways

Visit Mecklenburg County Parks and Recreation Department's Web site at **www.charmeck.org/Departments/Park+and+Rec/Home.htm** and click "**Greenways**" or "**Outdoor Activities**," then "**Biking**."

Airport

Charlotte/Douglas International Airport (CLT)
www.charlotteairport.com

Intercity Bus

Uptown Greyhound Terminal
601 West Trade Street
www.greyhound.com

FYI: A new Charlotte Gateway Station is planned at this location, a hub for Amtrak, Greyhound, and CATs bus and rail services.

Interstate Highways

I-77 (South/north from Columbia, South Carolina, to Charleston, West Virginia)
I-85 (South/north from Greenville, South Carolina, to Greensboro, North Carolina)

16

Memphis, Tennessee

Memphis, famous for its jazz and dry ribs, is also the birthplace of rock and roll, and of course, the home to Elvis Presley's Graceland. Fortunately and unfortunately, Memphis is recognized primarily by sound bites and anecdotes, a frequent answer to many trivia questions. But Memphis is one of the most substantial, high-quality downtowns in America and has a lot to offer new residents.

The city is unique, with its special brand of soul food and traditions. It enjoys a proud personality that celebrates its music and also mourns the death of Martin Luther King Jr. As one of the more historically relevant American cities, it will, with the growth and popularity of its already magnificent downtown, become even more so in the coming decades. Here are the top five reasons Memphis is easily a best sunbelt downtown.

1. Critical mass emerging

Local residents are enthusiastic downtown lovers who are very proud of the work and accomplishments of their center city. There's even a local television show called *Definitely Downtown*. This passion, dedication, and vitality is quickly noticed by newcomers.

2. Beale Street jazz

Beale Street was once a questionable area in the early 1900s when pawnshops, prostitutes, and people practicing voodoo vied with jazz as the main attractions. The street's storied history has even spawned an original— the Voodoo Fest, held in W. C. Handy Park. Beale Street's vibrant jazz clubs, shops, and the best barbecue Memphis has to offer was one of the major catalysts in downtown Memphis' redevelopment. Today, locals watch people, listen to music, and enjoy street performances here.

3. Allure of old Memphis

Imagine walking down a Main Street that still looks a lot like it did in the early 1900s. Many of the historic buildings display their original business names and old-fashioned logos still painted on their sides. Main Street is paved with red bricks, period street lamps, and shade trees. Antique trolleys with their original wooden seats, old fashioned light fixtures, and copper handles link five miles of track within downtown. The trolleys are powered by overhead electric lines, just as in olden days—even the thirty-cent fare is a throwback to days gone by. But it's not for show: These trolleys carry more than 1 million riders every year.

4. The Mississippi River

It's easy to imagine the old Delta paddle-wheelers and steamboats rolling down the Mississippi, especially when you catch a glimpse of a river cruise ship making its way toward Natchez or New Orleans. Downtown residents who live in apartments, condominiums, or bluff side houses can watch barges full of grain, train cars, or steel containers stacked high slowly floating to their destination. The riverfront is the home of many events, most notably the mammoth Memphis in May International Festival, where hundreds of thousands flock to Tom Lee Park and other open spaces along its banks. There's something special about having the largest and most famous river in America as a downtown neighbor.

5. City of light

Memphis is implementing one of America's most ambitious downtown lighting schemes called Light it Up: The Downtown Illumination Project. The objective is to draw attention to noteworthy architecture and showcase the city as full of radiance and energy.

Target Retirement Districts and Neighborhoods

Downtown Memphis's target retirement neighborhoods include the Downtown Core, the South Side Neighborhoods, and Mud Island's Harbor Town.

Downtown Core

The Court Square Center on Main Street offers retail, residential, and office space. South along Main, another major project called the "New Main Block" will also provide a new city neighborhood, and not far away, there's AutoZone Baseball Park where the Memphis Redbirds share the neighborhood with newly constructed loft apartments. The Beale Street Entertainment District, which includes the W. C. Handy Park and the nationally famous Gibson Guitar Plant, is also here. Other major landmarks include the Peabody Hotel, the new FedExForum (home to the NBA Memphis Grizzlies), and the historic Orpheum Theatre. One of several historic sub-districts includes Cotton Row, once America's cotton hub, and provides condominiums and apartments inside old warehouses and in newly constructed buildings.

Downtown is generally bounded by the Mississippi River (west), I-40 (north), Linden Avenue (south), and Danny Thomas Boulevard (east). See the Downtown Memphis Residents' Association at **www.memphisdna.org** and the Center City Commission Web site at **www.downtownmemphis.com** for more information.

Uptown

The northern section of downtown Memphis (north of I-40) near the Memphis Pyramid Arena and the gateway to Mud Island's Harbor Town is poised for new growth and development. This district is already called "Uptown," and there are plans to redevelop almost five-hundred-acres into more than 1,000 new residences and supporting businesses. See the Uptown Partnership's Web site for more information: **www.uptownmemphis.org**.

Medical District

With the expansion of the trolley line, the Medical District (to the east side of Danny Thomas Boulevard, east of the downtown core) will become an important new downtown neighborhood. This area has more than 30,000 medical employees and thousands of students who may eventually want to live and work in the same neighborhood. The Center City Commission has created a "Medical District Master Plan" that includes the historic Victorian Village, which is focusing momentum for new residential development.

South Side Neighborhoods

Many sections here have become the cool place to be in recent years, thanks to the South Main Street Historic Arts District. South Main Street, called the SoHo of the South, features interesting and varied restaurants, art galleries, theaters, and an active pedestrian scene. Art lovers can hop the trolley and take the Art Trolley Tour and go from gallery to gallery, or see outdoor cult films at Fresh Air Flicks. The area, also home to the National Civil Rights Museum, has easy access to the Mississippi Riverwalk. New residents now live here in restored warehouses, new condominiums, and apartments. To the west of Main Street, in the South Bluffs Warehouse District, old warehouses are currently undergoing a dramatic transformation into residential living opportunities.

The South Bluffs Community, further south, is a new development with nearly five hundred residential structures in an instant community setting. The generally industrial South End neighborhood is also under massive reconstruction and redevelopment. Look for thousands of new condos and apartments to be on the real estate market in the next few years.

For more information, visit the South Main Historic District's Web site at **www.southmainmemphis.org**.

Mud Island

The monorail goes from downtown across the river to an island park. Farther north on this island is also where over 5,000 people live in a community called Harbor Town. This place can provide a unique lifestyle for retirees: the serenity of a suburb yet a decidedly downtown lifestyle. Harbor Town provides gardens, grocery stores, walking paths, great river views, marinas, and a wide variety of housing choices from small apartments to enormous mansions. After nearly twenty years since the first home was built here, Mud Island is still growing. Neighborhoods on the northern section of the island are being constructed and will continue developing in the future.

There is no official Web site for Harbor Town. More information on Mud Island River Park can be found at **www.mudisland.com**.

Downtown Memphis Essentials

Dry ribs "Memphis style": Make sure to stock paprika, onion power, salt, and cayenne pepper so you can practice becoming a master at preparing the Memphis-style rib rub. No sauce is needed to create a dry outside and a moist inside for this Southern delicacy. Barbecuing Memphis ribs is a way of life in this city, and copied around the world.

Beale Street: You can take a stroll up Beale Street any night of the week, and have a marvelous time without spending a dime. The street shows, the people, the neon signs, and the music will electrify your spirit and make you proud to live here.

Trolley rides: Take the wonderful old-fashioned trolley to the South Main Historic Arts District or along the river to Mud Island. Even if you have no particular place to go, the ride only costs thirty cents.

The ducks: Although there are now several Peabody Hotels around the country, the original is still in Memphis. You'll definitely enjoy the hotel's twice-daily duck march, and your out-of-town visitors will too.

The spirit lives on: You can't be a Memphis resident and not feel the spirit of Elvis. Fans flock to Memphis for his birthday and to commemorate his death. And although Graceland is in the suburban Whitehaven area of Memphis, many tributes to Elvis and concerts are still held downtown.

Mud Island: It's an island getaway that's never far away if you're a downtown resident. Just hop on the monorail and escape into delightful reprieve from the city's commotion. Although the Mud Island Riverwalk portrays the history and significance of the entire Mississippi River system, the island also has hiking trails, bike trails, and even pedal-boat rentals.

General Statistics

Population: Downtown (core): 6,834; (2000); City: 671,929 (2003); Metro: 1,239,337 (2003)

Terrain: Downtown Memphis is flat along the Mississippi River with a steep bank rising up to the heart of downtown.

Climate Overview: cool winters/hot summers

Average January high/low temperature: 49/32F

Average July high/low temperature: 89/69F

Average annual total precipitation: 53 inches

Average annual snowfall: 5 inches

Number of cloudy days: 150

Cost of Living: Find out the current cost of living between Memphis and your community by visiting **www.homefair.com** and clicking "**Moving to a New State**" or "**Moving Locally**," then follow the prompts.

Cost of Housing:

Zip code: 38103 (Covers all of downtown, Harbor Town)

Price snapshot: $319,875; sq/ft: 1,258

Real estate prices fluctuate. For up-to-date neighborhood housing cost information, input the zip code above in the Homestore Web site (affiliated with Realtor.com) at **www.homestore.com/Cities**.

Rent Costs: If you want to rent, explore **www.rentnet.com** and also investigate the neighborhood Web sites for current rents and available properties.

Taxes

Property Tax: $3.30 per $100 of property assessment, and property assessment is 25 percent of the property appraisal for residential real estate. See the Shelby County Assessor's Web site at **www.assessor.shelby.tn.us** for updates.

Sales Tax: 9.25 percent 6 percent state tax on groceries; prescription drugs are exempt.

State Income Tax: No state income taxes. Limited to dividends and interest income.

Downtown Memphis Retirement Lifestyle Web Guide

Living

Visit the Center City Commission Web site for an extensive listing of current housing opportunities in downtown Memphis at **www.downtown memphis.com** and click "**Live**" for the most up-to-date listing of downtown apartments and condominiums. Also contact the Memphis Area Association of Realtors at **www.maar.org**.

City Hospitals

Methodist University Hospital
1265 Union Avenue
www.methodisthealth.org

University of Tennessee Medical Group
Various locations
www.utmedicalgroup.com

Regional Medical Center at Memphis
Various locations
www.the-med.org

Health Clubs

Fogelman Downtown YMCA
245 Madison Avenue
www.ymcamemphis.org

Volunteering

Volunteer Memphis
22 North Front Street, Suite 780
www.volunteermemphis.org

Hands on Memphis
630 Market Street
www.handsonmemphis.org

Educational opportunities

City Colleges and Universities

Christian Brothers University
650 East Parkway South
www.cbu.edu

Rhodes College
2000 North Parkway
www.rhodes.edu

Harding University Graduate
 School of Religion
1000 Cherry Road
www.hugsr.edu

Southwest Tennessee
 Community College
Various locations
www.southwest.tn.edu

LeMoyne-Owen College
807 Walker Avenue
www.loc.edu

The University of Memphis
Midtown, 3720 Alumni Drive
www.memphis.edu

Memphis College of Art
1930 Poplar Avenue
www.mca.edu

Library

Memphis Public Library (Central Library)
3030 Poplar Avenue
www.memphislibrary.org

Entertainment

Restaurants, Bars, and Nightclubs

Visit www.downtownmemphis.com and click "**Play**" for restaurants and nightclubs in downtown Memphis.

Professional Sports

Memphis Grizzlies (basketball)
FedExForum, 191 Beale Street
www.nba.com/grizzlies

Memphis Redbirds (baseball)
AutoZone Park, 200 Union Avenue
www.memphisredbirds.com

College Sports
The University of Memphis
Located on the east side of Memphis
Baseball, basketball, cross-country, football, golf, rifle, soccer, tennis, track
    and field, women's volleyball
www.memphis.edu

Performing Arts

Ballet Memphis
Orpheum Theatre,
    203 South Main Street
www.balletmemphis.org

The Memphis Symphony Orchestra
Cannon Center for the Performing
    Arts, 255 North Main Street
www.memphissymphony.org

Theatre Memphis
Perkins at Southern
www.theatrememphis.org

Opera Memphis
Clark Opera Memphis Center,
    6745 Wolf River Parkway
www.operamemphis.org

Playhouse on the Square
Professional Resident
    Theatre Company
51 South Cooper
www.playhouseonthesquare.org

Major Museums

Memphis Rock 'n' Soul Museum
191 Beale Street
www.memphisrocknsoul.org

STAX Museum of American Soul Music
926 East McLemore Avenue
www.soulsvilleusa.com

National Civil Rights Museum
450 Mulberry Street
www.civilrightsmuseum.org

National Ornamental Metal Museum
374 Metal Museum Drive
www.metalmuseum.org

Special Events (Best Bets)

Africa in April
Robert R. Church Park, downtown
www.africainapril.org

Beale Street Music Festival
May. Part of Memphis in
    May festival

Memphis in May
  International Festival
May. Memphis heritage.
  Riverfront and various locations
www.memphisinmay.org

Desti-Nations International
  Family Festival
May. Part of Memphis in May festival

Memphis Music and Heritage Festival
Labor Day weekends, downtown
www.southernfolklore.com

Elvis Tribute Week
August. Although held at Graceland,
  downtown concerts are featured
www.elvis.com

Favorite Downtown Parks

W. C. Handy Park
Beale Street Entertainment District

Court Square
The city's urban park on Madison
  Avenue

Tom Lee Park
The primary Mississippi Riverfront
  park, host to many festivals

Mud Island River Park
www.mudisland.com

For more information on all of Memphis' Parks, see the City of Memphis Park Services Web site at **www.cityofmemphis.org**.

Major Retail

Downtown Memphis offers a wide variety of shopping. For a current list of stores see **www.downtownmemphis.com** and click "**Play**," then "**Shopping**."

Major Grocery Stores

No major grocery stores exist in downtown Memphis, but several small grocery stores are available. Large grocery stores are located just east in the Medical District.

Miss Cordelia's
737 Harbor Bend Road

Alice's Urban Market
513 South Front Street

Jack's Food Store
76 North Main Street

Phillips Sundry
345 South 4th Street

Roxie's Grocery
520 North 3rd Street

South Second Market
6 South 2nd Street

City/Farmer's Markets
Butler Street Bazaar
11 West Butler Street

Getting around

City Bus Service/Trolley Service
Memphis Area Transit Authority (MATA)
www.matatransit.com

Airport
Memphis International Airport (MEM)
www.memphisairport.org

Intercity Bus
Greyhound Bus Terminal
1 Union Avenue
www.greyhound.com

Intercity Rail
Memphis Amtrak Station
"City of New Orleans" from New Orleans to Chicago
545 South Main Street
www.amtrak.com

Interstate Highways
I-40 (West/east Little Rock, Arkansas, to Nashville, Tennessee)
I-55 (South/north from Jackson, Mississippi, to St. Louis, Missouri)

Miami, Florida

Florida is the traditional, stereotypical retirement destination. Retirees and empty nesters flock here to enjoy sunny year-round warm weather. Now, however, there's a new Miami: sophisticated and vibrant urban destination. Here are five reasons why Miami should be on or near the top of your list.

1. **Exciting and impressive**
   Miami's downtown is quickly emerging as one of the most vibrant, exciting cities in the world. More than 20,000 new homes, mostly condominium skyscrapers, are popping up in its downtown neighborhoods and districts, and new retail establishments and entertainment venues are being built to serve these residents. According to the Miami Development Authority, around one hundred new tall buildings are either under construction or planned. It's an electrifying time to live in Miami.

2. **World city**
   Miami has more cultural flavor that most other American cities. The food, the arts, language, and customs are decidedly influenced by the countries to the south. The city also has America's highest population of foreign-born residents, mostly from Latin America. This mix of cultural influences is highly attractive for people seeking interesting neighbors and friends.

3. **A Florida alternative**
   Downtown Miami is the hot new Florida retirement resort where residents can live in a vibrant city and still have access to some of the world's

most famous beaches and other nearby oceanfront destinations. Residents can visit all the beaches and then retreat to their local urban havens.

4. **Fashionable**

Miami is now considered the new Hollywood: Many movie and pop music stars live here. Miami's nightlife is also a plus with its trendy music scene. If you want a vibrant, active lifestyle, Miami could be the perfect place.

5. **Design and style**

The city's art deco architecture is mostly associated with South Beach, but can also be found in the downtown area. It's that 1920s to 1940s look: retro boxy building with rounded corners, outlined with neon, and painted in flaming and bright pastel colors. Miami interiors are airy with terracotta or marble floors, palm plants, glass tables, and reproduction Spanish or Hollywood-deco furniture.

Target Retirement Districts and Neighborhoods

Downtown Miami is a long forty-block area that hugs Biscayne Bay. Target areas include the Central Business District, Downtown North neighborhoods, Brickell, and Park West.

Central Business District

Miami's central downtown area has thousands of new skyscraper condominiums. Bayside Marketplace is a shopping center that not only serves the current residents, but also heavily caters to cruise ship passengers. The area is building new shopping complexes, some with movie theaters and grocery stores, and thousands more residential units are currently under construction. You'll find the Bayfront Park and Amphitheater, the Miami Museum of Art, and the hub of the Metromover and Metrorail systems here.

The district is bounded by Biscayne Bay (east), 5th Street (north), I-95 (west), and the Miami River (south). For more information, visit the Downtown Miami Development Authority Web site at **www.miamidda.com**.

Brickell

Brickell Avenue, named for 1870s pioneers William and Mary Brickell, houses downtown Miami's most prestigious addresses. Long established as one of Miami's banking centers with over 115 banks and many of them international, this area, known as the "Wall Street of the South," is now undergoing an impressive condominium boom. Eight new high-rise towers ranging from thirty-four to seventy stories have recently been constructed, fifteen are under construction, and fifteen more are in the planning stages. In addition, Mary Brickell Village, a new retail area with a Publix supermarket, now provides locals their own pedestrian-friendly shopping center.

Brickell is bounded by SW 15 Road (south), I-95 (west), and Biscayne Bay (east). For more information, visit the Brickell Area Association's Web site at **www.brickellarea.com**.

Park West

Park West is north from the Central Business District and is named for its location west of Bicentennial Park. Park West is now going vertical—seven fifty- to seventy-five-story residential towers are either under construction or proposed. The new Museum Park (Bicentennial Park) will feature a maritime and a science museum, and will be the new home to the Miami Museum of Art. Park West is exciting because it is a growing district.

The area is bounded by 5th Street (south), I-395 (north), I-95 (west), and Biscayne Bay, the park, and the adjacent American Airlines Arena. For more information, visit the Downtown Miami Development Authority Web site at **www.miamidda.com**.

Downtown North—Media and Entertainment District

Several interesting neighborhoods and districts lie north of I-395. The Omni-Venetia District, a hot redevelopment area, is anchored by the spectacular Miami Performing Arts Center—the new home to the Florida Grand Opera and the Miami City Ballet. Nearby lofts, apartments, and more highrises are making it possible for locals to enjoy an evening of quality entertainment. Another area, known as the Wynnewood Arts District, is west of

North Miami Boulevard and north of 17th Street. It's an old industrial area that has emerged into a collection of artist-related businesses, galleries, and a "Fashion District" along NW Fifth Avenue. It's also south of Miami's Design District, famous for its furniture, interior design, and art establishments.

The north side of downtown all the way to 40th Street and beyond is getting more urban and more livable. For more information, see the Wynwood Arts District Web site at **www.wynwoodartdistrict.com**; the Design District at Miami Design District's Web site at **www.designmiami.com**; and the Miami Downtown Development Authority's Web site at **www.miamidda.com**.

Downtown Miami Essentials

Latin cuisine: "Latin Cuisine" is a fusion of great food from Latin America and the Caribbean: Brazil, Columbia, Peru, Argentina, Cuba, and other countries.

Living the sky life: Imagine the views you'll have from your fifty-story terrace. You could watch the gigantic cruise ships or enjoy the sunset over new skyscrapers. If you move to downtown Miami, you'll more than likely be living in the sky.

Salsa: You'll get hooked on the Caribbean and Latin music that can be heard in Miami's nightclubs, and sometimes on the streets.

Bayfront Park concerts: Enjoy the outdoors and the Miami skyline by attending the concerts at the Bayfront Park Amphitheater.

Beach excursions: As a resident, you'll be drawn to the warm blue-green waters of south Florida. Miami Beach is only a short drive across Biscayne Bay, or you could head south to Bill Baggs Cape Florida State Park's beautiful beaches on Key Biscayne. It is Florida, after all.

The Miami Performing Arts Center: It might be the country's most outstanding venue for opera, theater, and the symphony and you can live within walking distance to it all.

General Statistics

Population: Downtown core: 19,927 (2000); City: 379,724 (2003); Metro: 5,288,796 (2003)

Terrain: Generally flat, downtown Miami fronts Biscayne Bay and is bisected by the Miami River.

Climate Overview: warm winters/hot summers

Average January high/low temperature: 76/60F

Average July high/low temperature: 88/75F

Average annual total precipitation: 56 inches

Average annual snowfall: none

Number of cloudy days: 114

Cost of Living: Find out the current cost of living between Miami and your community by visiting **www.homefair.com** and clicking **"Moving to a New State"** or **"Moving Locally,"** then follow the prompts.

Cost of Housing:

Zip code: 33131 (Southern Central Business District, Brickell); price snapshot: $425,229; sq/ft: 1,842

Zip code: 33132 (Central Business District, Park West, Downtown North); price snapshot: $415,998; sq/ft: 1,412 sq/ft

Real estate prices fluctuate. For up-to-date neighborhood housing cost information, input the zip codes above in the Homestore Web site (affiliated with Realtor.com) at **www.homestore.com/Cities**.

Rent Costs: If you want to rent, explore **www.rentnet.com** and also investigate the following neighborhood Web sites for current rents and available properties.

Taxes

Property Tax: $2,548 per $100,000 of assessed value. Keep current by visiting the Miami-Dade County Property Appraiser site at **www.miamidade .gov/pa/home.asp**.

Sales Tax: 7 percent. Groceries and prescription drugs are exempt.

State Income Tax: No state income taxes.

Downtown Miami Retirement Lifestyle Web Guide

Living

For a current list of apartments and condominiums in downtown Miami, see the Miami Downtown Development Authority's Web site at **www.miamidda.com** and click "**Lifestyle and Culture**," then "**Downtown Miami Living**."

City Hospitals

Baptist Hospital
8900 North Kendall Drive
www.baptisthealth.net

Cedars Medical Center
1400 NW 12th Avenue
www.cedarsmedicalcenter.com

Jackson Memorial Hospital
1611 NW 12th Avenue
www.um-jmh.org

Mercy Hospital
3663 South Miami Avenue
www.mercymiami.com

Mt. Sinai Medical Center
4300 Alton Road
Miami Beach
www.msmc.com

Health Clubs

For a complete list, see the Miami Downtown Development Authority's Web site at **www.miamidda.com** and click "**Lifestyle and Culture**," then "**Shopping and Dining**" and follow the prompts for a continuously updated list.

Volunteering

Hands on Miami
www.handsonmiami.org

Miami Red Cross
www.miamiredcross.org/volunteer.html

Educational opportunities

City Colleges and Universities

Miami International University of
  Art and Design
1501 Biscayne Boulevard
www.ifac.edu

Miami Dade College Campuses
InterAmerican Campus
627 SW 27th Avenue
www.mdc.edu/iac

Mitchell Wolfson New World
  Center Campus
300 NE 2nd Avenue
www.mdc.edu/wolfson

Medical Center Campus
950 NW 20th Street
www.mdc.edu/medical

New World School of the Arts
25 NE 2nd Street
www.mdc.edu/nwsa

University of Miami
1306 Stanford Drive,
  Coral Gables, Florida
www.miami.edu

Library

Miami Dade Public Library System (Main Library)
101 West Flagler Street
www.mdpls.org

Entertainment

Restaurants, Bars, and Nightclubs

Over one hundred restaurants are located in downtown Miami. For a complete list, see the Miami Downtown Development Authority's Web site at **www.miamidda.com** and click "**Lifestyle and Culture**," then "**Shopping and Dining**," then "**Dining**" or "**Night Spots**" for continuously updated lists.

Professional Spectator Sports

Downtown:
Miami Heat (basketball)
American Airlines Arena, 601 Biscayne Boulevard
www.nba.com/heat

Suburban:

Miami Dolphins (football)
Dolphins Stadium in Miami Gardens
www.miamidolphins.com

Florida Marlins (baseball)
Dolphins Stadium in Miami Gardens
http://florida.marlins.mlb.com

College Sports

University of Miami (Coral Gables)
Basketball, cross-country, rowing, swimming and diving, tennis, track and
field, men's football, women's golf, soccer, and volleyball
http://hurricanesports.cstv.com

The Performing Arts

Concert Association of Florida
Miami Performing Arts Center
Sanford and Delores Ziff Ballet
   Opera House
1300 Biscayne Boulevard
www.concertfla.org

Miami City Ballet
Miami Performing Arts Center
Sanford and Delores Ziff Ballet
   Opera House
1300 Biscayne Boulevard
www.miamicityballet.org

Florida Grand Opera
Miami Performing Arts Center
Sanford and Delores Ziff Ballet
   Opera House
1300 Biscayne Boulevard
www.fgo.org

Miami Symphony Orchestra
Various venues
www.miamisymphony.org

*Ballet Gamonet Maximum
   Dance Company*
Gusman Theater of the
   Performing Arts
174 East Flagler Street
www.maximumdancecompany.com

New World Symphony
Miami Performing Arts Center
Sanford and Delores Ziff Ballet
   Opera House
1300 Biscayne Boulevard
www.nws.edu

Major Museums

Historical Museum of South Florida
101 West Flagler Street
www.historical-museum.org

Miami Art Museum-MAM
101 West Flagler Street
www.miamiartmuseum.org

Special Events (Best Bets)

Argentinean Festival
May. Bayfront Park Amphitheater. Music, culture, art
www.festivalargentino.com

Big Orange New Year's Eve Celebration
December 31. Watch the Big Orange ball drop from the Hotel Intercontinental

Calle Ocho
March. Little Havana street party celebrating Hispanic culture
www.carnavalmiami.com

International Ballet Festival
Presented by the Miami Hispanic Ballet Company
August/September. Various venues
www.miamihispanicballet.com

Miami Carnival
October. West Indian Carnival and parade through downtown
www.miamicarnival.net

Miami Hong Kong Dragon Boat Festival
March. Hong Kong dragon boat race and celebration on Brickell Key in
downtown
www.miamidragon.com

Miami International Film Festival
March. Various venues
www.miamifilmfestival.com

Miami Reggae Festival
August. Bayfront Park Amphitheater

Miami Wine and Food Festival
March. Huge downtown wine-tasting event
www.miamiwinefestival.org

Rasin Festival
November. Haitian music fest at Bayfront Amphitheater

Saint Sophia Greek Festival
February. Annual Greek fest at St. Sophia Greek Orthodox Cathedral
www.saintsophiagreekfestival.com

Soulfrito (Urban Latin Music Festival)
www.SoulFrito.net

Movie Theater
Proposed for Metropolitan Miami's incredible mixed-use development
300 South Biscayne Boulevard
www.metropolitanmiami.com

Favorite Downtown Parks
Bicentennial Park
1075 Biscayne Boulevard
www.ci.miami.fl.us/Parks/pages/park_listings/specialized.asp

Brickell Nature Park
501 Brickell Avenue
www.ci.miami.fl.us/Parks/pages/park_listings/specialized.asp

Jose Marti Park
351 SW 4th Street
www.ci.miami.fl.us/Parks/pages/park_listings/community.asp

Lummus Park
404 NW 3rd Street
www.ci.miami.fl.us/Parks/pages/park_listings/community.asp

Miamarina Bayfront Park
100 Biscayne Boulevard
www.ci.miami.fl.us/Parks/pages/park_listings/specialized.asp

Pace Park
NE 18th Street and North Bayshore Drive
www.ci.miami.fl.us/Parks/pages/park_listings/specialized.asp

Simpson Park
55 SW 17th Street
www.ci.miami.fl.us/cms/parks/15_16.asp

Southside Park
100 SW 11th Street
www.ci.miami.fl.us/Parks/pages/park_listings/community.asp

Shopping

Major Retail
For a complete list of all shops and retail in downtown Miami, see the Miami
Downtown Development Authority's Web site at **www.miamidda.com** and
click "**Lifestyle and Culture**," then "**Shopping and Dining**," then "**Dining**"
or "**Nightspots**" for a continuously updated list.

Groceries
Publix
134 SW and 13th Street
10th Street in Brickell
668 SW 3rd Street
4870 Biscayne Boulevard
www.publix.com

Whole Foods
300 South Biscayne Boulevard in the Metropolitan Miami condo development
www.wholefoods.com

City/Farmer's Markets

Seasonal farmer's market at Miami Avenue and Flagler Street
Sponsored by the Downtown Miami Development Authority
www.miamidda.com

Getting around

Public Transportation

Miami Transit System
Metrobus: A citywide public bus
Rail: Metromover, an overhead single-car "Peoplemover" train serving a
   4.5-mile fixed loop from Brickell to northern downtown Miami.
   Metromover links with the regional rail, Metrotrain, which serves greater
   Dade County on a north-south line.
www.co.miami-dade.fl.us/transit

Intercity Bus

Downtown Greyhound Terminal
36 NE 10th Street
www.greyhound.com

Airport

Miami International Airport (MIA)
www.miami-airport.com

Interstate Highways

I-75 (North to Naples, Florida)
I-95 (North to Fort Lauderdale, Florida)

Four-Season Downtowns

Many Ruppies automatically flock to the warm, sunny states, but others who enjoy hot, humid summers also can't do without cool, dry falls, exhilarating winters, and perfect springs. For them, retiring to a city that provides four distinct seasons is the best choice. Some of the finest cities are in colder climates, and in this section, the four best four-season downtowns are Columbus, Ohio; Denver, Colorado; Indianapolis, Indiana; and Milwaukee, Wisconsin.

18

Columbus, Ohio

Columbus, the fifteenth-largest American city, and the largest in Ohio, has more people than Seattle, Atlanta, Boston, Washington, D.C., Las Vegas, Denver, Minneapolis, and Miami. Even Cleveland and Cincinnati only have about half the population of Columbus. However, Columbus, with its "big-city status," always seems to be Ohio's "third city" and is overlooked by most people. Ironically, this is what gives the city its charm.

USA Today featured Columbus in an article called "The Everyman of America" because the city's population represents the average racial, ethnic, and income levels for the entire country. Companies from all over the world use residents here to test new products and services. Columbus is always a welcome surprise to newcomers, visitors, or Ruppies. Here are five great reasons to consider Columbus for your retirement.

1. **Big-city lifestyle, small-town feel**

   Columbus, with almost 750,000 residents, still has that small-town feeling because it's a friendly, tight-knit community—both in and around the city. Retirees will find the surrounding residential districts, for example, the German, Victorian, and Italian Villages, to be extremely laid-back. Neighborhoods are filled with parks and preserved historic homes. Columbus is the perfect city for people who want the best of a big-city atmosphere but insist on the comforts and familiarity of a small-town setting.

2. **Vibrant youth**

   The Ohio State University, only two and a half miles north of downtown, is the second-largest university in America, with around 50,000 students. The economic and cultural power of the university cannot be overstated—it's the largest employer in town, with 18,000 employees. This massive student presence has allowed Columbus to enjoy a personality and setting unlike most other large cities. The university guarantees Columbus a "city within a city" ensuring a high-level of youthful energy and spirit. There are *also* 30,000 students who attend the other colleges in downtown Columbus: Franklin University, Columbus State Community College, and Columbus College of Art and Design. So, if you want a place with a younger mindset, Columbus is it.

3. **The unfinished city**

   In the past few years the city has begun rebuilding many neglected areas of downtown to match its new self-image and expectations. This work-in-progress is encouraging because old buildings are now coming to life as new residential structures, and new construction has transformed surface parking lots, neglected mid-rise buildings, and vacant land.

4. **Design aware**

   The city has become innovative in America because of its strong architectural design review development controls and commitment to quality urban development. In nearly every downtown neighborhood and district, development proposals—including any new commercial and residential projects—must fit inside the city's urban fabric, and be scrutinized by design review commissions. Retirees and empty nesters who are searching for newly constructed homes will find a product that has been picked-over and commented on by many people. And as the city changes and builds up, retirees can be a part of the positive changes that are happening.

5. **Nice and tidy**

   The neighborhoods here are compact and tidy, and traffic generally flows freely. Residents will find clean, safe parks full of joggers and dog walkers among the backdrop of green gardens and flowing fountains. Simply put: Columbus is a very nice place to call home, and a high-quality city where you can retire.

Target Retirement Districts and Neighborhoods

Official downtown Columbus is bounded by the Scioto River on the west and the Innerbelt Freeway on all other sides. Within the Innerbelt is the official downtown core city with the many urban neighborhoods surrounding it.

Downtown Core

Four major areas make up the downtown core: Capitol Square and Uptown, Nationwide Arena District, the Discovery District, and the Market Exchange District.

Capitol Square and Uptown

Broad and High streets, the city's two major thoroughfares, intersect at Capitol Square, which is centered around the all-granite Ohio Statehouse. New condominiums and retail stores are being developed here, with high-tech runners that scroll underneath elaborate electronic signs. There's a new television station planned where pedestrians can watch the morning newscast through the four-story plate-glass windows. This will be the Columbus version of NBC's *Today*.

Capitol Square, the city's theater district, is also home to the following recently restored structures: the Ohio Theater, Palace Theater, Vern Riffe Center for the Arts, and the Southern Theater. Locals can attend Broadway shows, concerts, Columbus Ballet Met, vintage movies, the Columbus Symphony, and all the entertainment venues in one localized area.

Uptown, one of the oldest areas with the newest designation, blends into Capitol Square beginning at Lynn Alley just north of Broad Street, and is generally bounded by Front Street on the west and 4th Street on the east. The center of Uptown features the redevelopment of the Gay Street Corridor, an intact historic corridor of new restaurants, outdoor patios, coffee shops, and a new hotel. A few skyscrapers have been converted into housing facilities near modern new glass and steel residential mid-rise buildings. For more information, see the Downtown Columbus Web site at **www.downtowncolumbus.com**.

Arena District

The Arena District, the newest and fastest developing district in the downtown, features brand-new offices, entertainment venues, restaurants, coffee shops, and luxury condos near the new Nationwide Arena (home of the Columbus Blue Jackets, a National Hockey League team). It's easy to know that you're in this district because the primary building material is fresh red brick, everything is orderly, and the area even has its own maintenance crew and security team to serve residents and visitors.

The Arena District is bounded by the Scioto River (west), High Street (east), Spring Street (south), and I-670 (north). For more information, visit the Arena District's Web site at **www.arena-district.com**.

Discovery District

The Discovery District is a huge and varied area with shady streets, grand single-family homes, old apartment buildings, lush parks and topiary gardens, and a few quaint restaurants, small-town shops, and underdeveloped

In Capitol Square, tight Lynn and Pearl Alleys become urban markets during the summer months.

industrial and warehouse spaces. It's called "Discovery" because it's home to the following colleges: Franklin University, Columbus College of Art and Design, Capital University Law School, Columbus State Community College, as well as the Columbus Metropolitan Library, and the Columbus Museum of Art. Although a major cultural and educational destination, this area lacks the residential redevelopment momentum of other districts, but it's in the works and will probably increase in the future.

The Discovery District is bordered by I-670 (north), I-71 (east), I-70 (south), and 5th Street (west). See the Discovery District Development Corporation's Web site: **www.discoverydistrict.com**.

Near North Neighborhoods and Districts

This area begins at I-670 and along North High Street, the corridor to Ohio State University. Some of the most sought-after and celebrated local urban neighborhoods are located here.

Short North Arts District

Adorned by seventeen steel arches that span North High Street, this district is the city's premier gallery and specialty shopping area. Galleries are speckled with high-end sculpture and paintings, and there are also alternative theaters here. This is by far the most pedestrian-intensive area and the city's primary restaurant row, featuring all kinds of food for every mood and pocketbook, and a great place for an after-dinner walk. A condominium boom has occurred here along High Street, with high-end lofts and flats lining the corridor.

The Short North Arts District is a narrow strip bounded by I-670 (south), Fifth Avenue (north), and includes one block on either side of High Street. For more information, see the Short North Business Association's Web site at **www.shortnorth.org**.

Victorian Village

Victorian Village, due west of the Short North Arts District, is one of the most popular historic neighborhoods in downtown. Victorian mansions surround Goodale Park, and also line Neil Avenue, a beautiful corridor connecting the Arena District with the Ohio State University.

Victorian Village is bounded by Goodale Street (south), 5th Avenue (north), High Street (east), and Harrison Street (west). For more information, visit the Victorian Village Society's Web site at **www.victorianvillage.org**.

Harrison West

Harrison West is the rapidly redeveloping area adjacent and west of Victorian Village between Harrison Avenue and the Scioto River. Many of its streets are paved with bricks, and older homes are being restored to their late 1800s splendor. A large-scale residential development called Harrison Park is being built along the Scioto River that includes condominiums, lofts, flats, and single-family homes.

Harrison West is the area bounded by I-670 (south), 5th Avenue (north), Harrison Street (east), and the Olentangy River (west). For more information, visit Harrison West Association's Web site at **www.harrisonwest.org**.

Italian Village

Italian Village, the neighborhood with the highest home value appreciation in Columbus, is undergoing a rapid-fire transformation with new single-family homes being constructed within the existing historic housing stock. One of the most anticipated new developments, along 4th Street and on the easternmost side of the neighborhood (Jeffrey Place), will include 1,000 new lofts, apartments, town homes, single-family homes, parks, retail stores, and a new senior center.

Italian Village is east of High Street from 5th Avenue on the north and south to I-670. For more information, visit the Italian Village Society's Web site at **www.italianvillage.org**.

Near South Neighborhoods and Districts

The near south is one of the most preserved sides of downtown, featuring tidy neighborhoods east of High Street and restored historic warehouse districts on the west side. The following are target destinations for the near south side.

German Village

German Village has long been the city's "most finished" historic neighborhood. It includes 233 acres of cobblestone and brick streets, late 1880s carriage homes, park mansions, and a charm reminiscent of Savannah, Georgia, or Charleston, South Carolina. More than 1,600 buildings have been restored since 1960, making German Village the largest privately funded historic district on the National Register of Historic Places. It's a gorgeous area to retire to.

German Village is bounded by Interstate Livingston Avenue (north), High Street (west), and Jaeger Street and Grant Avenue (east). For more information, visit the German Village Society's Web site at **www.germanvillage.com**.

Brewery District

The Brewery District is both an old historic area and a quickly developing section on the southwest side of downtown. Its rich history began in the 1830s when German immigrants began brewing beer in the area and eventually built six breweries. Some of these old red brick buildings still exist today. Luxury apartments and condominiums are now being constructed around a new Kroger grocery store. The Brewery District has transitioned into a functional residential area and will continue westward onto the Whittier Peninsula along the Scioto River. Currently, Whittier is home to the city car impound lot and many remnant warehouses, but will become an environmentally friendly, sustainable "green development."

The Brewery District (with Whittier Peninsula) is bounded by I-70 (north), the Scioto River (west), Whittier Street (south), and High Street (east). For more information, visit the Brewery District's Web site at **www.brewery district.com**.

Merion Village

This appreciating neighborhood is located due south of German Village and sometimes called "German Village adjacent." Like its neighbor, it has mostly historic single-family homes, a few row houses, and apartment buildings that are set on delightful streets. Although the home prices are considerably lower than German Village, the amenities and lifestyle are very similar.

Merion Village is bounded by Nursery Lane, Jaeger and Whittier streets (north), Parsons Avenue (south), and E. Morrill Avenue and High Street (west). For more information, see the Merion Village Society's Web site at **www.merionvillage.org**.

Near East Side Neighborhoods

Just east of I-71 is a lovely neighborhood called Olde Towne East, featuring historic mansions along Bryden Road, and, increasingly, rehabilitated historic apartment buildings and condominiums on the East Broad Street corridor. Old Oaks, an enclave of mostly single-family homes, is especially attractive, and the King-Lincoln District offers condominiums and apartments near Long Street. The entire east side has been *much* slower to redevelop than the other outlying Near North or Near South neighborhoods, but momentum is building due to the dedication and tireless efforts of the area's strong neighborhood organizations.

Olde Towne East is bounded by Long Street (north), I-71 (west), I-70 (south), and Wilson Street (east). For more information, see Olde Towne East's Web site at **www.oldetowne.org**. Old Oaks is on the south side of I-70, west of South Ohio Avenue, north of Livingston, and west of Kimball Place. See **www.oldoaks.net**.

Downtown Columbus Essentials

43215—Urbanize your life: Downtown residents can meet neighbors and friends and become active in the improvement and evolution of the area by joining the Downtown Residents' Association. This group meets once a month wearing 43215 T-shirts, the zip code for downtown. Find out more at **www.dracolumbus.com**.

Buckeyes: You might wear buckeye nuts on a string around your neck at football games. Ohio State's mascot is Buckeyes, and sooner or later, you will probably become a Buckeye yourself. If you're not familiar with the Ohio State teams, you'll learn quickly. You'll also learn how to make and enjoy the chocolate and peanut butter buckeye candies during the holidays—and maybe even give them as gifts to your sports fanatic friends.

Becoming a market tester: Because Columbus represents the average demographics of America, Ruppies may have the opportunity to try new restaurants and new products before anyone else. Columbus residents sometimes see and then judge what's coming even before residents of New York or Los Angeles.

The Michigan game: It might seem trite to out-of-towners, but an unofficial holiday in Columbus (usually in late November or early December) is when the Ohio State University plays the University of Michigan—OSU's historic out-of-state rival and known as "that school from up north."

A ticket for the #2: Since Columbus is one of the biggest cities in America without a train, many people rely on its (sometimes lackluster) bus system. But whether you're a seasoned urban dweller or a country bumpkin, people know and many ride the #2, which services High Street to the far north and south reaches. It's actually a fun and interesting ride, and an urban legend in town.

Loving Cowtown: Columbus is generally (and lovingly) known throughout the state as the "Cowtown" of Ohio, or "Cowlumbus." Columbus never landed the major-league football or baseball teams and has endured a severe inferiority complex, even though it has become the largest city in the state with the most educated, computer savvy, and young population. A recent *Cleveland Plain Dealer* article, "Columbus Rocks!" tells of the city's new image in Ohio. Many locals are beginning to use the term "Nowtown."

Tolerance: Many cities in this book are tolerant, but Columbus is getting a lot of national attention for its accepting local population. A recent article in the *San Diego Union Tribune* sums this up:

> "Tolerence" is the name of the Columbus game—whether toward its ample Jewish community, gays (the third largest enclave in the country, after San Francisco and New York), Afro-Americans (BET, 2002: "the best city in America for Afro-American families"), Appalachians, who move from the mountains in Kentucky to the city, and of course the largest population of Amish in the world." (From the article "Columbus? Hip and Happening? Yes, It's True" by Laura Walcher, May 21, 2006.)

Many Ruppies looking to Columbus will appreciate this bonus perk.

General Statistics

Population: Downtown core: 6,198 (2000); City: 730,008 (2003); Metro: 1,674,589 (2003)

Terrain: Downtown Columbus is flanked by the Scioto River and is generally flat.

Climate Overview: cold winters/warm summers

Average January high/low temperature: 36/20F

Average July high/low temperature: 85/64F

Average annual total precipitation: 38 inches

Average annual snowfall: 28 inches

Number of cloudy days: 190

Cost of Living: Find out the current cost of living between Columbus and your community by visiting **www.homefair.com** and clicking **"Moving to a New State"** or **"Moving Locally,"** then follow the prompts.

Cost of Housing:

Zip code: 43201 (North: Victorian Village, Short North, Harrison West, Italian Village); price snapshot: $187,232; sq/ft: 1,654

Zip code: 43206 (South: German Village, Brewery District, and beyond); price snapshot: $153,784; sq/ft: 1,489

Zip code: 43215 (Downtown core including the southern sections of the Short North Arts District, Italian Village, and Victorian Village neighborhoods); price snapshot: $307,185; sq/ft: 1,593

Real estate prices fluctuate. For up-to-date neighborhood housing cost information, input the zip codes above in the Homestore Web site (affiliated with Realtor.com) at **www.homestore.com/Cities.**

Rent Costs: If you want to rent, explore **www.rentnet.com** and also investigate the following neighborhood Web sites for current rents and available properties. Also try **www.columbusretrometro.com.**

Taxes

Property Tax: $1,674 per $100,000 of assessed value. Keep up to date by visiting the Franklin County Auditor Web site at **www.franklincounty ohio.gov/auditor.** Many downtown residential developments have property tax incentives and exemptions, especially inside the "Innerbelt" freeway.

Sales Tax: 6.75 percent. Groceries and prescription drugs are exempt.

City Income Tax: 2 percent flat rate.

State Income Tax: .712 percent to 7.185 percent. (Nine tax brackets. Single: low $5,000 to high $200,000; personal exemption: $1,300. Married: $21,250 to $200,000; personal exemption: $2,600. Child exemption: $1,300.)

Downtown Columbus Retirement Lifestyle Web Guide

Living

Begin at the Downtown Columbus Resource Center at **www.downtown columbus.com** and click "**Living**," then "**for rent**" or "**for sale**" to research current and upcoming housing opportunities in downtown Columbus and the surrounding neighborhoods. Another excellent source is **www.columbus retrometro.com**.

City Hospitals

Grant Hospital
111 South Grant
**www.ohiohealth.com/facilities/
   maps/grant**

Mt. Carmel Medical Center
793 West State Street in the
   Franklinton neighborhood
www.mountcarmelhealth.com

Ohio State University Medical Center
370 West 9th Avenue
www.medicalcenter.osu.edu

Riverside Hospital
3535 Olentangy River Road
**www.ohiohealth.com/facilities/
   maps/riverside**

Health Clubs

Arena District Athletic Club
325 McConnell Boulevard
www.arenadistrictathleticclub.com

Athletic Club of Columbus
136 East Broad Street,
   Capitol Square
www.accolumbus.com

Lifestyle Family Fitness Center
Fifth Third Center, 21 East
   State Street, Capitol Square
www.calfit.net

Capital Club
Huntington Center, 41 South
   High Street, Capitol Square
www.capitalcolumbus.com

Curves (women only)
Huntington Plaza, 37 West
  Broad Street, Capitol Square
www.curves.com

World Gym
9 East Long Street in Uptown
www.worldgymcolumbus.com

Grant Health and Fitness Center
111 South Grant Avenue
  in the Discovery District
**www.ohiohealth.com/body
  .cfm?id=1541**

YMCA of Central Ohio
65 South Fourth Street in Uptown
www.ymcacolumbus.org

Volunteering

United Way of Central Ohio
360 South Third Street
www.uwcentralohio.org and click
  "Finding and Giving Help," then
  "Volunteer"

American Red Cross of Greater
  Columbus
995 East Broad Street
http://columbus.redcross.org and
  click **"volunteer"**

Educational opportunities

City Colleges and Universities

Capital University
1 College and Main Street,
  Bexley, east of downtown
www.capital.edu

Capital University Law School
303 East Broad Street
  in the Discovery District
www.law.capital.edu

*The New Center for Professional
  Development*
215 North Front Street
  in the Arena District
http://thenewcenter.capital.edu

Columbus College of Art and Design
107 North 9th Street
  in the Discovery District
www.ccad.edu

Columbus State Community College
550 East Spring Street
  in the Discovery District
www.cscc.edu

Franklin University
201 South Grant Avenue
  in the Discovery District
www.franklin.edu

The Ohio State University
North High Street, near Short North Arts District
www.osu.edu

Library

Columbus Metropolitan Library
96 South Grant Avenue in the Discovery District
www.cml.lib.oh.us

Entertainment

Restaurants, Clubs, Bars, and Nightclubs

Visit **www.downtowncolumbus.com** and click "**See and Do**" for the latest listing of more than two hundred restaurants and nightclubs in downtown Columbus.

Professional Spectator Sports

Columbus Blue Jackets (hockey)
Nationwide Arena, 200 West
    Nationwide Boulevard in the
    Arena District
www.bluejackets.com

Columbus Clippers (baseball)
New Huntington Park, opens in
    2008 at the corner of Neil Avenue
    and Nationwide Boulevard
www.clippersbaseball.com

Columbus Crew (soccer)
Crew Stadium, 1 Black and Gold
    Boulevard
www.thecrew.com

Columbus Destroyers (football)
Nationwide Arena, 200 West
    Nationwide Boulevard
www.columbusdestroyers.com

College Sports

The Ohio State University
Men's and women's basketball, cross-country, fencing, golf, gymnastics, ice
    hockey, lacrosse, rowing, soccer, swimming and diving, tennis, track and
    field, volleyball, men's baseball, football, wrestling, women's field hockey,
    softball, synchronized swimming
www.ohiostatebuckeyes.com

The Performing Arts

Ballet Met Columbus
Ohio Theater, 39 East State Street
  in Capitol Square
www.balletmet.org

*Columbus Symphony Orchestra
  and Chorus*
Ohio Theater, 39 East State Street
  in Capitol Square
www.columbussymphony.com

Opera Columbus
Mershon Auditorium,
  1871 North High Street,
  OSU Campus
www.operacolumbus.org

*The Columbus Association for
  the Performing Arts*
Various venues and performances
www.capa.com

Major Museums

The Columbus Museum of Art
480 East Broad Street in
  Capitol Square
www.columbusmuseum.org

*Columbus Ohio's Center of
  Science and Industry (COSI)*
333 West Broad Street
www.cosi.org

The Wexner Center at OSU
1871 North High Street
www.wexarts.org

Special Events (Best Bets)

Columbus Arts Festival
June. One of the largest arts festivals in the country along the Scioto River
  in downtown Columbus
www.gcac.org

Columbus Jazz and Rib Fest
July. More than 500,000 attendees enjoy jazz performances and can sample thirty ribbers' ribs from ten states
www.musicintheair.org/jazzfest.htm

Community Festival
June. Called "ComFest" for short, this self-proclaimed "hippie" music and
    art festival is an incredible people-watching experience
www.comfest.com

The Columbus Marathon
October. One of the top U.S. marathons by *Runner's World* and *USA Today*
www.columbusmarathon.com

DooDah Parade
July 4. A silly, topical, sometimes stupid but always fun parade through
    the Short North Arts District and Victorian Village neighborhood
www.doodahparade.com

Festival Latino
June. One of the premier Hispanic/Latino festivals in the Midwest with
    300,000 attendees. Held in Bicentennial Park
www.festivallatino.net

The Short North Gallery Hop
Held on the first Saturday of every month, rain or shine, along High Street
    in the Short North Arts District. The premier people-watching event in
    Columbus for twenty years
www.shortnorth.org

Stonewall Columbus Pride Holiday
June. 100,000-plus participate in the second-largest gay pride parade in the
    Midwest
www.stonewallcolumbus.org

Via Colori
September. Street painting (chalking) festival in the Short North Arts District
www.shortnorth.org/viacolori

Movie Theaters

The Arena Grand Theatre
175 West Nationwide Boulevard
www.arenagrand.com

Drexel Gateway
East 9th Avenue and North High Street
www.gatewaytheater.com

Favorite Downtown Parks

For information on downtown parks, see the City of Columbus Department of Parks and Recreation at **http://recparks.columbus.gov**

Batelle Riverfront Park
25 Marconi Boulevard along the Scioto River in the River South District

Bicentennial/Galbreath Park
233 Civic Center Drive
Riverfront Park featuring outdoor amphitheater, gardens, and sculptures in the River South District

Deaf School Park and Topiary Garden
408 East Town Street in the Discovery District

Franklin Park and the Franklin Park Conservatory
1777 East Broadway, one mile east of downtown
Features botanical collections, gardens, and a butterfly exhibit
www.fpconservatory.org

Goodale Park
Goodale and Front streets in Victorian Village
Bounded by Park Street, Goodale Boulevard, Dennison Avenue, and Buttles Avenue in Victorian Village. Goodale Park is the city's most popular urban oasis and a heaven for dog walkers. Many special events are held here, including the Community Festival

McFerson Commons/Arch
195 West Nationwide Boulevard in the Arena District
A public commons featuring the Daniel Burnham–designed Union Station Arch, preserved from Columbus' demolished train depot, Union Station

North Bank Park
301 West Spring Street in the Arena District

Schiller Park
1069 Jaeger Street in German Village
The beautiful southern equivalent to Goodale Park with similar amenities.
Features a large pond, dog walking, picnic areas, and jogging trails

Sensenbrenner Park
300 North High Street in Uptown
Hardscape park and fountain named after M. E. Jack Sensenbrenner, former
  mayor

SHOPPING

Major Retail

City Center Mall (on the decline
  but big redevelopment ideas
  are forthcoming)
111 South Third Street,
  Capitol Square
www.shopcitycenter.com

Short North Arts District
The region's premier alternative
  shopping district, features art
  galleries and specialty boutiques
North High Street
www.shortnorth.org

Groceries

Giant Eagle
600 Neil Avenue, Victorian Village
562 Whittier Avenue in German Village
www.gianteagle.com

Whole Foods: Proposed
Vine Street between Neil Avenue and Front Street in the Arena District
www.wholefoods.com

Kroger
South Wall Street in the Brewery District
www.kroger.com

City/Farmer's Markets
The North Market
Shop for meats, cheeses, fish, baked goods, produce, ethnic foods, gourmet products, flowers, and unique gifts, while enjoying some of the best people watching in the city.
59 Spruce Street in the Arena District
www.northmarket.com

Pearl Alley Market
Pearl Alley and Lynn Alley, Capitol Square
www.downtowncolumbus.com

Getting around

Public Bus Service
Central Ohio Transit Authority (COTA)
www.cota.com

Bike Trails
Olentangy/Scioto Trail
Linking downtown to northern and southern suburbs
http://recparks.columbus.gov

Intercity Bus
Downtown Greyhound Terminal
111 East Town Street
www.greyhound.com

Airports
Port Columbus International Airport (CMH)
www.port-columbus.com

Rickenbacker International Airport (LCK)
www.columbusairports.com

Interstate Highways
I-70 (East/west from Dayton, Ohio, to Pittsburgh, Pennsylvania)
I-71 (South/north from Cincinnati, Ohio, to Cleveland, Ohio)

19
Denver, Colorado

The city and county of Denver begins where the High Plains end, and where the peaks of the Rocky Mountains appear. Take away the mountains and Ruppies would still have plenty of reasons to settle in Denver's gorgeous in-town neighborhoods. Comfortable and inviting new loft condominiums are currently being constructed in redeveloping districts.

Denver is a world-class city home to the impressive Denver Art Museum featuring an "explosion of glass and titanium" addition by famed architect Daniel Libeskind, the Millennium Bridge, the most elaborate footbridge in the world, and the fifth-busiest airport in the country. In many ways, Denver, perhaps even more so than Dallas, acts like America's "Big D."

Following are the top five reasons why living in downtown Denver easily lands on the best of the four-season downtowns list.

1. **New urban Old West**

   Denver celebrates history and culture with its horse shows, rodeos, steer-wrestling competitions, and the entire gamut of traditionally Western-themed events. Downtown's National Western Complex features the near century-old Stock Show and a still-used stadium arena built in the early 1900s. There's even a "Bronco Buster" monument that portrays a cowboy seconds from being thrown off a wild bucking bronco. The setting is reminiscent of the Old West, and it's easy to imagine the horses of yesterday drinking in troughs and tied up to the hitching posts of the old historic buildings in Lower Downtown and on upper Larimer Street.

2. **Fabulous parks system**

Denver has an impressive city park system. Parks are numerous, exceedingly beautiful, and meticulously manicured. City Park, east of downtown, has more than three hundred acres of greenery with clear views of the skyline and the Rocky Mountains, and offers paddle boats, walking trails, flower gardens, and an in-town golf course. Civic Center Park, a giant expanse of park in the middle of tall buildings is reminiscent of Boston Common, and anchored by the city/county building, the futuristic Denver Art Museum, the public library, and the elaborate State Capitol. The new Commerce Park in the Central Plate Valley area feels like the nearby Great Plains has been imported into the middle of town. Kayakers take on the waters of the Platte in Confluence Park, joggers pass by fountains, and picnickers delight in the countless places to park their baskets. Denver is a city park lover's heaven.

3. **Pedestrian pleasure**

Although Denver is a car culture, a lot of the neighborhoods are great places to take a long stroll. The 16th Street Mall is a good example, with an urban promenade that offers newer retail shops, street performers, and a lot of pedestrians. The Lower Downtown (LoDo) neighborhood's sidewalks are wide and welcoming, with a host of outdoor cafés and shops. Capitol Hill is also a fun place to walk with its intimate little business districts and tree-lined sidewalks. Cars will always rule here, and the city doesn't provide the coziness of Center City Philadelphia or Boston, but walking in Denver is still a pleasure.

4. **Sports city**

Downtown is a sports center through and through—with seven professional teams. Sport venues are either downtown or very nearby, making it quick and easy to attend a Broncos football game or a Rockies doubleheader. (A residential/commercial neighborhood called Ballpark has even been built around Coors Field.) Avalanche hockey is big here, and so are the basketball Nuggets. Factor in the Rapids, professional soccer, and the Mammoths, professional lacrosse, and downtown sports fans can look forward to a new game or match all year. And for Ruppies who choose to live here—it's all in the neighborhood.

5. **Bright days, clear nights**

Most days are sunny and dry year-round. While weather has little to do with the quality of urban environments, residents are able to enjoy the outdoors more here than in almost any other large city. Because of Denver's mile-high elevation, humidity will rarely impede a jog or a picnic, and couch potatoes will have no excuse for staying indoors.

Target Retirement Districts and Neighborhoods

Downtown Denver's target retirement neighborhoods include the Downtown Core neighborhoods, the fast redeveloping North Neighborhoods, and the wide variety of the East and West Neighborhoods.

Downtown Core

The middle of downtown provides the typical big-city experience: tall skyscrapers, architecturally significant museums, such as the cutting-edge Denver Art Museum, and the old Denver Public Library. The highlight of the area is the nearly twenty-block long 16th Street Mall, a pedestrian retail area with a multiplex movie theater that serves the entire downtown area and beyond. This corridor stretches from Broadway to Union Station, and is heavily served by public transit. During the last decade, the spillover success of the adjacent district's residential popularity has sparked the construction of new condominiums and apartments here.

This area is a narrow section northwest of Civic Center Plaza (home of City Hall and the State Capitol), west of Broadway, east of Speer Boulevard, and south of 20th Street, and blends into the Lower Downtown area (LoDo) toward the Platte River. Visit the Downtown Denver Residents' Association's Web site at **www.ddro.org** for more information.

Lower Downtown (LoDo)

This is the most revered neighborhood in Denver, built in and around a thirty-block historic industrial warehouse section that straddles the Platte River. The wide cobblestone streets, old street lamps, and hitching-post railings give this enclave a strong Old West feeling. Residents here usually live in condominium lofts in the old warehouse buildings, but new apartments and condos are also being constructed. LoDo has numerous restaurants (especially the Larimer Square area) and is a major entertainment district for the region, with plenty of art galleries, shops, nightclubs, and pubs. The area is near bike trails and outdoor parks in the adjacent Central Platte Valley and only steps away from the 16th Street Mall.

LoDo is generally bounded by 20th Street, Wewatta Street, Speer Boulevard, and Larimer Street. For more information, see the Lodo Downtown District, Inc.'s Web site at **www.lodo.org**.

The Central Platte Valley (CPV)

The emerging Central Platte Valley begins around the railroad tracks between the historic northwest neighborhoods and Lower Downtown. It's Denver's most notable transformation story. Although the area around the South Platte River was formerly barren, a host of new lofts are being constructed there today, and this is becoming a highly sought-after urban neighborhood. The Central Platte Valley has almost one hundred acres of parks, including the expansive Commons Park, a huge skate park, and miles of bike trails. It also includes the Pepsi Center (where professional basketball, hockey, arena football, and professional lacrosse teams play), and the Millennium Bridge that spans the river and the railroad tracks linking LoDo and Union Station (Amtrak and local light rail). This neighborhood is on its way to becoming one of Denver's best places to live.

The Central Platte Valley's general boundaries are I-25, Wewatta Street, Auraria Parkway, and 23rd Street. For more information, visit the Downtown Denver Partnership's Web site at **www.downtowndenver.com** and click "**Urban Living**," then "**Neighborhood Profiles**."

North Neighborhoods (NoDo)

Eight neighborhoods combine to create NoDo, but the two most prominent are Ballpark and Curtis Park. The Ballpark neighborhood has quickly redeveloped around and north of Coors Field, which is located a few blocks northeast of LoDo. New condominium and apartment buildings, mimicking the architecture of the old warehouse buildings, have been constructed in recent years. Residents can shop at the Ballpark Market, advertised as a European, open-air style market, where vendors converge to sell their wares during the summer months. The Ballpark neighborhood also features the Larimer Street Market—the neighborhood's fresh farmer's market. On the northern edge of this area is an artists' district and a strong Latin community along Larimer Avenue commonly known as Upper Larimer where there are new restaurants and businesses. Curtis Park, a historic district with a diverse, mixed-income population and a variety of housing opportunities, is east of the Ballpark area. Grand historic homes with oversized front yards are interspersed among the large apartment buildings and new condominiums. To the east of Curtis Park is Five Points, Denver's historically African American business district, which has become a hotspot of jazz clubs and restaurants.

The NoDo neighborhoods are on the north side of downtown beginning at 18th Street on the southwest, Blake Street on the northwest, Downing Street on the east, and Tremont Place on the southeast.

For more information on the entire Northern Downtown area, see the Northern Downtown Alliance's Web site at **www.nodoalliance.com**. Also visit the Upper Larimer Neighborhood Association at **www.upperlarimer.org** and the See Curtis Park Neighbors' Web site at **www.curtispark.com**.

East Neighborhoods

The Capitol Hill and Uptown neighborhoods offer a contrast from the core enclaves with a variety of housing choices and a diverse mix of neighbors.

Capitol Hill

This neighborhood's businesses and housing opportunities are widely varied; for example, tattoo parlors and alternative galleries mix with high-end boutiques and expensive clothing stores. Tiny apartments in old brownstones are not that far away from some of the city's largest mansions in established historic districts. There are small business districts with theaters, artists' studios, and parks embedded throughout. Capitol Hill is also considered the bohemian area of Denver, with a large artists' and alternative cultural community, making this an exciting place to live.

Capitol Hill forms a giant square between Lincoln Street, 7th Avenue, York, and Colfax Avenue and is located east of the State Capitol Building. For more information, see the Capitol Hill United Neighbors' Web site at **www.chundenver.org**.

Uptown

Uptown is on a hill just east of downtown Denver and north of Capitol Hill in an area north of the historically seedy but now redeveloping Colfax Avenue. This is a diverse area that's attracting new restaurants along 17th Street and has interesting shops and many newcomers.

Uptown's boundaries are Broadway, Colfax Avenue, 23rd Avenue, and York Street. Visit the Uptown On The Hill Neighborhood Association's Web site at: **www.uptownonthehill.org**.

West Neighborhoods

Jefferson Park/Highland

These sister neighborhoods sit on a hill west of the Central Platte Valley with great views of the downtown skyline. They are diverse in population, housing styles, and commercial districts, and many new development projects are complementing the existing historic structures. Jefferson Park is also home to the Invesco Mile High Stadium and is within walking distance to LoDo and downtown.

Jefferson Park is between I-25, Speer Boulevard, Federal Boulevard, and West Colfax Avenue. Visit the Jefferson Park United Neighbors' Web site at **www.jpun.org**. Highland's boundaries are Federal Boulevard, 38th Avenue, I-25, and 23rd Avenue. See Highland United Neighbors at **www.neighbor hoodlink.com/denver/huni**.

Downtown Denver Essentials

Spending time in LoDo: You'll find yourself browsing books at the Tattered Cover Bookstore, one of the largest independent bookstores in the Western United States, drinking a beer at a local pub, and strolling the streets along outdoor cafés. LoDo is a top attraction and a premier urban neighborhood.

5,280: There are 5,280 feet in a mile. In fact, you'll be reminded in various places all around town. Just in case, to refresh your memory: on the west steps of the Capitol, at Coors Field, and at Invesco Field at Mile High. Since you'll be living a mile above the ocean, the city will never let you forget how far up that is.

City park afternoons: What a great experience: an early summer day in the three-hundred-acre City Park east of downtown. Feed the ducks, jog, enjoy nature in one of America's best big-city parks, or spend time in any of Denver's other wonderful urban open spaces.

Rocky Mountain oysters: No, you probably won't want to eat them, but it sure is fun to talk about ordering them as an appetizer when your family comes to visit from out of town. This local delicacy (cow testicles) is specially battered up and deep-fried like mushrooms, crispy outside, juicy inside.

General Statistics

Population: Downtown core: 4,320 (2000); City: 556,835 (2003); Metro: 2,301,116 (2003)

Terrain: Greater downtown Denver has slightly rolling hills beginning the ascent to the Rocky Mountain foothills to the west.

Climate Overview: cold winters/warm summers

Average January high/low temperature: 43/16F

Average July high/low temperature: 88/59F

Average annual total precipitation: 15 inches

Average annual snowfall: 59 inches

Number of cloudy days: 120

Cost of Living: Find out the current cost of living between Denver and your community by visiting **www.homefair.com** and clicking **"Moving to a New State"** or **"Moving Locally,"** then follow the prompts.

Cost of Housing:

Zip code: 80202 (Central Denver, Lower Downtown); price snapshot: $464,529; sq/ft: 1,434

Zip code: 80203 (Western Capitol Hill, Western Uptown, Near Southeast); price snapshot: $257,801; sq/ft: 1,221

Zip code: 80204 (West, sections of Jefferson Park); price snapshot: $224,229.63; sq/ft: 1,369

Zip code: 80205 (NoDo neighborhoods and Near Northeast, East); price snapshot: $240,900; sq/ft: 1,443

Real estate prices fluctuate. For up-to-date neighborhood housing cost information, input the zip codes above in the Homestore website (affiliated with Realtor.com) at **www.homestore.com/Cities**.

Rent Costs: If you want to rent, explore **www.rentnet.com** and also investigate the following neighborhood Web sites for current rents and available properties.

Taxes

Property Tax: Current residential tax rate is 7.96 percent of actual value multiplied by a local mill value, depending on location. Keep up to date on the city and county of Denver's Assessor's Office Web site at **www.denver gov.org/dephome.asp?depid=23**.

Sales Tax: 6.4 percent. Groceries and prescription drugs are exempt.

State Income Tax: 4.63 percent flat rate.

Downtown Denver Retirement Lifestyle Web Guide

Living

Visit the Downtown Denver Partnership's Web site for an extensive listing of current housing opportunities in downtown Denver at **www.downtown denver.com**, click "**Urban Living**," then "**For Sale**" or "**For Rent**." Also visit the "**Downtown Brokers**" link for a listing of downtown Realtors and brokers who specialize in the urban housing market.

City Hospitals

The Children's Hospital
1056 East 19th Avenue, Uptown
  neighborhood
www.thechildrenshospital.org

Denver Health and Hospital Authority
777 Bannock Street
www.denverhealth.org

Exempla Saint Joseph Hospital
1835 Franklin Street,
   Uptown/Whittier
www.exempla.org

National Jewish Medical
   and Research Center
1400 Jackson Street, East Denver
www.nationaljewish.org

Presbyterian/St. Luke's Medical Center
1719 East 19th Avenue,
   Uptown neighborhood
www.pslmc.com

St. Anthony Central Hospital
4231 West 16th Avenue,
   West Denver
www.stanthonyhosp.org

University of Colorado Hospital
4200 East Ninth Avenue,
   East Denver
www.uch.edu

Health Clubs

Athletic Club at Denver Place
1849 Curtis Street
www.acdp.com

Colorado Athletic Club Downtown
1630 Welton Street
www.coloradoac.com/downtown

Denver Athletic Club
1325 Glenarm Place
www.denverathleticclub.cc

Downtown YMCA
25 East 16th Avenue
www.denverymca.org

Oxford Club Spa Salon
   and Fitness Center
1600 17th Street, LoDo
www.theoxfordhotel.com

Riverfront Athletic Club
1610 Little Raven,
   Central Platte Valley/LoDo
www.terwilligerfitness.com

Twentieth Street Gym
   Recreation Center
1011 20th Street
City of Denver Parks
   and Recreation
www.denvergov.org

Volunteeering

Metro Volunteers (United Way)
444 Sherman Street, Suite 100
www.metrovolunteers.org

Educational opportunities

City Colleges and Universities

Art Institute of Colorado
1200 Lincoln Street
www.artinstitutes.edu/denver/

Community College of Denver
  (Auraria Campus)
1111 West Colfax Avenue
http://ccd.rightchoice.org

Denver School of Nursing
1401 19th Street
www.denverschoolofnursing.org

Metropolitan State College of Denver
900 Auraria Parkway
www.mscd.edu

University of Colorado at Denver
  and Health Services Center
900 Auraria Parkway
www.cudenver.edu

University of Denver
1870 South High Street
www.du.edu

Library

Denver Public Library (Central Library in downtown)
10 West Fourteenth Avenue
www.denverlibrary.org

Entertainment

Restaurants, Bars, and Nightclubs

Downtown Denver Partnership makes sure this list is always up-to-date
at **www.downtowndenver.com/visitors**. Click "**Shopping and Dining**" or
"**Nightclubs and Entertainment**" for the complete list.

Professional Spectator Sports

Colorado Avalanche (hockey)
Pepsi Center, 1000 Chopper Circle,
　Central Platte Valley
www.coloradoavalanche.com

Colorado Crush (arena football)
Pepsi Center, 1000 Chopper Circle,
　Central Platte Valley
www.coloradocrush.com

Colorado Mammoth (lacrosse)
Pepsi Center, 1000 Chopper Circle,
　Central Platte Valley
www.coloradomammoth.com

Colorado Rapids (soccer)
Invesco Field at Mile High
　in Jefferson Park
1701 Bryant Street
www.coloradorapids.com

Colorado Rockies (baseball)
Coors Field, 2001 Blake Street in
　NoDo/Ballpark
www.coloradorockies.com

Denver Broncos (football)
Invesco Field at Mile High
　in Jefferson Park
1701 Bryant Street
www.denverbroncos.com

Denver Nuggets (basketball)
Pepsi Center, 1000 Chopper Circle,
　Central Platte Valley
www.nba.com/nuggets

The Performing Arts

Colorado Ballet
Ellie Caulkins Opera House
14th and Curtis streets
www.coloradoballet.org

Opera Colorado
Ellie Caulkins Opera House
14th and Curtis streets
www.operacolorado.org

Colorado Symphony Orchestra
Boettcher Concert Hall,
　Denver Performing Arts Complex
1000 14th Street
www.coloradosymphony.org

Major Museums

Byers-Evans House Museum
1300 Bannock Street in the
   Golden Triangle
www.coloradohistory.org

Children's Museum of Denver
2121 Children's Museum Drive
   in Jefferson Park
www.cmdenver.org

Colorado History Museum
1300 Broadway in the
   Golden Triangle
www.coloradohistory.org

Denver Art Museum
100 West 14th Avenue Parkway
www.denverartmuseum.org

*Denver Museum of Nature
   and Science*
2001 Colorado Boulevard,
   City Park
www.dmns.org

Museum of Contemporary Art
1275 19th Street
www.mcartdenver.org

Special Events (Best Bets)

Capitol Hill People's Fair
June. Huge street fair
   celebrating the diversity of the
   Capitol Hill Neighborhood
www.peoplesfair.com

Cherry Creek Arts Festival
July. Popular arts and crafts shows
   held near the University of
   Denver with "Festival Nights:
   Music on Filmore" on
   Filmore Avenue
www.cherryarts.org

Cinco de Mayo
May 5. 16th Street Mall
   Extravaganza in downtown
www.newsed.org

Great American Beer Festival
September. 1,500 beer brewers at
   the Denver Convention Center
www.beertown.org

Juneteenth
Mid-June in Five Points.
   Celebrating the end of slavery
   in Texas (now Colorado)

LoDo Music Festival
June in Lower Downtown and/or
   Ballpark neighborhoods

OktoberFest
September in Larimer Square.
   German music, food, beer,
   and costumes
www.oktoberfestdenver.com

PrideFest
Late June. 200,000 attendees,
one of the big gay pride parades
in America
www.pridefestdenver.org

Taste of Colorado
September in Civic Center Park.
Food, food, and more local food
(and music)
www.atasteofcolorado.com

St. Patrick's Day Parade
March. Downtown Denver
**www.saintpatricksdayparade.com
/denver.htm**

Movie Theater
Denver Pavilion (fifteen-screen)
16th Street Mall and Glenarm
www.denverpavilions.com

Favorite Downtown Parks
To explore the following parks and many more, go to **www.denvergov.org**,
click on "**Neighborhoods**," then the "**Parks**" link.

Cheesman Park in Capitol Hill
Franklin Street and 8th Street

Confluence Park
Cherry Creek and the South
Platte River

City Park
Three-hundred-acre park east of
downtown
2500 York Street

Skyline Park
Three-acre urban open space
on Arapahoe Street

Civic Center Park
Intersection of Colfax and
Broadway

Mestizo/Curtis Park
Curtis Street and 31st Avenue

Commons Park
Thirty-acre park in Central Platte
Valley includes the nation's
largest skating park

Amusement Parks
Six Flags Elitch Gardens Theme Park (in downtown)
2000 Elitch Circle
www.sixflags.com

Shopping

Downtown Denver Partnership makes sure their shopping list is always up-to-date at **www.downtowndenver.com/visitors**. Click "**Shopping and Dining**" for the complete list of grocery stores, drug stores, and all types of specialty and conventional retail stores. The other neighborhood links in the target neighborhood sections also have current local shopping information.

Major Retail
Denver Pavilions
16th Street Mall and Glenarm
www.denverpavilions.com

Larimer Square
1430 Larimer Square between
   14th and 15th streets
www.larimersquare.com

Writer Square in LoDo
www.writer-square.com

Tabot Center
Between Arapahoe and
   Larimer streets
www.taborcenter.com

Lower Downtown Area
Shops and boutiques line the
   streets of the neighborhood
www.lodo.org

Getting around

Public Bus and Light Rail Train Service
The Regional Transportation District (RTD)
www.rtd-denver.com and **www.rtd-denver.com/LightRail**

City Bike Trails/Routes
City and County of Denver's Bicycle Program
www.denvergov.org/Bicycle_Program

Intercity Train

Amtrak
Denver Union Station, 1701 Wynkoop Street in downtown
www.amtrak.com

Intercity Bus

Greyhound Bus Terminal
1055 19th Street
www.greyhound.com

Airport

Denver International Airport (DIA)
www.flydenver.com

Interstate Highways

I-70 (West/east from Utah to Kansas)
I-80 (East to Nebraska)
I-25 (South/north from Santa Fe, New Mexico, to Cheyenne, Wyoming)
To see traffic updates on the city and county of Denver freeways: **www.denver gov.org/traffic**

Indianapolis, Indiana

It's America's twelfth largest city, and boasts one of the most livable, note-worthy downtowns. The city's perfectly shaped angular blocks have begun to fill up with enthusiastic urban dwellers who have transformed Indianapolis into a thriving American city. Here are the top five reasons that downtown Indy is a truly wonderful place to retire.

1. Model downtown

In the 1980s, leaders set on a new course for urban revitalization. The city bricked the streets, polished their renowned Monument Circle, and opened up a visitors' center there. The downtown theaters were spruced up to encourage more artists and then declared official arts districts. A world-class downtown zoo, sports venues, shopping districts, and entertainment destinations were also added to the mix. The city even conceived a downtown program called "Building Better Neighborhoods" and allotted $500 million to improve parks, streets, sidewalks, and bike paths. Mayors, city planners, convention center managers, and other leaders from all over the world come to Indianapolis to learn how the city turned itself around. Although Indy began working thirty years ago, there's still a lot of work to be done—and Ruppies can definitely help make more good things happen here.

2. Lemonade out of lemon landscapes

Since the area surrounding Indianapolis is a flat, agrarian landscape, city planners have gone out of their way to make sure that downtown "wows" with its revitalized historic neighborhoods, the elaborate professional sport venues, and their surrounding spin-off businesses. The neatest improvements have been made to the Indianapolis Canal—an otherwise boring man-made ditch that assists the city's drainage into the White River. Today, the Canal Walk, with amazing city views and urban pedestrian paths, attracts locals and tourists to enjoy the Midwest's Venice. Unlike so many other Midwestern cities that don't realize the importance of making lemonade out of lemon environments, Indianapolis is a champion of implementing high-quality man-made extras.

3. **Monument Circle**

Walking in Monument Circle in the middle of downtown will make you feel like you're walking in Paris. This large traffic circle is surrounded by giant buildings and features an elaborate three-hundred-foot tall monument and surrounding fountains. The monument depicts various aspects of American history, including the Revolutionary War, the Mexican American War, and the Civil War. Monument Circle is also important because it represents the very soul of Indianapolis, setting the aesthetic example for the city, and making a big impact on the quality of life in the entire downtown area.

4. **White River State Park**

Mammoth White River State Park is what you'd expect in a rural state park—wide-open spaces and a lot of room to spread out, but this urban park is decidedly different. It features art museums, the NCAA Hall of Champions, a downtown zoo, and even a butterfly garden. Residents don't need a car to get away from the bustle of the city, because a peaceful day at the state park is just a short walk to the west.

5. **Urban sports center**

Since every sports venue is located in the middle of downtown, not far away from the Monument Circle, sports fans can walk to the game. Pro men's and women's basketball, pro football, and hockey are all played in the same neighborhood. And don't forget the nearby Indy 500, which puts the city of Indianapolis in a class all its own.

Target Retirement Districts and Neighborhoods

Downtown's target retirement neighborhoods include the Downtown Core, the historic and arty neighborhoods of the Northeast Quad, and the canal-themed Northwest Quad.

Downtown Core

Downtown Indianapolis is laid out as a square and split into four equal squares. Monument Circle is in the very middle, the very center of Indianapolis, where Meridian and Market streets intersect, splitting the downtown into the four distinct "quads."

The Wholesale District

The newly dubbed Wholesale District (still widely known as downtown's Warehouse District) is the sports activity hub of the city. Men's and women's professional basketball fans enjoy the many pre- and postgame restaurants and bars that are scattered around the Conseco Fieldhouse. The Colts' RCA Dome and the Indiana Convention Center is also here. In addition, this area has the highest concentration of hotels in downtown. Shoppers can visit the Circle Center Mall, an indoor shopping mall that is still going strong since its opening in the mid-1990s. This south core neighborhood also hosts the Indianapolis Symphony Orchestra, and the Indiana Repertory Theatre. Scattered around the district are old warehouses and office buildings that have been converted into condominiums and apartments, and new housing development is being planned.

The Wholesale District is south of Monument Circle and includes the surrounding blocks of Meridian Street and ends at South Street. For more information, visit the Wholesale District's Web site at **www.discoverwhole saledistrict.com**.

Northeast Quad

Highlighted by the city's premier arts district, this area is dotted throughout with lovely historic residential enclaves, and has the most intact existing neighborhoods and new development momentum. The four square blocks near the downtown core have experienced a boom of newly constructed urban condominiums and town homes. These have been built on surface parking lots or otherwise vacant property and have transformed the neighborhood.

The Central Library on Ohio Street and the Indianapolis City Market, a fresh farmer's market located inside a pavilion-style building, are both located here. University Park, on the corner of Pennsylvania and New York streets, is also a popular place for locals to walk their dogs and meet neighbors.

Mass Ave Arts District—"45 degrees from ordinary"

Massachusetts Avenue, the most important street in the Northeast Quad, bisects the area perfectly in a southwest to northeast diagonal. This district, which takes up about five blocks of Massachusetts Avenue between New York Street and St. Clair Street, is a growing, emerging concept. It features an array of restaurants, bars, nightclubs, theaters, and the highest concentration of art galleries in Indianapolis. This corridor and the surrounding area is also the hub of new condominiums and apartment development in the city.

Massachusetts Avenue, called the "urban art gallery," features permanent and rotating public art on prominent corners and in small parks located up and down the corridor. It's a great is the place to have coffee at an outdoor café and people watch during scheduled art gallery walks. For more information, see the Mass Ave Arts District's Web site at **www.discovermassave.com**.

Lockerbie Square and Chatham Arch Historic Districts

Lockerbie Square, a hidden gem in the middle of the Northeast Quad, is a residential historic district. It has quaint historic homes and a few old commercial structures located within an eight square block area immediately south and east of Massachusetts Avenue, and has become one of the city's most recognized and successful historic enclaves. For more information, visit the Lockerbie Square People's Club Web site at **www.lockerbiesquare.org**.

The Chatham Arch Historic District, much larger than Lockerbie, reaches north all the way to I-70, and features showplace historic cottages, row houses, and century-old middle-class homes. See the Chatham Arch Neighborhood Association at **www.chathamarch.org**. Both districts have enjoyed a healthy share of downtown's new residential construction. Large-scale mid-rise condominiums and smaller town homes are rising alongside older warehouses that are transforming into lofts. It's worth a trip to these sister neighborhoods to see the blend of new and old taking shape.

Northwest Quad

Not nearly as developed as the Northeast Quad, this area, west of Meridian and north of Market, features the Indianapolis Canal and Canal Walk. There's also Indiana University/Purdue University at Indianapolis, a shared campus, and White River State Park, which includes the city's primary festival park, "Military Park."

Canal Walk District

The straight-line Indianapolis Canal features a bike path and walkway system that surrounds the residential district. It hums in the summertime with joggers and strollers moving alongside gondolas and paddleboats. Outdoor enthusiasts can observe great unobstructed downtown skyline views from the Canal Walk, and are also treated to a linear urban park full of design surprises: intricate murals and public art centerpieces, intriguing pedestrian bridges and underpasses, and a dramatic seventeen-foot waterfall at "McCormick's Rock," the birthplace of Indianapolis. It's also possible to live directly on the canal in several new or recently constructed apartments. Lucky locals can also enjoy the canal's parks and trails, visit the Indianapolis Museum of Contemporary Art and nearby restaurants, and then get lost in the wilds of White River State Park. For more information, see **www.discovercanal.com**.

Downtown Indianapolis Essentials

Canal walks: The moment you arrive in Indianapolis, put on your walking shoes and take advantage of the Canal Walk—it might become your exercise route.

The Indy 500: The Indy 500 is a sporting event so huge that the entire city holds a month-long celebration in its honor. It's not in a convenient downtown location, so you'll need your car—but you know you'll enjoy it.

Naptown?: Indianapolis still can't shake those old derogatory nicknames before it became the fantastic city of today: *Indian-**nap**-olis* and "Naptown," meaning that the city will put you to sleep. But those days are long gone. When you retire to downtown Indy, stick to "Circle City" and "Indy."

The Circle of Lights: Don't miss Monument Circle at Christmastime with its thousands of lights. This event, appropriately called "The Circle of Lights," can become the beginning of your holiday tradition.

African American heritage: The Indiana Black Expo Summer Celebration is one of the largest cultural festivals held here. The Eli Lily Civil War Museum on Monument Circle is a wonderful place to learn about Indianapolis' important role in shaping the history of black America.

Becoming a Hoosier: Indiana is the "Hoosier" state, and you'll become an urban Hoosier when you arrive. What does it mean? Everyone will tell you a different story. Even though the debate on its meaning is rarely discussed by locals, the word "Hoosier" is deeply rooted in Indiana folk lore.

General Statistics

Population: Downtown core: 17,907 (2000); City: 784,242 (2003); Metro: 1,595,377 (2003)

Terrain: Downtown Indianapolis is generally flat.

Climate Overview: cold winters/warm summers

Average January high/low temperature: 35/19F

Average July high/low temperature: 85/65F

Average annual total precipitation: 40 inches

Average annual snowfall: 23 inches

Number of cloudy days: 180

Cost of Living: Find out the current cost of living between Indianapolis and your community by visiting **www.homefair.com** and clicking **"Moving to a New State"** or **"Moving Locally,"** then follow the prompts.

Cost of Housing:

Zip code: 46202 (Northeast Quad, Northwest Quad, and near North Neighborhoods north of downtown); price snapshot: $195,357; sq/ft: 2,479

Zip code: 46203 (Downtown Core, Wholesale District, western sections of Northeast Quad, eastern sections of Northwest Quad); price snapshot: $232,991; sq/ft: 1,656

Real estate prices fluctuate. For up-to-date neighborhood housing cost information, input the zip codes above in the Homestore Web site
(affiliated with Realtor.com) at **www.homestore.com/Cities**.

Rent Costs: If you want to rent, explore **www.rentnet.com** and also investigate
the neighborhood Web sites for current rents and available properties.

Taxes

Property Tax: $1,530 per $100,000 of assessed value. Keep current at the Marion County Treasurer's Web site at **www.indygov.org/eGov/County/
Treasurer/home.htm**.

Sales Tax: 7 percent. Groceries and prescription drugs are exempt.

State Income Tax: 3.4 percent flat rate. (Personal exemption for single:
$1,000; married: $2,000; child exemption: $1,000.)

Downtown Indianapolis Retirement Lifestyle Web Guide

Living

A good place to begin to find out more about residential opportunities in
downtown Indianapolis is to visit Indianapolis Downtown Incorporated's
Web site at **www.indydt.com**, then click "**New Residential Products**" for a
list of the latest choices. Also see the Metropolitan Indianapolis Board of
Realtor's Web site at **www.mibor.com**.

City Hospitals

Community Hospitals Indianapolis
Various locations
www.ecommunity.com

St. Vincent Hospitals and Health Services
Various locations
www.stvincent.org

The Heart Center of Indiana
10580 North Meridian Street
www.theheartcenter.com

Health Clubs

Curves Fitness Center Downtown Indy
135 North Pennsylvania Street
www.curvesinformation.com

The Columbia Club
121 Monument Circle
www.columbia-club.org

Indianapolis Athletic Club
350 North Meridian Street
www.iacindy.com

YMCA at the Athenaeum
401 East Michigan Street
www.indyymca.org

Volunteering

United Way of Central Indiana
   Volunteer Center
3901 North Meridian Street
www.uwci.org

American Red Cross of
   Greater Indianapolis
441 East 10th Street
www.redcross-indy.org
and click "**Volunteer**"

Educational opportunities

City Colleges and Universities

Indiana Business College
550 East Washington Street
www.ibcschools.edu

Ivy Tech Community College
   of Indiana
50 West Fall Creek Parkway
www.ivytech.edu

Indiana University/
   Purdue University Indianapolis
425 University Boulevard
www.iupui.edu

University of Indianapolis
1400 East Hanna Avenue
www.uindy.edu

Library

Indianapolis-Marion County Interim Central Library
202 North Alabama Street
Central Library
40 East St. Clair Street
www.imcpl.org

Entertainment

Restaurants, Bars, and Nightclubs

Visit **www.indydt.com** and click "**Find It**," then "**Dining**" for the latest complete listing for downtown restaurants.

Professional Spectator Sports

Indiana Blast (soccer)
Kuntz Stadium,
   1502 West 16th Street
www.indianablast.com

Indianapolis Colts (football)
Lucas Oil Stadium
www.colts.com

Indiana Ice (hockey)
Pepsi Coliseum,
   1202 East 38th Street
www.indianaice.com

Indiana Fever (women's basketball)
Conseco Fieldhouse,
   125 South Pennsylvania Street
www.wnba.com/fever

Indiana Pacers (basketball)
Conseco Fieldhouse,
   125 South Pennsylvania Street
www.nba.com/pacers

Indianapolis Indians (baseball)
Victory Field, 501 West Maryland
www.indyindians.com

The Performing Arts

Indiana Repertory Theatre
140 West Washington Street
www.indianarep.com

Indianapolis Symphony Orchestra
32 East Washington Street
www.indianapolissymphony.org

Philharmonic Orchestra of Indianapolis
32 East Washington Street
www.philharmonicindy.org

Major Museums

Historic Ransom Place Museum
830 Dr. Martin Luther King Jr.
   Street, Northwest Quad
www.ransomplace.org

Freetown Village, Inc.
625 Indiana Avenue,
   Northwest Quad
www.freetown.org

Colonel Eli Lilly Civil War Museum
Soldiers and Sailors Monument
  Lower Level, Monument Circle
www.state.in.us/iwm/civilwar/
  index.html

Eiteljorg Museum of American Indians
  and Western Art
500 West Washington Street
www.eiteljorg.org

Indiana Historical Society
450 West Ohio Street
www.indianahistory.org

Indiana State Museum
650 West Washington Street,
  Northeast Quad
www.indianamuseum.org

Indiana War Memorial Museum
431 North Meridian Street
www.in.gov/iwm/warmemorial

Indianapolis Museum of Art
4000 Michigan Road,
  far north Indianapolis
www.ima-art.org

Indianapolis Museum of
  Contemporary Art
340 North Senate Avenue,
  Northwest Quad
www.indymoca.org

James Whitcomb Riley Home
528 Lockerbie Street,
  Northeast Quad
www.rileykids.org/museum

Morris-Butler House Museum
1204 North Park Avenue,
  Northeast Quad
www.historiclandmarks.org/
  what/mbhouse.html

National Art Museum of Sport
University Place Conference Center,
  Northwest Quad
850 West Michigan Street
www.namos.iupui.edu

NCAA Hall of Champions
700 West Washington Street
www.ncaahallofchampions.org

President Benjamin Harrison Home
1230 North Delaware Street,
  Northeast Quad
www.presidentbenjamin
  harrison.org

Special Events (Best Bets)

500 Festival
The entire month of May with
all kinds of events to celebrate
the Indy 500
www.500festival.com

Brew-Ha-Ha
June. Beer tasting extravaganza
at the Phoenix Theatre,
749 North Park Avenue in the
Northeast Quad
www.phoenixtheatre.org

Italian Street Festival
June. Holy Rosary Catholic Church
at 520 Stevens Street,
Southeast Quad
**www.italianheritage.org/
streetfestival.htm**

Indian Market
June. Native American cultural
festival at the Eiteljorg Museum,
downtown
www.eiteljorg.org

*Indiana Black Expo Summer
Celebration*
July. African American culturefest
www.indianablackexpo.com

Indy Jazz Fest
June. Military Park
www.indyjazzfest.net

Rib America Festival
Labor Day. Huge barbecue in
Military Park
www.ribamerica.com

Taste of Freedom
July 4th food fest at White River
State Park in downtown
www.inwhiteriver.org

*Vintage Indiana Wine
and Food Festival*
June. Military Park
www.vintageindiana.com

Movie Theaters

United Artists Theatre (Circle Centre)
49 West Maryland Street
www.uatc.com

Hollywood Bar and Filmworks
247 South Meridian Street
www.filmworksonline.com

IMAX Theater
Indiana State Museum
650 West Washington Street
www.imax.com/indy

Favorite Downtown Parks

University Park
New York and Meridian streets
www.in.gov/iwm/historical

White River State Park
  (includes Military Park)
801 West Washington Street
www.inwhiteriver.com

Shopping

Visit **www.indydt.com** and click "**Find It**," then "**Shopping**" for the latest complete listing for every store in downtown.

City/Farmer's Markets

Indianapolis City Market
Historic public market featuring fresh food, art, and crafts
222 East Market Street
www.indianapoliscitymarket.com

Getting around

Public Bus Service

"IndyGo" Indianapolis Public
  Transportation Corporation
www.indygo.net

Airport

Indianapolis International Airport
  (IND)
www.indianapolisairport.com

Bike Routes and Trails

www.indyfitness.net/Facilities/
  bike.htm

Intercity Bus

Downtown Greyhound Terminal
350 South Illinois Street
www.greyhound.com

Interstate Highways

I-70 (East/west from Dayton, Ohio, to St. Louis, Missouri)
I-74 (From Bloomington, Illinois, to Cincinnati, Ohio)
I-65 (South/north from Louisville, Kentucky, to Chicago, Illinois)
I-69 (North to Fort Wayne, Indiana)

Milwaukee, Wisconsin

Milwaukee is a genuine, straightforward kind of city with a steady focus on downtown redevelopment. For example, it's currently knocking down the monolithic pillars that elevated the Park East Freeway above the city, and replacing them with boulevards along with new condominiums and apartments. Milwaukee prides itself on Midwestern sensibility and an abundance of small-town courtesy and friendliness, but with a slower pace than nearby Chicago. Here are five more reasons why Milwaukee is a prime four-season retirement destination.

1. Dramatic natural setting

Milwaukee gets its name from the Algonguian Indian word *millioki*, meaning "gathering place by the waters." Locals can enjoy the views of Lake Michigan, take advantage of the miles of public beaches, Rollerblade, ride bikes, or just walk along the beach and soak up the scenery. The close lakefront proximity even makes it possible to take up sailing. It's no wonder that one of the city's slogans is "A Great Place on a Great Lake."

Downtown Milwaukee is also set on the Milwaukee River and features the urban Riverwalk and trail connecting the East Side southward to the Historic Third Ward neighborhood. The area is a great way to enjoy the outdoors, and it's also a popular spot for dining and entertainment, with lots of restaurants, shops, and bars. Walkers can stroll above tour boats that meander down the river and among colorful public artwork. In addition, outdoor enthusiasts can explore the rest of Milwaukee's 20,000 acres of public parks, and miles of hiking trails.

2. **Historic preservation**

Old exquisite government buildings are constructed with "cream city stone," huge, historic mansions line Lake Drive just northeast of downtown, and old church steeples still dot the landscape. Many of the nineteenth-century neighborhoods have been revitalized.

3. **Architectural innovation**

The architecture of some new structures may mimic the breweries and old warehouses along the riverfront, while others, including sparkling new modern forty-story condominiums, rise above the old neighborhoods. The new Milwaukee Art Museum is a dramatic building with "wings" that open as if the building were flying, but then fold down when the museum is closed. The idea might seem too unique for other cities, but not in Milwaukee. It's a new architectural icon like the stately Allan Bradley clock tower.

4. **Old World charm**

Milwaukee is known for the large population of German and Polish people who settled there, and it's also known for sauerkraut, polka, and accordion music. It's a highly ethnic city, full of cultural heritage and

Milwaukee's expanded Riverwalk lends itself to prime dining, promenades, boat docks, and spectacular views of downtown. (Photo courtesy of the City of Milwaukee—Department of City Development; photographer David Lattaye.)

expression. The city has a strong Arab, African American, Chinese, Hispanic, Italian, Native American, Russian Jew, Scandinavian, Scottish, and Slovenian population, all of whom still practice many homeland traditions, customs, and religions.

5. **Unreal festivals**

Many colorful festivals are held in downtown Milwaukee, where residents can experience different cultures, music, and food during every season. Churches here also hold a variety of incredible celebrations and big community get-togethers. While it's not unusual for cities to offer a number of festivals, Milwaukee brings them all together as no other city can. In fact, one of its nicknames is "The City of Festivals."

Target Retirement Districts and Neighborhoods

Downtown Milwaukee's target neighborhoods include East Town, Historic Third Ward, the East Side, and Westown.

East Town

Milwaukee's central business district encompasses the East Town neighborhood, and is home to city hall, old-world narrow streets, tall skyscrapers, and the magnificent Cathedral Square Park. It also features the Horace Maier Festival Park, and Summerfest, the city's biggest outdoor celebration. The Water Street Entertainment District is here, and a major theater district is located along the Milwaukee River that includes the historic Pabst Theater, the Marcus Center for the Performing Arts, and many other smaller venues. The Milwaukee Arts Museum is also in the downtown core. This area is enjoying incredible residential growth, with new condominium towers and loft condominiums.

East Town is bounded by Lake Michigan (east), I-794 (south), the Milwaukee River (west), and a loosely defined northern boundary around Ogden Street. For information on entertainment, shops, bars, churches, and services, visit the East Town Neighborhood Association's Web site: **www.east town.com**. Don't miss the Milwaukee Downtown Web site at **www .milwaukeedowntown.com**.

South (of downtown): Historic Third Ward

Immediately south and across the tangled I-794 freeway is perhaps the most celebrated of the Milwaukee neighborhoods—the Historic Third Ward. It's a large collection of old industrial warehouses that have turned into art galleries, restaurants, and specialty stores. Artists have shops here and keep them open for the popular "Gallery Night and Day" event—a huge celebration of art held once a month. The Christmas holidays are never without cookie baking, dancing, caroling, and a tree-lighting ceremony. The Ward is also home to many off-Broadway and alternative theater productions.

There are several condominiums and apartments that front Water Street where the Riverwalk extends from the downtown core. The homes are near the newly constructed Public Market, featuring art, entertainment, and fresh food vendors.

The Historic Third Ward is bounded by I-794 to the north; south and west by the Milwaukee River; and Lake Michigan to the east. For more about shopping, living, dining and entertainment, visit the Historic Third Ward Association's website at **www.historicthirdward.org**.

The East Side Neighborhoods

There are a variety of housing choices here, including single-family homes, apartments, and condominiums. Residents can enjoy a short walk to the parks and beaches of Lake Michigan, or take a walk down Brady Street. This street and the entire East Side is a popular haven for all kinds of artists, coffee houses, vintage clothing stores, unusual boutiques, and specialty shops. Feeding off the youthful energy of the nearby University of Wisconsin–Milwaukee, the East Side extends its special flair northeasterly along Prospect Avenue, where even more unique shops, restaurants, and services are located. There are also drug stores, restaurants, and small grocery stores here.

The East Side neighborhoods are generally located north of the downtown core, east of the Milwaukee River, and south of the University of Wisconsin–Milwaukee campus area. See the service directory provided by the East Side Business Improvement District at **www.theeastside.org**.

Westown

This active downtown neighborhood is chock-full of restaurants, nightclubs, and new condominiums and apartment construction. Residents here will be close to the shops on Grand Avenue—the destination for shoppers throughout downtown Milwaukee. The newly refurbished mall on Wisconsin Avenue offers a wide variety of retail stores that would ordinarily only be found in the suburbs. Westown is home to the Bradley Center (Milwaukee Bucks) and the U.S. Cellular Arena (indoor soccer). Westown's Third Street, one of Milwaukee's signature streets, is also located here. The street is still paved with cobblestones and features many German shops and restaurants, and straddles the Milwaukee River. Westown also hosts RiverFlicks, a free outdoor movie festival during the summer, the huge St. Patrick's Day Parade, and one of the largest farmer's markets in the city.

It's located west of the Milwaukee River and north of I-794 north to around Juneau Avenue. See the Westown Business Improvement District #5's Web site at **www.westown.org** for more information.

Downtown Milwaukee Essentials

Cream City Brick: Yet another of Milwaukee's nicknames (other than City of Festivals, the Genuine American City, and the Great City by a Great Lake) is "Cream City." Many of the city's old historic buildings are constructed with cream city brick, a milky colored brick that makes Milwaukee's buildings immediately recognizable.

Milwaukeese: If you happen to be thirsty in downtown, ask someone to point you to the nearest *bubbler.* A bubbler is a water fountain in Milwaukeese. And if you're searching for an ATM machine, it's a Tyme machine. And for some reason, even though Milwaukee is in the Midwest, locals use the more northeastern term "soda" instead of what you'd expect—a "pop."

Lakefront walks: It's one of America's most beautiful urban waterfronts—strolling the walkways along Lake Michigan's blue waters during the summertime.

Learning to polka: Why not learn to polka? Take advantage of all the diverse nationalities that are celebrated in Milwaukee and have fun learning about other cultures.

The Public Market: Spend a day here and listen to music, thump just-picked melons, and pick out organic poultry—or any other thing you want. Although it's new, it's already a cherished downtown destination.

MAM wings: Become acquainted with the new symbol of Milwaukee, the "wings" of the new Milwaukee Art Museum. Some locals call it the "Calatrava" because it was designed by the famous Spanish architect Santiago Calatrava. It's a marvelous structure and embodies the spirit of a city that soars.

General Statistics

Population: Downtown: 16,359 (2000); City: 583,624 (2003); Metro: 1,514,313 (2003)

Terrain: Downtown Milwaukee features the Milwaukee River and the Lake Michigan waterfront. The surrounding area contains gently rolling hills.

Climate Overview: cold winters/warm summers

Average January high/low temperature: 27/13F

Average July high/low temperature: 80/62F

Average annual total precipitation: 32 inches

Average annual snowfall: 47 inches

Number of cloudy days: 175

Cost of Living: Find out the current cost of living between Milwaukee and your community by visiting **www.homefair.com** and clicking **"Moving to a New State"** or **"Moving Locally,"** then follow the prompts.

Cost of Housing:

Zip code: 53202 (East Town, the East Side neighborhoods, Historic Third Ward); price snapshot: $339,875; sq/ft: 1,585

Zip code: 53203 (Westown); price snapshot: $268,824; sq/ft: 1,811

Real estate prices fluctuate. For up-to-date neighborhood housing cost information, input the zip codes above in the Homestore Web site (affiliated with Realtor.com) at **www.homestore.com/Cities**.

Rent Costs: If you want to rent, explore **www.rentnet.com** and also investigate the neighborhood Web sites for current rents and available properties.

Taxes

Property Tax: Ranging from $19 to up to $30 per $1,000 full value. Find latest assessments at the City of Milwaukee's Web site, **www.city.milwaukee .gov**, and click **"Departments,"** then **"Assessor."**

Sales Tax: 5.6 percent. Groceries and prescription drugs are exempt.

State Income Tax: 4.6 percent to 6.75 percent. (Four tax brackets. Single: low $8,840 to high $132,580 and over; exemption: $700. Married filing jointly: $11,780 to $176,770; exemption: $1,400. Child exemption: $400. An additional $250 exemption is provided for each taxpayer or spouse age 65 or over.)

Downtown Milwaukee Retirement Lifestyle Web Guide

Living

Visit the Milwaukee Downtown Web site at **www.milwaukeedown town.com** and click **"Own the Home of Your Dreams,"** then "Housing" for a listing of downtown residential properties. Also visit **www.realtor.com** and input downtown's 53202 and 53203 zip codes to explore current residential listings, and visit the Greater Milwaukee Association of Realtors at **www.gmar.ws**.

City Hospitals

Aurora Sinai Medical Center
945 North 12th Street, Westown
www.aurorahealthcare.org

Clement J. Zablocki VA Medical Center
5000 West National Avenue
www.va.gov

Froedtert Memorial Lutheran Hospital
9200 West Wisconsin Avenue
www.froedtert.com

St. Francis Hospital
3237 South 16th Street
www.stfrancishospital.net

Columbia St. Mary's, Inc.—
Milwaukee campus
2323 North Lake Drive
www.columbia-stmarys.org

Health Clubs

Bally Total Fitness
1237 North Van Buren Street
www.ballyfitness.com

YMCA of Metropolitan Milwaukee
161 West Wisconsin Avenue
www.ymcamke.org

Curves
123 East Wells Street
www.curves.com

Wisconsin Athletic Club
411 East Wisconsin Avenue
www.thewac.biz

Milwaukee Athletic Club
758 North Broadway Street
www.macwi.org

Volunteering

The Volunteer Center of Greater Milwaukee
2819 West Highland Boulevard
www.volunteermilwaukee.org

Educational opportunities

City Colleges and Universities

Marquette University
Wisconsin Avenue and
   North 16th Street, Westown
www.marquette.edu

Milwaukee Institute for
Art and Design
273 East Erie Street,
   Historic Third Ward
www.miad.edu

Milwaukee School of Engineering
1025 North Broadway,
   downtown Milwaukee
www.msoe.edu

Milwaukee Area Technical College
Downtown Milwaukee Campus
700 West State Street
www.matc.edu

University of Wisconsin–Milwaukee
2200 East Kenwood Boulevard
www.uwm.edu

Library
Milwaukee Public Library
814 West Wisconsin Avenue in Westown
www.mpl.org

Entertainment

Restaurants, Bars, and Nightclubs
For complete, up-to-date listings see the neighborhood Web sites:
Downtown/East Town: **www.easttown.com** and **www.milwaukeedown town.com**
Historic Third Ward: **www.historicthirdward.org**
Brady Street: **www.bradystreet.com**
The East Side: **www.theeastside.org**
Westown: **www.westown.org**

Also visit **www.onmilwaukee.com** for the best restaurant and nightclub search in downtown Milwaukee.

Professional Spectator Sports
Milwaukee Bucks (basketball)
Bradley Center, 1001 North Fourth
   Street in Westown
www.nba.com/bucks

Milwaukee Brewers (baseball)
1 Brewers Way
http://milwaukee.brewers.mlb.com

Milwaukee Admirals (hockey)
Bradley Center, 1001 North
   Fourth Street in Westown
www.milwaukeeadmirals.com

Milwaukee Wave (soccer)
U.S. Cellular Arena, 400 West
   Kilbourn Avenue in Westown
www.milwaukeewave.com

College Sports
Marquette University
Wisconsin Avenue and 16th Street in Westown
Marquette's most popular sports include men's basketball, women's basketball, cross-country, men and women's soccer, men and women's tennis,
   track, and volleyball. Spectators welcome
www.gomarquette.com

University of Wisconsin, Milwaukee
2200 East Kenwood Boulevard, East Side
Baseball, basketball, cross-country, soccer, swimming, diving, track and field
www.uwm.edu/UWM/Athletics

The Performing Arts
Florentine Opera
Marcus Center for the Performing Arts
929 North Water Street
www.florentineopera.org

Milwaukee Ballet
Marcus Center for the Performing Arts
929 North Water Street
www.milwaukeeballet.org

The Milwaukee Symphony Orchestra
Marcus Center for the Performing Arts
929 North Water Street
www.milwaukeesymphony.org

Milwaukee Chamber Theatre
Broadway Theatre Center in the
   Historic Third Ward
www.chamber-theatre.com

Milwaukee Repertory Theater
Various venues
www.milwaukeerep.com

Major Museums
Discovery World at Pier Wisconsin
Downtown on the Lakefront
www.discoveryworld.org

Milwaukee Public Museum
800 West Wells Street
www.mpm.edu

Milwaukee Art Museum
700 North Art Museum Drive
www.mam.org

Captain Frederick Pabst Mansion
2000 West Wisconsin Avenue
www.pabstmansion.com

Special Events (Best Bets)

African World Festival
August. Music, talent shows, dance, and food
Held at Henry Maier Festival Park, 200 North Harbor Drive
www.africanworldfestival.com

Arab World Fest
August. Celebrating Middle Eastern culture. Entertainment, food, dancing
Held at Henry Maier Festival Park, 200 North Harbor Drive
www.arabworldfest.com

Asian Moon Festival
June. Celebrating Asian culture
Held at Henry Maier Festival Park, 200 North Harbor Drive
www.asianmoonfestival.com

Bastille Days
July. Celebrating the French Revolution with a huge downtown block party
    and featuring a walk/run called "Storm the Bastille," food, entertainment
Held in East Town's Cathedral Square Park
www.easttown.com

Festa Italiana
July. Italian cultural festival
Held at Henry Maier Festival Park, 200 North Harbor Drive
www.festaitaliana.com

German Fest
July. German culture festival with German food and beer, entertainment, dancing
Held at Henry Maier Festival Park, 200 North Harbor Drive
www.germanfest.com

Irish Fest
August. Billed as "The world's largest Irish cultural festival"
Held at Henry Maier Festival Park, 200 North Harbor Drive
www.irishfest.com

Jazz in the Park, East Town
Free jazz concerts in Cathedral Square Park, Thursdays in summer
www.easttown.com

Lakefront Festival of Arts
June. Sponsored by the Milwaukee Art Museum and held on Art Museum Drive

Mexican Fiesta
August. Mexican culture festival
Held at Henry Maier Festival Park, 200 North Harbor Drive
www.mexicanfiesta.org

Milwaukee International Film Festival
October. Independent film festival with showings in theaters around the city
www.milwaukeefilmfest.org

Polish Fest
Billed as the largest Polish festival in America
Held at Henry Maier Festival Park, 200 North Harbor Drive
www.polishfest.org

Pride Fest
June. Milwaukee's gay, lesbian, bisexual, and transgendered festival
www.pridefest.com

RiverFlicks
August. Outdoor movies in Westown along the Milwaukee River
www.westown.org

River Rhythms
June. Westown's music festival along the Milwaukee River
www.westown.org

St. Patrick's Day Parade
March. Parade route starts in Westown and ends up across the Milwaukee River
www.saintpatricksparade.org

RiverSplash
June. Kicks off Milwaukee's festival season with food, "River Sculpting"
   concerts on the river, and fireworks
Held at various locations along the Milwaukee River
www.riversplash.com

Summerfest
Late June/early July. Thirteen stages of all kinds of music and a million
   spectators
Held at Henry Maier Festival Park, 200 North Harbor Drive
www.summerfest.com

Movie Theaters

Center Theatre Corp
214 West Wisconsin Avenue

Landmark Downer
2589 North Downer Avenue

Oriental Landmark III Theatres
2230 North Farwell Avenue

Prospect Mall Cinemas
2239 North Prospect Avenue

Humphrey Imax Dome Theater
800 West Wells Street

Favorite Downtown Parks

Henry W. Maier Lakefront Festival Park
Festival Central,
   200 North Harbor Drive

Cathedral Square Park
North Jefferson and East Wells

Pere Marquette Park
West State and Old World Third

Union Square
West Michigan between 3rd and
   4th streets

Riverwalk
East Town to Historic Third Ward

Shopping

For complete, up-to-date listings see the neighborhood Web sites:

Downtown/East Town: **www.easttown.com** and **www.milwaukeedown town.com**

Historic Third Ward: **www.historicthirdward.org**

Brady Street: **www.bradystreet.com**

The East Side: **www.theeastside.org**

Westown: **www.westown.org**

Also visit **www.onmilwaukee.com** for shopping in downtown Milwaukee.

Major Grocery Stores

Metro Market
1123 North Van Buren Street

Pick and Save
Various locations

City/Farmer's Markets

East Town Farm Market
Cathedral Square Park
www.easttown.com

Westown Farmer's Market
Zeidler Union Square
www.westown.org

Milwaukee Public Market
400 North Water Street in the Historic Third Ward
www.milwaukeepublicmarket.org

Getting around

Public Bus Service

Milwaukee County Transit System
www.ridemcts.com

Bike Lanes and Routes

City of Milwaukee
www.ci.mil.wi.us/display/router.asp?docid=14143

Intercity Train Service

Milwaukee Train Station

Amtrak train station located at 4th Street and St. Paul Avenue. Cross-country service and the "Hiawatha Service" runs fourteen trains daily between Chicago and Milwaukee to Chicago.

www.amtrak.com

Intercity Bus

Downtown Bus Terminal

111 East Town Street

www.greyhound.com

Ferry Service

Lake Express Ferry (to Muskegon, Michigan)

Milwaukee Terminal

2330 South Lincoln Memorial Drive

www.lake-express.com

Airport

General Mitchell International Airport (MKE)

5300 South Howell Avenue

www.mitchellairport.com

Interstate Highways

I-43 (South/north from Rockford, Illinois, to Green Bay, Wisconsin)

I-94 (South from Madison, Wisconsin, to Chicago, Illinois)

Downtowns to Watch

Since many downtowns are experiencing tremendous gains in housing, some deserve special attention either because they have momentum that warrants watching, or they are on the verge of becoming exceptional urban places to live. In the following chapters, discover the four most impressive downtowns on the rise that merit your consideration: Chattanooga, Tennessee; Los Angeles, California; Oklahoma City, Oklahoma; and Omaha, Nebraska. (And don't forget to browse the appendix for a few dozen more!)

Chattanooga, Tennessee

Chattanooga, nicknamed the Scenic City, is known for its high-quality of life and scenic beauty, especially with its panoramic views from downtown. Not only does the Tennessee River, which flows through downtown, contribute to its picturesque geography, but the city has also developed itself around its outdoor amenities.

Chattanooga has long been a tourist destination. Twenty-three-hundred-foot Lookout Mountain, in the southern view from downtown, features Ruby Falls, a waterfall inside of a cave, and "Rock City," where you can supposedly "see seven states." There's also the Incline Railroad, a cable car that climbs the side of the mountain. With the addition of the Tennessee Aquarium in the early 1990s, the spruced-up downtown joined Lookout Mountain as a tourist stop.

Although almost 14,000 people live around the city core, the newly rebuilt downtown with its solid employment base and quality outdoor amenities is a strong plus for attracting new residents. This is a small, comfortable, homey city that's becoming ever vibrant. Here are five more reasons Chattanooga is a downtown to watch.

1. Environmental city

Today, Chattanooga is known as one of the world's turnaround cities. It cleaned up its air to standards higher than most Southern cities. The mountain views from downtown are stunning and clear. This was one of the first cities in the country that understood the importance of "going green." It boasts "green parking orchards," parking lots that collect and recycle rainwater, and a series of greenway trails throughout downtown.

The city also features a fleet of quiet-running, zero-emission and free electric buses that whirl around downtown. In addition, the Tennessee Riverfront has been cleaned up, an ambitious recycling program has been implemented, wetland restoration parks have been established, and new "green buildings" that take advantage of sunlight and glass for heating and cooling have also been built. Many cities are "going green," but it's Chattanooga's persistence and dedication to correct past mistakes that have made it such a beautiful, clean city today. Downtown Chattanooga is building on this environmental progress, and becoming a place for people who care about the environment and want to be a part of the city's success story.

2. National model downtown

Chattanooga has a twenty-year head start on downtown revitalization compared to other cities its size, and even much larger cities. A big part of downtown Chattanooga's success is due to its new status as a clean and "green" city, but an even bigger reason is because of the incredible capital improvements that have been implemented: the Tennessee Aquarium Park, dynamic streetscape improvements and street furniture, and the Miller Park Concert Pavilion, among others.

3. Splendid urban waterfront

A huge draw for people who live in Downtown Chattanooga is the revitalized waterfront, especially the Tennessee Riverpark, a ten-mile linear bicycle/walkway along the Tennessee River. There's also Ross's Landing, where a large music pavilion hosts concerts and the city's biggest festival, Riverfest. In addition, there's a pedestrian pier and a large park with giant stairs leading down to the river where people picnic while watching the boats go by. The Riverpark features an underground passageway leading to the river and marking the beginning of the Cherokee Indians' "Trail of Tears." Heading east, there's an ingenious amphitheater underneath a four-lane street bridge, a pedestrian's version of San Francisco's Lombard Street, and the Hunter Arts Museum. Then the trail extends through natural wetlands, rolling hills, and occasionally opens up into other large parks.

4. **The Walnut Street Bridge**

The 2,340-foot Walnut Street Bridge is the longest pedestrian bridge in the world. For many who experience the bridge's magic, it alone would be reason enough to want to move to downtown Chattanooga. The bridge is connected to the Tennessee Riverpark and links the downtown core and the Bluff View Arts District with the dynamic North Shore area. It was originally an old Model-T bridge, barely wide enough for one of today's cars, which was saved from demolition in the early 1990s. It's been restored and painted "Chattanooga Blue" to match the sky and the water, and is for pedestrians only. Although the bridge is used every day, it's especially popular at night. The city and mountain views draw downtown walkers, joggers, Rollerbladers, and bike riders to enjoy one of the most inspiring places to exercise and experience the urban outdoors. Residents love this bridge and consider it an invaluable asset to their city.

5. **Sports and the urban outdoors**

Downtown Chattanooga is steadily building a reputation for its wide array of outdoor sports offerings. The Tennessee River and its tributaries attract fishermen, kayakers, and sailboat enthusiasts who can dock from various downtown locations, including Ross's Landing and Coolidge Park. Hikers can hit the mountain paths while walkers can follow nature trails from their starting point in downtown. Even rock climbers are encouraged to use the one-hundred-foot-tall stone bases that support the Walnut Street Bridge. Downtown Chattanooga is for outdoor enthusiasts, offering both city benefits and access to a variety of outdoor activities.

Target Retirement Districts and Neighborhoods

Downtown Chattanooga's neighborhoods include the Downtown Core, the North Shore/North Chattanooga area, and the emerging Southside.

Downtown Core

The core is a long, narrow area bisected by two main north-south streets, Broad Street and Market Street, and east-west by Martin Luther King Boulevard. Miller

Plaza, a smartly designed concert park with an open brick yard with benches and picnic tables is one of the highlights of downtown. It's home to music festivals including the Nightfall Concert Series and weekday lunch concerts. You'll find shops and restaurants sprinkled within the office buildings and hotels in the central business district. The northern end of downtown is currently the liveliest, especially the Jack's Alley area where outdoor patios, cafés, and bars dominate the landscape. The northernmost end along the Riverfront features the Tennessee Aquarium, Bijou Movie Theater, the Creative Discovery Museum, and a variety of restaurants that are frequented by both tourists and locals. New high-end condominium buildings are also being constructed here.

Chattanooga's Downtown Core is bounded by the Tennessee River on the west and the north, 11th Street on the south, and Houston Street around the University of Tennessee-Chattanooga on the east. For more information, visit the River City Company, the public-private downtown development corporation at **www.rivercitycompany.com**, and Downtown Chattanooga Partnership at **www.downtownchattanooga.org**.

North Shore

The North Shore, a district of North Chattanooga, is now a hotbed of urban living. It's also the home to Coolidge Park at Walnut Street Bridge's northern terminus. Coolidge Park is known for its restored carousel, a major destination for kids and their families. The area is highlighted by the four bustling city blocks of Frazier Avenue, featuring bookstores, clothing boutiques, tattoo parlors, coffee houses, and outdoor sports stores. The North Shore is also the home of the Chattanooga Theatre Center, which features Broadway shows and other plays, as well as concerts. The area in the hills north of Frazier Avenue (North Chattanooga) has mature trees, historic bungalows with front porches, and elaborate gardens. The riverfront here also includes new condominium buildings and apartments, where residents are mere steps away from enjoying the park, the bridge, and the shops along Frazier Avenue.

The North Shore/North Chattanooga area's southern boundary is Cherokee Boulevard/Frazier Avenue/Barton Avenue and extends into the northern hills. See the North Chattanooga Neighborhood Association's Web site for more information at **www.northchatt.com**.

Southside

The Southside, home of the old industrial plants, is starkly different from the other downtown neighborhoods. Much of this area is either vacant property or preserved industrial shells. New construction, including the Chattanoogan Hotel, the Chattanooga Conference Center, and a new elementary school were all designed in a style similar to the old Southside factories. There are also excellent restaurants, art galleries, an antique row along Cowart and Market streets, and a row of shops and restaurants along Market Street near the Chattanooga Choo Choo. There are single-family homes and town homes, and new condominium lofts are emerging in the old historic warehouse buildings. The Southside also features the Chattanooga Market where the rest of the city can shop for homegrown produce, or arts and crafts, and listen to live music. This market, located in one of the old factory shells, makes for a dramatic and enjoyable shopping experience. The new University of Tennessee–Chattanooga football stadium is also here, where football fans can enjoy tailgaiting parties, and music lovers can enjoy outdoor concerts. There's still work to do here, but activity and development is definitely on the rise.

The Southside is generally bounded by Highway 27, Market Street, I-24, and 12th Street. There is currently no Web site reference available.

Downtown Chattanooga Essentials

Walnut Street Bridge: You have to actually walk the world's longest pedestrian bridge to understand how wonderful it is, then you'll easily become addicted to this experience.

An outdoor hobby or two (or three): Residents of Chattanooga can take full advantage of the tremendous outdoor amenities that the city offers. Head for the Tennessee Riverpark and kayak or Rollerblade. Or start walking and enjoy the many urban greenways that criss-cross the city.

The electric shuttle: Hop on the little white electric buses on the north side of downtown to the Chattanooga Choo Choo Hotel in the south. The buses are free and will come in handy when you want to try out a new restaurant or go to a new shop. The Bijou Movie Theater anchors the northern shuttle stop, so you can take in a movie and a walk along the river before you ride home.

The Coolidge Park carousel: When grandchildren come to visit, wow them with a trip to this local icon for a spin on an intricately carved wooden ostrich or unicorn. Then head next door to the fountain where turtles and lions "spit" on children frolicking in the long sprays of water.

Bluff View Arts District: For a romantic evening with your spouse or a fun night with friends, take the Riverwalk and zigzag up to the Bluff View Arts District. Enjoy the interesting public art, and perhaps even visit the latest exhibits at the Hunter Museum of Art. Try a variety of outdoor cafés that are hidden within the trees and gardens for a glass of wine or a cup of cappuccino.

Bessie Smith Strut: The must-be-experienced Strut offers a large procession in memory of the late jazz great and native of Chattanooga, Bessie Smith. It's an unusual people-watching experience in downtown.

General Statistics

Population: Downtown: 13,529 (2000); City: 154,853 (2003); Metro: 485,927 (2003)

Terrain: Downtown Chattanooga begins generally flat from the Southside with rolling hills in the Downtown Core, steep bluffs on the Tennessee River, and then becomes very hilly in North Chattanooga.

Climate Overview: cool winters/hot summers

Average January high/low temperature: 49/30F

Average July high/low temperature: 90/69F

Average annual total precipitation: 54 inches

Average annual snowfall: 5 inches

Number of cloudy days: 155

Cost of Living: Find out the current cost of living between Chattanooga and your community by visiting **www.homefair.com** and clicking **"Moving to a New State"** or **"Moving Locally,"** then follow the prompts.

Cost of Housing:

Zip code: 37402 (Downtown Core); price snapshot: $455,926 (limited housing supply); sq/ft: 2,530

Zip code: 37402 (Southside); price snapshot: $140,556; sq/ft: 1,587

Zip code: 37405 (North Shore/North Chattanooga); price snapshot: $186,721; sq/ft: 1,711

Real estate prices fluctuate. For up-to-date neighborhood housing cost information, input the zip codes above in the Homestore Web site (affiliated with Realtor.com) at **www.homestore.com/Cities**.

Rent Costs: If you want to rent, explore **www.rentnet.com** and also investigate the neighborhood Web sites for current rents and available properties.

Taxes

Property Tax: Typical tax bill is $2,520 for $100,000 home. Visit the City of Chattanooga Treasurer's Office Web site at: **www.chattanooga.gov**, click **"Departments,"** then **"Finance."**

Sales Tax: 9.25 percent. Groceries and prescription drugs are exempt.

State Income Tax: No state income taxes.

"Nightfall," the free outdoor concert series at Miller Plaza, has become a Friday night tradition. Drink a cocktail and join your neighbors to enjoy rock, blues, jazz, reggae, zydeco, funk, bluegrass, and folk music every weekend from May to the end of September. (Photo courtesy of the Chattanooga Downtown Partnership.)

Downtown Chattanooga Retirement Lifestyle Web Guide

Living

Visit the Downtown Chattanooga Partnership at **www.downtownchatta nooga.org** and click "**Get a Place of Your Own**" for the most up-to-date listing of downtown apartments and condominiums. Also contact the Chattanooga Association of Realtors at **www.chattrealtors.com**.

City Hospitals

Erlanger Hospital
975 East Third Street
www.erlanger.org

Memorial Hospital
2525 de Sales Avenue
www.memorial.org

Parkridge Hospital
2333 McCallie Avenue
www.parkridgemedicalcenter.com

Health Clubs

YMCA of Metropolitan Chattanooga
301 West Sixth Street
www.chatt-ymca.org

The Sports Barn
301 Market Street
www.sports-barn.com

Volunteering

United Way of Greater Chattanooga
630 Market Street
www.uwchatt.org

Chattanooga-Hamilton County Red Cross
801 McCallie Avenue
www.chattanooga-redcross.org

Downtown Chattanooga Partnership
850 Market Street
www.downtownchattanooga.org and click "**Volunteer**"

Educational opportunities

City Colleges and Universities

The University of Tennessee
  at Chattanooga
615 McCallie Avenue
www.utc.edu

Chattanooga State Technical
  Community College
4501 Amnicola Highway
  (three miles east of downtown)
www.chattanoogastate.edu

Library

Chattanooga Hamilton County Bicentennial Library
1001 Broad Street, downtown
www.lib.chattanooga.gov

Entertainment

Restaurants, Bars, and Nightclubs

Downtown Chattanooga has an array of restaurants, bars, and nightclubs.
Unfortunately, there is no official Web site dedicated to this kind of directory. Chattanooga's alternative and arts newspaper the *Pulse* provides the
best current listing. Visit **www.chattanoogapulse.com**.

Professional Sports

Chattanooga Lookouts (baseball)
BellSouth Park on Hawk Hil
www.lookouts.com

College Sports

The University of Tennessee at Chattanooga
Located on the northeast side of downtown on Martin Luther King Boulevard.
  Men's and womens' tennis, and golf, men's baseball, football, women's
  volleyball soccer, cross-country, and softball
www.utc.edu

The Performing Arts

Chattanooga Opera
Performs in the Tivoli Theater,
   709 Broad Street
www.chattanoogasymphony.org

Chattanooga Symphony Orchestra
Performs in the Tivoli Theater,
   709 Broad Street
www.chattanoogasymphony.org

Chattanooga Theatre Centre
400 River Street, North Shore
www.theatrecentre.com

UTC Fine Arts Center
Corner of Vine and Palmetto streets
www.utc.edu/Administration/
   FineArtsCenter

Major Museums

Hunter Museum of American Art
10 Bluff View, Bluff View Arts District
www.huntermuseum.org

Creative Discovery Museum
321 Chestnut Street
www.cdmfun.org

Chattanooga African American History Museum
200 East Martin Luther King Boulevard
www.caamhistory.com

Special Events (Best Bets)

Bella Sera
June. Food, wine tasting, fundraisers. Held in the Bluff View Arts District
www.bellaseraevent.com

Chattanooga Bluegrass Experience
September/October. National bluegrass headliners, held at Miller Plaza
www.downtownchattanooga.org

Chattanooga's CultureFest
Summer, check for dates. Multicultural celebration in Coolidge Park
www.culturefest.org

Four Bridges Arts Festival
May. A celebration of the visual arts. Held at various venues each year
www.avartist.org

Independence Day Pops on the River
July 3 at Coolidge Park
www.downtownchattanooga.org

Nightfall Concert Series
May through September, Friday nights. Concerts, music events, and dancing
www.downtownchattanooga.org

Riverbend Festival
June/July. The granddaddy of Chattanooga festivals. Eight days of music,
   five stages, fireworks. Held on the Tennessee Riverfront in downtown
www.riverbendfestival.com

Rhythm at Noon
May through August. Free concerts at Miller Park during lunch hour
www.downtownchattanooga.org

Southern Brewers Festival
September. A celebration of beer on the Riverfront
www.southernbrewersfest.org

Street Musicians
Arts and entertainment from Memorial Day through Labor Day,
weekends on the downtown sidewalks
www.downtownchattanooga.org

Wine over Water
September. Set on the Walnut Street pedestrian bridge. Sampling wines from
   over one hundred world wineries, music
www.wineoverwater.org

Winter Days and Lights
Celebration of lights all winter in downtown, featuring Christmas on the
   river with a Grand Illumination (light show), and the Holiday Star Light
   Parade
www.downtownchattanooga.org

Movie Theater

Bijou Movie Theater
215 Broad Street in downtown

Favorite Downtown Parks

Aquarium Plaza
Located outside the
Tennessee Aquarium

Coolidge Park
In North Shore on the river,
features restored carousel, kids'
interactive fountains, green space,
and a music pavilion

Miller Park
910 Market Street
Urban park with large fountains
and grassy areas

Miller Plaza
850 Market Street
Major site for concerts and
festivals with park benches
and picnic tables

Renaissance Park—
Adjacent to Coolidge Park
Twenty-three-acre urban wetlands
park with nature trails

Ross's Landing Park
Across from Tennessee Aquarium in
downtown. Features marina, boat
piers, and a natural amphitheater

Tennessee Riverwalk/Riverpark
Ten-mile river walk stretching from
downtown to the Chickamauga
Dam

Walnut Street Bridge
Pedestrian-only bridge, a favorite
spot for walkers and joggers,
linking downtown to North
Shore/Coolidge Park

Shopping

Warehouse Row (outlet mall)
1110 Market Street in downtown

Fraizer Avenue in the North Shore
Specialty shops, boutiques, and restaurants

Grocery Stores

No major grocery stores except for two very small food marts. Grocery stores are located two miles away in any direction.

City/Farmer's Markets

The Chattanooga Market
1826 Carter Street at the First Tennessee Pavilion
www.chattanoogamarket.com

Getting around

City Bus

Chattanooga Area Regional Transit Authority
City bus, downtown electric shuttle with free service serving downtown
www.carta.org

Bike Routes/Trails

See Outdoor Chattanooga's Web site at **www.outdoorchattanooga.com**

Airport

Chattanooga Metropolitan Airport (CHA)
www.chattairport.com

Intercity Bus

Greyhound Bus Terminal
960 Airport Road/Shepherd Street
www.greyhound.com

Interstate Highways

I-24/59 (West to Nashville, Tennessee, south to Birmingham, Alabama)
I-75 (South/north from Atlanta, Georgia, to Knoxville, Tennessee)

23 Los Angeles, California

Behind New York, Los Angeles is America's second-largest city, but historically has not offered much for urban living enthusiasts. The city grew in the age of urban sprawl and concentrated on building freeways and large homes with backyard swimming pools and not a great city center. During the last decade, however, Los Angeles has aggressively revitalized its unique and attractive downtown areas, filled vacant properties with new residential towers, reused old warehouse buildings and converted them to loft spaces, and generated interest and enthusiasm about urban living. "Metro" trains have also arrived, bringing the city into the transit big leagues. Downtown Los Angeles is becoming the downtown to watch. Here are five reasons why it's a great place to consider for your retirement.

1. Diversity

Downtown Los Angeles enjoys a diverse mix of cultures. Mexican influences can be seen in many of its districts, for example, Olvera Street, the El Pueblo Historic Monument, and Mexican Marketplace. Then there's Chinatown, a district adjacent to the core of downtown on the north side, and Little Tokyo, with its prominent Japanese American National Museum. Here, wealthy and middle-class residents live near their poorer neighbors on the east side of downtown (and Skid Row's large homeless population)—allowing many volunteer opportunities for locals who care. Mostly, however, downtown Los Angeles is a celebratory interaction of cultures, ethnic shops and restaurants, and bustling sidewalks.

2. City markets

There may not be a full-service downtown grocery store, but a planned Ralph's is upcoming and several more will surely follow in the future. Downtown residents still have places to shop for fresh food, especially in several high-quality city markets: the City Market, Grand Central Market, Seventh Street Produce Market, and Farmer's Market. Grocery stores are needed, but these markets make shopping for food an adventurous experience.

3. Performing arts world center

Residents can take advantage of the world-renowned Los Angeles Philharmonic and the Los Angeles Master Chorale at the new Walt Disney Concert Hall, or the opera at the Dorothy Chandler Pavilion. Downtown's Theater District provides rousing productions, and the cultural arts festivals in the city are too long to list. With Hollywood up the street, it's no wonder that musical and theatrical performances abound in this town.

4. Spectacular architecture

Los Angeles is the film capital of the world, and directors here know that they don't have to go to New York to provide a Manhattan backdrop. Tight streets with rows and rows of tall historic banks, theaters, old mercantile structures, and other buildings, especially along and near Broadway, are gloriously preserved. New buildings, such as the aforementioned Frank Gehry–designed Walt Disney Concert Hall and the Cathedral of Our Lady of the Angels, are equally dramatic.

5. Growing and emerging

According to the Downtown Los Angeles Center Business Improvement District, almost 10,000 residential units have been constructed since 1999, 4,500 are currently under construction, and 12,000 more are being planned. This is a great time to be part of downtown's makeover.

Target Retirement Districts and Neighborhoods

Downtown Los Angeles is bounded by the Hollywood Freeway 101, Harbor Freeway, I-110, Santa Monica Freeway, I-10, and the Los Angeles River. The following are downtown's primary neighborhoods and districts.

Historic Downtown

The Historic Downtown, often referred to as the Historic Core, is a twenty-five-square-block collection of beaux arts and art deco–style mid-rises. It's the city's turn-of-the-century hub for business and retail, and today's most charming urban district. Broadway, the main street, is home to the Theater District and features historic theaters and old movie palaces. On 4th Street, between Spring and Main is the Old Bank District, where a collection of hundred-year-old commercial and bank buildings have been turned into residential lofts. The neighborhood features Grand Central Market near Broadway, which was the old city produce market established in 1917.

On the southwest boundary is the Jewelry District, a concentration of jewelry businesses and wholesalers, featuring the St. Vincent Jewelry Center, a historic landmark. Pershing Square, with a plaza, trees, a large reflecting pool, and a fountain, is one of downtown's premier parks, and provides outdoor movie nights and a popular winter ice skating rink. The eastern end borders the Little Tokyo neighborhood and the Toy District. Apartments and condominiums can be found in many of the old buildings above the retail stores.

Historic Downtown is between Hill Street (west), 1st Street (north), 5th Street (south), and Los Angeles Boulevard (east). For more information, see the Historic Downtown Los Angeles Business Improvement District's Web site at **www.historicdowntownla.com**.

Bunker Hill

Bunker Hill, new downtown Los Angeles, is up the hill and to the west of Historic Downtown. Best known for its modern skyscrapers and as an employment center, this area is now the home to the city's cultural and performing arts venues, including the Walt Disney Concert Hall, Dorothy Chandler Pavilion, Mark Taper Forum, Ahmanson Theatre, Wells Fargo Museum, and the Museum of Modern Art. Because of the vast cultural opportunities, the area has begun to provide an increasing number of housing opportunities.

Bunker Hill lies between 1st Street (north), Hill Street (east), Harbor Freeway (west), and 4th Street (south). See **www.downtownla.com** for more information.

Artists District

This large collection of industrial warehouses, also called the Arts District, is separated from the downtown core by Little Tokyo and the Toy District, and bordered on the south and east by the industrial land Warehouse District. Many of the old buildings have been converted into New York–style lofts, offering excellent views of the Bunker Hill skyline to the west. The Artists District also hosts the Los Angeles Arts Festival.

The Artists District is between the Los Angeles River, Alameda Street, 1st Street, and 7th Street. To learn more, visit the Los Angeles Downtown Arts District's Web site at **www.ladad.com**.

Fashion District

The area draws top fashion designers and students, but also shoppers seeking a bargain—especially along Wall Street and Santee Alley. One of the city's largest flower markets is located on Wall Street between 7th and 8th streets. The Fashion District has begun to offer new residential housing opportunities and is building more every year.

It's a huge eighty-two-square-block area south of the downtown core, east of Broadway, and north of the Santa Monica Freeway. For more information, visit the LA Fashion District Business Improvement District at **www.fashiondistrict.org**.

South Park

South Park, a residential growth pole, has enjoyed a boom of new residential development in recent years. The area, known for the Staples Center and the Los Angeles Convention Center, is also home to the Museum of Neon Art.

South Park is south of Bunker Hill, east of the Harbor Freeway, west of the Fashion District, and north of the Santa Monica Freeway. See **www.down townla.com** for more information.

Downtown Los Angeles Essentials

Holiday shopping in the Toy District: You'll shop for all kinds of knick-knacks in this remarkable twelve-square-block area: toys, video games, die-cast trinkets, etcetera.

A Metro card: Take the clean, new Metro trains for day trips: to Old Pasadena, or to Long Beach, or Redondo Beach, or even to Hollywood and Vine for a star-sighting.

Chinatown days: Take the Metro Gold from Union Station to the Chinatown Station for a day of shopping at Central Plaza. Browse at the Chinatown Farmer's Market, and then have a big Chinese feast in America's third-largest Chinatown. Don't miss the Chinese New Year Parade and Festival. See **www.chinatownla.com**.

Santee Alley: Put a twenty in your pocket on any Saturday, and head up to Santee Alley in the heart of the Fashion District and see how much you can buy. Fashion bargain-hunting is addictive and might fast become one of your favorite hobbies.

Fresh produce and just-cut flowers: Take a walk to the Flower District to create your own bouquet and then to the Seventh Street Produce Market to choose a wide array of fruits and veggies. Get there early before the best selection is gone.

Downtown on ice: It might be 80 degrees in December, but that will not stop you from enjoying a winter wonderland while skating in Pershing Square Park in downtown.

General Statistics

Population: Downtown: 36,360 (2000); City: 3,845,541 (2000); Metro: 12,829,272 (2000)

Terrain: Downtown Los Angeles is flat to slightly rolling from east to west where the terrain rises abruptly at the Bunker Hill ridge on the far west side.

Climate Overview: mild winters/warm summers

Average January high/low temperature: 65/48F

Average July high/low temperature: 82/62F

Average annual total precipitation: 14 inches

Average annual snowfall: zero

Number of cloudy days: 101

Cost of Living: Find out the current cost of living between Los Angeles and your community by visiting **www.homefair.com** and clicking **"Moving to a New State"** or **"Moving Locally,"** then follow the prompts.

Cost of Housing:

Zip code: 90013 (North Historic Core, Toy District, Little Tokyo); price snapshot: $518,400; sq/ft: NA

Zip code: 90014 (South Historic Core, Northern fringe of South Park, and Fashion District); price snapshot: $855,140; sq/ft: N/A

Zip code: 90015 (Fashion District, most of South Park); price snapshot: $488,301; sq/ft: 1,682

Zip code: 90021 (Southeast, Warehouse District, Southern Artists District); price snapshot: $646,136; sq/ft: 1,278

Real estate prices fluctuate. For up-to-date neighborhood housing cost information, input the zip codes above in the Homestore Web site (affiliated with Realtor.com) at **www.homestore.com/Cities**.

Rent Costs: If you want to rent, explore **www.rentnet.com** and also investigate the neighborhood Web sites for current rents and available properties.

Taxes

Property Tax: Varies according to location. Please visit Los Angeles County Property Tax Portal at **http://lacountypropertytax.com**.

Sales Tax: 8.25 percent. Food and prescription drugs exempted.

State Income Tax: 1.0 percent to 9.3 percent. (Six income tax brackets. Single: low $6,319 to high $41,477 and over, with additional 1 percent over $1,000,000. Filing jointly: Joint returns taxes are twice the tax imposed on half the income.)

Downtown Los Angeles Retirement Lifestyle Web Guide

Living

The best place to find out more about the housing in downtown Los Angeles is by visiting the Downtown Business Center Improvement District's Web site at **www.downtownla.com** and clicking "**Living Here.**" You'll find current and detailed information about downtown apartments, condos, lofts, new construction, and a variety of other housing links.

City Hospitals

Good Samaritan Hospital
1225 Wilshire Boulevard
www.goodsam.org

California Hospital Medical Center
1401 South Grand Avenue
www.chmcla.org

USC University Hospital
1500 San Pablo Street
www.uscuh.com

USC/Norris Comprehensive
  Cancer Center and Hospital
1441 Eastlake Avenue
www.norriscancerhospital.com

Orthopedic Hospital
  Outpatient Medical Center
2400 South Flower Street
www.orthohospital.org

Health Clubs

Stuart M. Ketchum Downtown YMCA
401 South Hope Street
www.ymcala.org

Los Angeles Athletic Club
431 West 7th Street
www.laac.com

Volunteering

American Red Cross of Greater
  Los Angeles
2700 Wilshire Boulevard
www.redcrossla.org/volunteer

United Way of Greater Los Angeles
523 West 6th Street
www.unitedwayla.org

Educational opportunities

City Colleges and Universities

University of Southern California
University Park campus
Exposition Boulevard and
   Pardee Way
www.usc.edu

Loyola University School of Law
919 Albany Street
www.lls.edu

*Fashion Institute of Design
   and Merchandising*
919 South Grand Avenue
www.fidm.com

Colburn School of Performing Arts
200 South Grand Avenue
www.colburnschool.edu

Library

Central Library
630 West 5th Street
www.lapl.org

Entertainment

Restaurants, Bars, and Nightclubs

Over two hundred restaurants are located in downtown Los Angeles. For a complete list, see **www.downtownla.com** and click "**Shopping and Dining Here**" or "**Arts and Entertainment.**"

Also see Chinatown's Web site at **www.chinatownla.com** and click "**Shopping, Dining, & Businesses**"; and Little Tokyo Business Association's Web site at **www.visitlittletokyo.com** and click "**Restaurants and Nightlife.**"

Professional Spectator Sports

Los Angeles Avengers (football)
Staples Center, 1111 South
   Figueroa Street
www.laavengers.com

Los Angeles Clippers (basketball)
Staples Center, 1111 South
   Figueroa Street
www.nba.com/clippers

Los Angeles Dodgers (baseball)
Dodger Stadium,
  1000 Elysian Park Avenue
www.dodgers.com

Los Angeles Galaxy (soccer)
Home Depot Center, 18400 Avalon
  Boulevard in Carson, California
www.lagalaxy.com

Los Angeles Kings (hockey)
Staples Center,
  1111 South Figueroa Street
www.lakings.com

Los Angeles Lakers (basketball)
Staples Center,
  1111 South Figueroa Street
www.nba.com/lakers

Los Angeles Sparks
  (women's basketball)
Staples Center,
  1111 South Figueroa Street
www.wnba.com/sparks

College Sports

University of Southern California
Trojan Athletics: men's and women's basketball, golf, swimming and diving,
  tennis, track, volleyball, water polo, men's baseball, football, women's cross-
  country, rowing, and soccer
www.usctrojans.com

The Performing Arts

Los Angeles Chamber Orchestra
Zipper Concert Hall
Colburn School of Performing Arts
200 South Grand Avenue
www.laco.org

Los Angeles Philharmonic
Walt Disney Concert Hall
111 South Grand Avenue
www.laphil.org

Center Theatre Group in Los Angeles
Various venues
www.taperahmanson.com

Los Angeles Opera
Dorothy Chandler Pavilion
135 North Grand Avenue
www.losangelesopera.com

Los Angeles Master Chorale
Walt Disney Concert Hall
111 South Grand Avenue
www.lamc.org

Music Center/Performing Arts Center of Los Angeles County
135 North Grand Avenue and various other venues
www.musiccenter.org

Major Museums

African American Firefighter Museum
1401 South Central Avenue
www.aaffmuseum.org

California African American Museum
600 State Drive (Exposition Park)
www.caammuseum.org

California Science Center
700 State Drive (Exposition Park)
www.californiasciencecenter.org

Chinese American Museum
425 North Los Angeles Street
www.camla.org

Japanese American National Museum
369 East First Street
www.janm.org

Museum of Contemporary Art
250 South Grand Avenue
www.moca.org

The Geffen Contemporary at MOCA
152 North Central Avenue
www.moca.org

Museum of Neon Art
501 West Olympic Boulevard
www.neonmona.org

Natural History Museum
900 Exposition Boulevard
www.nhm.org

USC Fisher Gallery
823 Exposition Boulevard
www.usc.edu/org/fishergallery

Wells Fargo History Museum
333 South Grand Avenue
www.wellsfargohistory.com

Special Events (Best Bets)

Downtown Los Angeles holds many special events and festivals every year. For a complete listing of daily and monthly festivals, visit Downtown Los Angeles Business Improvement District's Web site at **www.downtownla.com/ events_calendar.asp** and **www.downtownla.com/arts_entertainment.asp** for a complete listing of galleries and special stops for arts and entertainment.

Movie Theaters

Flagship Theatres
3323 South Hoover Street
www.flagshipmovies.com

Laemmle Theaters Grande 4 Plex
345 South Figueroa Street
www.laemmle.com

Favorite Downtown Parks

Biddy Mason Park
Between 3rd and 4th streets on Broadway

Pershing Square
Ice skating rink, outdoor movies in Pershing Square
532 South Olive Street
www.laparks.org/pershingsquare/pershing.htm

Exposition Park
Rose Garden, Natural History Museum, California African American Museum,
    Memorial Coliseum, and Sports Arena
Just south of downtown near the University of Southern California campus
600 State Drive

El Pueblo de Los Angeles Historic Park
Consists of forty-four acres, bounded by Alameda, Arcadia, Spring, and Macy
    streets; it contains the oldest church in Los Angeles and twenty-five other
    historic buildings.
845 North Alameda Street

Shopping

Los Angeles has incredible shopping opportunities: Jewelry District, Fashion
District, Flower Market, Toy District, and specialty retailers spread throughout the city. For more information, visit **www.fashiondistrict.org**, **www
.centralcityeast.org** (Toy District), **www.downtownla.com** and download
the "**How to Shop**" brochure.

Groceries
Ralph's
9th Street between Hope and Flower streets
www.ralphs.com

City/Farmer's Markets
City Market
Between San Julian and San Pedro
   streets and 9th and 11th streets
www.citymarketla.com

Grand Central Market
317 South Broadway
www.grandcentralsquare.com

Seventh Street Produce Market
1318 East 7th Street

*Los Angeles Wholesale
   Produce Market*
1601 East Olympic Boulevard

Getting around

Public Transit
Los Angeles County Metropolitan Transportation Authority
City bus and trains
The Red Line (train through downtown to North Hollywood) and Gold Line
   (north train through Chinatown to Pasadena) lines join at Union Station
   Transit Plaza, 800 North Alameda Street. The Blue Line to Long Beach
   joins the Red Line at 7th/Metro Station.
www.metro.net

City Bus
Los Angeles Department of Transportation
www.ladottransit.com

Intercity Train
Amtrak
Union Station Transit Plaza
800 North Alameda Street
www.amtrak.com

Airport

Los Angeles International Airport (LAX)
www.los-angeles-lax.com

Intercity Bus

Downtown Greyhound Terminal
1716 East 7th Street
www.greyhound.com

Interstate Highways

I-5 (South/north from San Diego, California, to Bakersfield, California)
I-10 (East/west from Santa Monica, California, to Ontario, California)
I-110 (South/north from Long Beach to downtown)

Oklahoma City, Oklahoma

The Oklahoma City skyline is a mix of tall modern buildings with splashes of historic hotels and old warehouses. Streets are tidy, shaded by trees with canopies that cool down the scorching summer sun. Oklahoma City is a nice place, and a lot has happened here in the past ten years. But the future is truly what makes downtown Oklahoma City a place to watch. Here are five reasons why.

1. **Metropolitan Area Projects (MAPS) campaign**

   In the 1980s, the city decided to rebuild downtown and devised a highly progressive plan—a "blueprint to revise downtown Oklahoma city through building, renovation, expansion, and development." Residents voted and approved a $238 million tax increase, and downtown's transformation began in 1993. Since then, MAPS funds has collected $309 million to build the impressive Bricktown Canal, a new Bricktown baseball park, one of the nation's best downtown libraries, and a new convention center and arena. A total of $1.5 billion has been invested in downtown, and the area continues to spur private development.

2. **Development has only just begun**

   In addition to MAPS, more innovations are happening behind the scenes. There are plans to construct hundreds of downtown homes and retail establishments in the northeast side of downtown (the Triangle Development). I-40, the major east-west freeway that flanks the south side of downtown, will reconnect the southern Riverside neighborhood, with the possibility of new residential boulevards and other future capital improvements. There's a lot of excitement about future possibilities here.

3. The Bricktown Canal

The Bricktown Canal is one of the most successful and ingenious MAPS projects. The first segment, a mile-long stretch that begins at a park near I-40, passes by a giant monument that represents the great land rush of 1889. The canal then meanders past Bricktown's restaurants, shops, and nightclubs, fronting what used to be the basements of old warehouse buildings and ends up at the new baseball park. There are bike trails and greenways that flank the canal, and auto and pedestrian bridges. Water taxis also provide rides down the canal.

4. A new river runs through it

A damming project of the North Canadian River, a stream by most people's standards, was completed in 2004, and created lakes on the south side of downtown south of I-40. The wider stream was dubbed the "Oklahoma River," and enhanced with bike and walking paths, and parks on either side, allowing boats to navigate the seven-mile stretch of deeper water (without creating wakes). The river is indicative of the spirit of a city that continues to use what it has and build what it needs. No one can say that Oklahoma City is not innovative.

5. Rich Western culture

It's a place rich with cultural heritage, full of Native American history, and marked with the pioneers' paths as they ventured West. Newcomers may even "become" urban cowboys or cowgirls, and have fun celebrating the city's Western culture.

Focus on the Future:
Up-and-Coming Neighborhoods

All of Oklahoma City's downtown residential neighborhoods are up-and-coming, including the central business district. Bounded by 4th, Hudson, Sheridan, and E. K. Gaylord streets, the central square contains most of Oklahoma City's tall skyscrapers. It's interesting to note the thirty-three-story First National Center that looks like a mini Empire State Building. This area generally houses offices and commercial buildings and currently offers few residential opportunities.

Bricktown (with Deep Deuce)

Bricktown, east of the central business district and north of I-40, is named for its predominant red brick buildings, and is the premier entertainment district. Restaurants, nightclubs, and a multiplex movie theater flank the Bricktown Canal and Southwestern Bell Bricktown Ballpark, and there are several shops in historic reconstructed warehouses. There are scant residences here, but there are lofts in several of the old warehouse buildings and plans for new housing near and along the canal.

A lot of full-time city dwellers live in the adjacent Deep Deuce neighborhood that blends into Bricktown from the north. It was historically African American and a jazz hotbed during the 1940s, and the first major residential development during the 1990s. A large town house and apartment complex allows residents easy walking access to the downtown core. Additional residential development is on the drawing board, and talks continue about reviving the historic entertainment district. See Bricktown's Web site at **www.bricktownokc.com** for more information.

Automobile Alley/Triangle District

This budding neighborhood was named for car dealerships that once lined North Broadway Avenue, but today, the area is home to art galleries, retail businesses, and residential lofts. The blocks surrounding the intersection of Harrison Avenue, North Oklahoma Avenue, and NE 5th Street are known as the historic Flat Iron District, and will be the midpoint for a plan to create downtown's largest residential neighborhood. The Triangle District, named for its shape, will feature 1,000 condominiums. A full-service grocery store, parks, "art walks," sculpture gardens, and all kinds of other urban amenities are also planned. The Triangle District will eventually provide a streamlined city neighborhood from Deep Deuce to the northern fringe of Automobile

Alley, and become one of America's newest examples of quality urban redevelopment.

The Automobile Alley District is bounded by 13th Street (north), NE 4th Street (south), Robinson Avenue (west), and I-235 (east). For more information on all of these downtown districts, visit the Downtown Oklahoma City Inc.'s Web site at **www.downtownokc.com**. Also see the Triangle's Web site at **www.thetriangleokc.com**.

Arts District

It's home to the Oklahoma City National Memorial, the Oklahoma City Museum of Art, the Stage Center for Performing Arts, Myriad Botanical Gardens, Civic Center Music Hall, a number of other theaters, and the new Ronald J. Norick downtown library. This entire area is peppered with apartments and condominiums, including new large-scale residential complexes, and the restored Montgomery Ward building, which now contains lofts.

The Arts District cradles the central core on the south, west, and northwest sides. For more information on all of these downtown districts, visit the Downtown Oklahoma City Inc.'s Web site at **www.downtownokc.com**.

Downtown Oklahoma City Essentials

Water taxis: You can catch a baseball game, take in dinner and a movie, and enjoy the mile-long water taxi ride through the warehouse district.

The National Memorial: The memory of April 19, 1995 will always haunt downtown Oklahoma City after Timothy McVeigh bombed the Alfred P. Murrah Federal Building on the north side of the city, killing 168 people. Each of the 168 lives that were lost is represented by a chair made of bronze, stone, and glass.

The underground: Oklahoma City doesn't have a subway system, but in 1931, the city built an intricate series of underground pedestrian concourses. It's possible to walk from the Convention Center on Sheridan Avenue and make your way to Kerr Park or Kerr McGhee Center and Plaza, then west to the Norick Library and the city and county buildings, then northward, emerging near the National Memorial Park. Of course, urbanites enjoy being outside, but during a hot summer day or a biting winter wind, these concourses will come in handy. There are new plans for turning the underground into a series of tunnels housing art galleries.

Native America: A $100 million Native American Museum and Cultural Center will be constructed south of downtown. When completed it will be the largest museum of its kind. Although Oklahoma's official nickname is the "Sooner State," it is also known as "Native America." When you retire to Oklahoma City, you'll be able to appreciate its rich history at this splendid new museum.

The Crystal Bridge: You'll want to take frequent trips to the Crystal Bridge at the Myriad Botanical Gardens, a showplace nature museum. The bridge is a glass tunnel filled with a tropical rainforest environment, with reptiles, birds, orchids, and a cascading waterfall. The surrounding grassy park is filled with lakes and vegetation, a nice backdrop to the southern face of the downtown skyline.

General Statistics

Population: Downtown: 4,165 (2003); City: 528,042 (2003); Metro: 1,132,652 (2003)

Terrain: Downtown Oklahoma City has flat land and gently rolling hills.

Climate Overview: cool winters/very hot summers

Average January high/low temperature: 47/26F

Average July high/low temperature: 93/71F

Average annual total precipitation: 32 inches

Average annual snowfall: 9 inches

Number of cloudy days: 130

Cost of Living: Find out the current cost of living between Oklahoma City and your community by visiting **www.homefair.com** and clicking **"Moving to a New State"** or **"Moving Locally,"** then follow the prompts.

Cost of Housing:

Zip code: 73102 (Central Business District, Arts District, southern half of Automobile Alley); price snapshot: $98,310; sq/ft: 1,657

Zip Code: 73104 (Bricktown, Deep Deuce northeastward); price snapshot: $138,527; sq/ft: 2,791

Real estate prices fluctuate. For up-to-date neighborhood housing cost information, input the zip codes above in the Homestore Web site (affiliated with Realtor.com) at **www.homestore.com/Cities**.

Rent Costs: If you want to rent, explore **www.rentnet.com** and also investigate the neighborhood Web sites for current rents and available properties.

Taxes

Property Tax: Varies widely by millage/location. Please see Oklahoma County Assessor's Web site at **www.oklahomacounty.org/assessor**.

Sales Tax: 7.25 percent. Prescription drugs are exempt. City: 2.75 percent.

State Income Tax: 0.5 percent to 6.65 percent. Rate applies to single persons not deducting federal income tax. (Low $1,000 to high $10,000 and over.) Personal exemption: $1,000. Those who are married filing jointly use the single percentage rates for income brackets twice as high as the single dollar amount. Taxpayers deducting federal income taxes use separate schedules, with rates ranging from 0.5 percent to 10 percent deducted before federal taxes. See the Oklahoma Tax Commission on the specifics of this system at **www.oktax.state.ok.us/oktax/incomtax.html**.

Downtown Oklahoma City Retirement Lifestyle Web Guide

Living

The best place to start looking for your urban home in Oklahoma is at Downtown Oklahoma City Inc.'s Web site: **www.downtownokc.com** and click "**Downtown Living**." You'll find new interactive location maps and contact information for developers and realtors.

City Hospitals

Bone and Joint Hospital
1111 North Dewey Avenue
www.boneandjoint.com

St. Anthony Hospital
1000 North Lee Avenue
www.saintsok.com

Oklahoma University Hospital
1200 Everett Drive
www.oumedcenter.com

Health Clubs

Edward L. Gaylord Downtown YMCA
1 NW 4th Street
www.ymcaokc.org

Check for current listings of health and fitness clubs in downtown by visiting the Downtown Oklahoma City Inc. Web site at **www.downtownokc.com** and click "**Shopping and Services**," then scroll to the "**Fitness**" category.

Volunteering

The Volunteer Center of Central Oklahoma
1501 North Classen Boulevard
http://volunteerok.net

Educational opportunities

City Colleges and Universities

Greater Oklahoma City Downtown Consortium:
Oklahoma City Community College, Oklahoma State University–Oklahoma City, Redlands Community College, Rose State College, University of Central Oklahoma
Ronald J. Norick Library/Learning Center
300 Park Avenue
www.downtowncollege.com

Langston University
4205 North Lincoln Boulevard
www.lunet.edu/okcweb

Mid-America Christian University
3500 SW 119th Street
www.macu.edu

Oklahoma City Community College
  (Main Campus)
777 South Main Street
www.occc.edu

Oklahoma City University
2501 North Blackwelder
www.okcu.edu

Oklahoma State University–
  Oklahoma City
900 North Portland Avenue
www.osuokc.edu

University of Oklahoma Health
  Sciences Center–Oklahoma City
1100 North Lindsay
www.ouhsc.edu

Library
Ronald J. Norick Library
300 Park Avenue
www.metrolibrary.org

Entertainment

Restaurants, Bars, and Nightclubs
Restaurants are always changing. Visit **www.downtownokc.com** and click "**Dining**" or "**Events/Entertainment**" for dining and nightclubs in downtown Oklahoma City.

Professional Spectator Sports
Oklahoma RedHawks (baseball)
Southwestern Bell Bricktown Ballpark
  at East Sheridan and North Walnut
  streets
www.oklahomaredhawks.com

Oklahoma City Blazers (hockey)
Oklahoma City Ford Center,
  100 West Reno Avenue
www.okcblazers.com

Oklahoma City Yard Dawgz (arena
  football)
Oklahoma City Ford Center,
  100 West Reno Avenue
www.okcyarddawgz.com

The Performing Arts

Ballet Oklahoma
Oklahoma City Civic Center
  Music Hall
201 North Walker Avenue
www.balletoklahoma.com

Black Liberated Arts Center (BLAC)
Oklahoma City Civic Center
  Music Hall
201 North Walker Avenue
**www.kennedy-center.org/
  education/partners/profiles/
  BLACInc.html**

Oklahoma City Philharmonic
Oklahoma City Civic Center
  Music Hall
201 North Walker Avenue
www.okcphilharmonic.org

Oklahoma City Repertory Theatre
Oklahoma City Civic Center
  Music Hall
201 North Walker Avenue
www.cityrep.org

Oklahoma City Theatre Company
Oklahoma City Civic Center
  Music Hall
201 North Walker Avenue
www.okctheatrecompany.org

For more performing arts information visit **www.downtownokc.com** and click "**Events/Entertainment**," then "**Stage and Screen**."

Major Museums

American Indian Cultural Center
SE corner of I-35/I-40 junction
www.nacea.com

Harn Homestead Museum
313 NE 16th Street
www.harnhomestead.com

*International Gymnastics
  Hall of Fame*
120 North Robinson Avenue
www.ighof.com

*Myriad Botanical Gardens
  and Crystal Bridge*
301 West Reno Avenue
www.myriadgardens.com

National Cowboy and
  Western Heritage Museum
1700 NE 63rd Street
**www.nationalcowboy
  museum.org**

Oklahoma City Zoo
2101 NE 50th Street
www.okczoo.com

Oklahoma Heritage Center
201 NW 14th Street
www.oklahomaheritage.com

Special Events (Best Bets)

An Affair of the Heart at Bricktown
June. One of the United States'
  largest arts and crafts shows
www.aaoth.com

Bricktown Downtown Salute
  Fourth of July Celebration
Three days of music, fun, and food
  in Bricktown
www.bricktownokc.com

deadCENTER Film Festival
June. Downtown in various venues
www.deadcenterfilm.org

Downtown in December
Holiday lights and New Year's Eve
  celebration in Bricktown
www.downtownokc.com

Oklahoma City Museum of Art
Donald W. Reynolds
  Visual Arts Center
415 Couch Drive
www.okcmoa.com

Oklahoma City National
  Memorial and Museum
620 North Harvey Avenue
**www.oklahomacitynational
  memorial.org**

Festival of the Arts
April. Huge downtown festival
  featuring art, crafts, music,
  and food
www.artscouncilokc.com

International Finals Rodeo
January. Annual championship
  rodeo for the International
  Pro Rodeo Association
www.iprarodeo.com

Paseo Arts Festival
Memorial Day in the Historic Paseo
  District (north of downtown)
www.thepaseo.com

Movie Theater

Harkins Bricktown 16
150 East Reno Avenue in Bricktown
www.harkinstheatres.com

Favorite Downtown Parks

State Capitol State Park
2221 Culbertson Drive

The Mat Hoffman Action Sports Park of Oklahoma City
1700 South Robinson, (SW 17 and Robinson)

Special Attractions

Water Taxi
On the Bricktown Canal
www.watertaxi.com

Six Flags Frontier City Amusement Park
Far north Oklahoma City on I-35, between Hefner Road and NE 122nd Street
www.sixflags.com/parks/frontiercity/index.asp

Shopping

Major retail

Visit **www.downtownokc.com** and click "**Shopping and Services**."

Groceries

No major grocery store in downtown Oklahoma City—yet.

City/Farmer's Markets

Farmer's Public Market
311 South Klein Avenue—west of downtown near I-40 (out of walking distance)
www.okcfarmersmarket.com

Getting around

Public Bus Service

Metro Transit
www.gometro.org

Airport

Will Rogers World Airport (OKC)
www.flyokc.com

Intercity Bus

Downtown Bus Terminal
421 West Sheridan Avenue
www.greyhound.com or www.trailways.com

Interstates

I-40 (East/west from Amarillo, Texas, to Fort Smith, Arkansas)
I-44 (East/west from Lawton, Oklahoma, to Tulsa, Oklahoma)
I-35 (South/north from Dallas/Fort Worth, Texas, to Wichita, Kansas)

25

Omaha, Nebraska

"**O**!" is a campaign designed by the Omaha Chamber of Commerce, the Greater Omaha Convention and Visitors Bureau, and the city of Omaha to represent the "passion for progress and excitement about the future." The *Boston Globe* recently ran a story titled, "Unexpected Omaha: 'Mystery tour' travelers are surprised at what they find." New residents of Omaha will catch the personality, promise, and spirit of O! and enjoy the advantages of living in the middle of a city that is continuously improving and becoming more exciting every year.

Omaha is rising from the Nebraska plains. Downtown now boasts a shiny new convention center, an arena that lights up the night sky, and the tallest structure between Denver and Minneapolis: the Tower at First National Center, a forty-five-story gleaming 634-foot skyscraper. It's becoming an exciting city with a keen focus on redeveloping its downtown. It's certain that Omaha has long been an ignored city, but it's also certain that Omaha's downtown is one to watch. Here are five reasons why.

1. The Old Market

This area is an impressive downtown historic district with about twenty square blocks. With a number of beautiful historic warehouses still intact, this district has become a nationwide model for utilizing old buildings for new purposes. The Old Market now anchors the rest of downtown Omaha.

2. Omaha's brand of urbanism

Omaha leaders are doing much to re-create their city and make it more urban. A group called Omaha by Design is first addressing how urban design and the improvement of public spaces impacts the quality of life and then implementing the necessary changes. The group is now considering landscape and environmental issues, for example, improving street landscaping and public art, preserving buildings, making more pedestrian-friendly neighborhoods, and establishing guidelines for the design of new construction. Urban developers and Realtors are also getting into the spirit with increased interest in downtown development. This is important to retirees who want to see their downtown improve and develop with quality construction.

3. Empty downtown land

Omaha's empty land will be a springboard for new growth and development. All eyes are on an eighty-square-block area north of I-480 between Creighton University and the new Riverfront, called North Downtown, or NoDo. This area will be developed into Omaha's new hot neighborhood: an entertainment district with nightclubs, restaurants, stores, and shops and potentially hundreds of residential opportunities. Although this will take years to fully develop, even a few concentrated blocks can provide a great place to live.

4. Gene Leahy Mall and Missouri Riverfront

Gene Leahy Mall is a ten-acre park that extends six blocks between Douglas Street and Farnam Street. It's considered an urban oasis, and provides lagoons, stair-step water fountains, walking paths, horseshoe-throwing areas, public art, and even a playground. Spend summer afternoons here and attend the Holiday Lights Festival in the winter. The park extends east into the Heartland of America Park, a thirty-one-acre park on the banks of the Missouri where Lewis and Clark stopped during their trek west. Walkers and bike riders will enjoy a boardwalk along the river wall, festivals during the summer, a large lake, and fountains—one shoots water into the air with a light show at night. Downtown Omaha residents have a giant park to enjoy as their front yard.

5. **Location**

Omaha is an urbane city with big-city amenities, but without the high-costs and hassles of a coastal metropolis. Luxury condominiums here can cost one-fifth as much as those in California or New York and yet still offer a mid-continent urban retreat. Newcomers will find the locals here to be vintage Midwesterners—sensible, friendly, and accommodating.

Target Retirement Districts and Neighborhoods

Omaha has only a few defined urban districts in its downtown—generally located between the banks of the Missouri River west to about 24th Street. Target retirement neighborhoods include the Old Market and the rest of the downtown core.

The Old Market

The Old Market, known locally as the Market, is the most urban neighborhood in Omaha. Lofts here are rehabilitated showplaces with exposed beams and utility pipes, towering ceilings, and huge windows. Many are concentrated around Jones Street, just far enough from the middle of downtown to provide wonderful views of the impressive Omaha skyline. This area has the finest restaurants, a farmer's market, specialty shops, boutiques, pubs, and nightclubs. A number of art galleries, bookstores, bakeries, and fun stores are also here, but a big, full-service grocery store is still to come.

Old Market is bounded on the north/south by Farnam and Leavenworth and east/west by 15th Street and the Missouri River. For more information, view Old Market's Web site at **www.oldmarket.com**.

Downtown Core

The Old Market was the first area in downtown to establish a concentration of residential housing. More housing opportunities are, however, popping up all the time, particularly near the heart of the central business district on Douglas Street, where there's new rehabilitated condominiums and the historic fourteen-story First National Bank building. Residents do not have a full-service neighborhood yet, but they can enjoy the historic architecture and anticipate a more vibrant city center in the near future. Locals here also have immediate access to the pleasures of the Old Market, the Gene Leahy Mall, the Missouri Riverfront, and the Quest Center Arena. For more information, visit Downtown Omaha Inc. at **www.downtownomaha.org**.

North Downtown (NoDo)

NoDo is a rapidly redeveloping former industrial area and rail yard north of I-480. Thousands of new residential homes and stores are proposed for this area. There is no official Web site for NoDo, but type "North Downtown NoDo Omaha" in a search engine to find out all about this new neighborhood.

Downtown Omaha Essentials

A good steak: Omaha steaks are shipped all over the world. In fact, Omaha in general is synonymous with perfect cuts of juicy steak grilled to order. Of course, there are plenty of ethnic restaurants and gourmet fare here, but Omaha steak is the specialty.

Many evenings in the Old Market: Whether it's holding a piping-hot chocolate during the Dickens Christmas, watching carolers and actors perform *A Christmas Carol*, dining out on the town, or exploring the shops on a hot summer day, you'll enjoy spending a lot of time in the Old Market.

The NCAA College Baseball World Series: Every year the best college baseball teams in the country converge on Omaha—the mecca of collegiate baseball. Making it to Omaha means playing in the College World Series, and it's as big of a deal for the locals as it is for the visiting players. This tradition, for almost sixty years now, has become the longest continuing location for any NCAA championship series. Catch a series pass and then attend the celebrations and festivities surrounding Rosenblatt Stadium, such as Fanfest. The stadium is only a thirty-minute walk down 13th Avenue.

Conversations in the park: Crowds gather at lunchtime in the Leahy Mall—a favorite spot to chat under the shadow of the city skyline.

Art hopping: Downtown Omaha has a dynamic arts community waiting for you to explore. Check out the Bemis Center with its art showings of paintings, sculptures, or mixed media. You'll recognize the building's painted windows, a permanent fixture since local fund-raisers established the center by selling each window for $5,000. See **www.bemiscenter.org** for more information. The Hot Shop Arts Center in the new NoDo area north of I-480 also provides galleries and exhibition spaces focusing on welding, ceramics, and forges for metalworking. See **www.hotshopsartcenter.com**.

Bracing for weather extremes—and loving it: Omaha weather is politely called "continental," which can mean bitterly cold and brutally hot. Fierce blizzards, although not common, can cripple the city (but rarely do) and a hot summer day in Omaha can easily top 100 degrees. Since Omaha's weather is changeable, it's exhilarating for people who enjoy the four seasons to the extreme.

General Statistics

Population: Downtown: 5,240 (2000); City: 409,416 (2003); Metro: 793,172 (2003)

Terrain: Downtown Omaha is slightly rolling throughout, sloping eastward toward the Missouri River.

Climate Overview: cold winters/warm summers

Average January high/low temperature: 31/11F

Average July high/low temperature: 88/66F

Average annual total precipitation: 30 inches

Average annual snowfall: 31 inches

Number of cloudy days: 160

Cost of Living: Find out the current cost of living between Omaha and your community by visiting **www.homefair.com** and clicking **"Moving to a New State"** or **"Moving Locally,"** then follow the prompts.

Cost of Housing:

Zip code: 68102 (Downtown Core, Old Market, North Downtown); price snapshot: $198,517; sq/ft: 1,425

Real estate prices fluctuate. For up-to-date neighborhood housing cost information, input the zip code above in the Homestore Web site (affiliated with Realtor.com) at **www.homestore.com/Cities**.

Rent Costs: If you want to rent, explore **www.rentnet.com** and also investigate the neighborhood Web sites for current rents and available properties.

Taxes

Property Tax: Typical payment of $2,148 per $100,000 assessed value. Keep current by visiting the Douglas County Assessor's office at **www.dc assessor.org**.

Sales Tax: 7.0 percent. Groceries and prescription drugs are exempt.

State Income Tax: 2.56 percent to 6.84 percent. (Four tax brackets. Single: low $2,400 to high $26,500 and over; personal exemption: $1,300. Married filing jointly: $4,000 to over $46,750.)

Downtown Omaha Retirement Lifestyle Web Guide

Living

There are no Web sites that cater exclusively to the thriving downtown Omaha real estate market. The best bet is to visit **www.realtor.com** and input downtown's 68102 zip code to explore current residential listings. Also visit the Omaha Board of Realtors' Web site at **www.oabr.com**.

City Hospitals

Immanuel Medical Center
6901 North 72nd Street
www.alegent.com

UNMC/University Hospital
42nd and Emile streets
www.unmc.edu

Creighton University Medical Center
601 North 30th Street
www.creightonhospital.com

Children's Hospital
8200 Dodge Street
www.chsomaha.org

Methodist Hospital
8303 Dodge Street
www.bestcare.org

Bergan Mercy Medical
7500 Mercy Road
www.alegent.com

Health Clubs
YMCA: Downtown
430 South 20th Street
www.metroymca.org

Volunteering

United Way of the Midlands
1805 Harney Street
www.uwmidlands.org/volunteer

Educational opportunities

City Colleges and Universities
Creighton University
2500 California Plaza
www2.creighton.edu

Grace University
1311 South 9th Street
www.graceuniversity.edu

Metropolitan Community College
Various locations around Omaha
www.mccneb.edu

*University of Nebraska's Peter Kiewit
   Institute of Information Science,
   Technology, and Engineering*
1110 South 67th Street
www.pki.nebraska.edu

University of Nebraska at Omaha
60th and Dodge streets
www.unomaha.edu

Library
Omaha Public Library
215 South 15th Street
www.omahapubliclibrary.org

Entertainment

Restaurants, Bars, and Nightclubs

See the Old Market's Web site at **www.omahaoldmarket.com**.

Professional Spectator Sports

Omaha Royals (baseball)
Rosenblatt Stadium, 1202 Bert Murphy Avenue
www.oroyals.com

College Sports

Creighton University
2500 California Plaza
www2.creighton.edu

University of Nebraska at Omaha
60th and Dodge streets
www.unomaha.edu

College Baseball World Series (June)
Rosenblatt Stadium
1202 Bert Murphy Avenue
www.cwsomaha.com

The Performing Arts

Omaha Symphony
Holland Performing Arts Center
13th and Douglas streets
www.omahasymphony.org

Opera Omaha
The Orpheum Theater
409 South 16th Street
www.operaomaha.org

For a complete schedule of local events, see Omaha Performing Arts' Web site at **www.omahaperformingarts.org**.

Major Museums

Joslyn Art Museum
2200 Dodge Street
www.joslyn.org

Hot Shops Art Center
1301 Nicholas Street
www.hotshopsartcenter.com

Bemis Center for Contemporary Arts
724 South 12th Street
www.bemiscenter.org

Special Events (Best Bets)

Holiday Lights Festival
December 31. Gene Leahy Mall
www.holidaylightsfestival.org

Leahy Mall Concert Series
Thursdays, May to September.
  Gene Leahy Mall
www.omahaperformingarts.org

Omaha Film Festival
March. Various venues
www.omahafilmfestival.org

Omaha Lit Fest
September. Various venues
www.omahalitfest.com

Omaha Jazz and Blues Festival
July. Omaha Riverfront
www.omahajazzandblues.com

Omaha Summer Arts Festival
June. Downtown on Farnam Street
www.summerarts.org

Favorite Downtown Parks

Gene Leahy Mall
1302 Farnam Street

Heartland of America Park
800 Douglas Street

SHOPPING

The Old Market: **www.omahaoldmarket.com**

Groceries

A trip outside downtown is usually required for large-scale grocery shopping, especially to the Food Bonanza in the Park East neighborhood. Otherwise, Cubby's at 601 South 13th Street provides staple groceries in a large convenience store and gas station.

City/Farmer's Markets

Omaha Farmer's Market
11th and Jackson streets and 11th and Howard streets
www.omahafarmersmarket.org

Getting around

Public Bus Service
Metro Area Transit
www.metroareatransit.com

Bike Routes/Trails
City of Omaha Parks and Recreation
www.ci.omaha.ne.us/parks

Airport
Eppley Airfield (OMA)
4501 Abbott Drive
www.eppleyairfield.com

Intercity Train
Amtrak Station
1003 South 9th Street
www.amtrak.com

Intercity Bus
Downtown Greyhound Terminal
601 South 13th Street
www.greyhound.com

Interstate Highways
I-80 (East/west from Des Moines, Iowa, to Lincoln, Nebraska)
I-29 (South/north from Kansas City, Missouri, to Sioux City, Iowa)

EXPLORE MORE OF AMERICA'S DOWNTOWNS

A major theme throughout this book has been finding a miniature New York lifestyle. Today, even small cities far from the coasts are either offering or working on providing fine dining, fun nightlife, public transportation, employment and volunteer opportunities, and increasingly, shopping. If you're flexible, you will be surprised to find your ideal downtown lifestyle, within your price range, in any number of cities. *All* downtowns are downtowns to watch, and they are adding new and exciting improvements every year. Explore the following cities' downtowns and their Web sites for a wide-variety of residential possibilities. (This is *not* an exhaustive list!)

ALABAMA

Birmingham

See all the good things happening here by visiting Operation New Birmingham's Web site at **www.yourcitycenter.com** and click **"Looking for a Loft."**

Huntsville

Although slow to develop, downtown Huntsville is finally on its way to building an urban center, perhaps just in time for your retirement. Visit Downtown Huntsville Inc.'s Web site at **www.downtownhuntsville.com** for more information.

Mobile

This good-sized but still quaint city is just beginning to revitalize. See Main Street Mobile, Inc.'s Web site at **www.mainstreetmobile.org**.

ARIZONA

Flagstaff

This high-elevation university town is a great place to retire. See the Flagstaff Downtown Business Alliance's Web site at **www.flagdba.com**.

Mesa

Mesa, a sprawling suburb of Phoenix, is establishing an all-around downtown with 3,000 residents and 7,000 employees. See the Downtown Mesa Association Web site at **www.downtownmesa.com**.

Phoenix

A great deal of new downtown housing is underway in an exciting downtown revitalization effort. Visit Downtown Phoenix Partnership's Web site at **www.coppersquare.com** and click **"Living Here"** for rental and for sale properties.

Scottsdale

Posh Scottsdale's downtown is on the move. See the Downtown Scottsdale Partnership's Web site at **www.scottsdaleaz.gov/projects/downtown**.

Tempe

Although technically a suburb of Phoenix, Tempe has received rave reviews for its downtown revitalization. Ruppies also have immediate access to huge Arizona State University. See Downtown Tempe Community, Inc.'s Web site at **www.downtowntempe.com**.

Tucson

A lot is happening in downtown Tucson, including a housing boom. See the Tucson Downtown Alliance's Web site at **www.downtowntucson.org** and click **"Living"** for rental and for sale residential opportunities.

ARKANSAS

Fayetteville

Home of the University of Arkansas, this small town is promoting "healthy and unique downtown living." See what's happening by contacting Downtown Fayetteville Partners at **www.fayettevilledowntown.org**.

Little Rock

Little Rock is becoming more of a big rock with its impressive downtown skyline and new influx of residential housing. See the Downtown Little Rock Partnership Web site at **www.downtownlr.com** and click **"Live"** for residential opportunities.

CALIFORNIA

Pasadena

A Los Angeles suburb, the city boasts "Old Pasadena" historic district with housing available nearby. See the Old Pasadena Management District's Web site at **www.oldpasadena.org**.

Sacramento

An $11 billion high-rise boom is underway and so is a bona fide (and cheaper) alternative to nearby Bay Area urban living. There's nothing quite like K-Street, a fabulous pedestrian and train-only corridor. See the Downtown Sacramento Partnership's Web site at **www.downtown sac.org** and click "**Live**."

San Diego

Heading toward "dynamic" status, rapidly urbanizing San Diego is one of the most impressive development stories in the United States. Visit the Downtown San Diego Partnership's Web site at **www.dtsd.org** and click "**Living Downtown**."

San Jose

America's tenth-largest city is in the famed Silicon Valley just south of San Francisco Bay, with a lot going on in downtown. See the San Jose Downtown Association Web site at **www.sjdowntown.com** for more information.

COLORADO

Boulder

Boulder is a quintessential college town with a lively downtown. See Downtown Boulder Business Improvement District's Web site at **www.dbi.org** for more information.

Colorado Springs

The number of residents and businesses is growing here each year. Visit Downtown Colorado Springs Partnership's Web site at **www.down towncs.com**.

CONNECTICUT

Danbury

Small and quaint, downtown Danbury is filled with restaurants and shops, and surrounding residential neighborhoods. See CityCenter Danbury's Web site at **www.citycenterdanbury.com**.

Hartford

Although much work is needed, Hartford could be the next big thing in New England. See Hartford Proud & Beautiful's Web site at **www.connect thedots.org/hpb/hpb.html**.

Stamford

Close to New York City, downtown Stamford is positioning itself as a city all its own. Visit the Stamford Downtown Special Services District's Web site at **www.stamford-downtown.com**.

DELAWARE

Wilmington

Bustling and dense, downtown Wilmington is a big city in a small-town package, and it's proximity to dynamic Philadelphia is a huge plus. See the Wilmington Renaissance Corporation's Web site at **www.wilmington renaissance.com**.

DISTRICT OF COLUMBIA

Expensive for the average retiree, downtown Washington provides a glorious, one-of-a-kind urban experience. See downtown D.C.'s Web site at **www.downtowndc.org** and click **"living here"** for more information.

FLORIDA

Fort Lauderdale

Downtown development is unbelievable here, with new high-rises and new residents. See the Downtown Development Authority's Web site at **www.ddaftl.org**.

Gainesville

This big college town has an emerging downtown square, and it's worth considering. See Main Street Gainesville's Web site at **www.downtown gainesville.com**.

Hollywood

The boom of nearby downtown Miami and Fort Lauderdale is rubbing off on Hollywood. Monitor the progress at Downtown Hollywood CRA's Web site at **www.downtownhollywood.com**.

Jacksonville

It's the less expensive alternative to south Florida and still very much Florida. Check the Downtown Vision, Inc.'s Web site at **www.downtown jacksonville.org** and click **"Living"** for more information.

Orlando

It's transforming into a great full-time city with plenty of new homes to purchase or rent. See the Downtown Development Board's Web site at **www.downtownorlando.com**.

St. Petersburg

Tampa's little sister is growing up fast. Explore the St. Petersburg Downtown Partnership's Web site at **www.stpetepartnership.org** for more information.

Tallahassee

It's the panhandle, the least expensive area in the state, and downtown Tallahassee has big plans. See the Tallahassee Downtown Improvement Authority Web site at **www.tallahasseedowntown.com** for more information.

Tampa

Downtown Tampa's big-city excitement is contagious, and its residential development continues. See the Tampa Downtown Partnership's Web site at **www.tampasdowntown.com**.

Panama City

Watch for impressive residential development happening here in the coming years. See the Downtown Improvement Board (DIB) Web site at **www .panamacitydowntown.com**.

Pensacola

It's one of the most ambitious small-city downtowns in America. See the Downtown Improvement Board's Web site at **www.downtownpensacola.com** and click **"Living Downtown."**

Sarasota

This small but booming arts city is growing an increasingly vibrant downtown. See the Sarasota Downtown Association's Web site at **www.down townsarasota.com**.

West Palm Beach

With a tremendous push for center city revitalization, West Palm Beach, although small, offers high-quality urban living—especially along the new Clematis Street. See West Palm Beach Downtown Development Authority's Web site at **www.westpalmbeachdda.com** and click **"Real Estate."**

GEORGIA

Decatur

The east suburb of Atlanta offers a walkable downtown full of restaurants, shops, and nearby housing. See the Decatur Downtown Development Authority Web site at **www.decaturga.com**.

Macon

Macon, an hour's drive south of Atlanta, is poised for growth. It offers a smaller, quainter urban setting. See NewTown Macon, Inc.'s Web site at **www.newtownmacon.com** and click **"Initiatives"** for more information.

Savannah

Beautiful historic Savannah remains much the same as it was one hundred years ago. See the Savannah Development and Renewal Authority's Web site at **www.sdra.net**.

IDAHO

Boise

It's emerging into a western dynamo with a rapidly rising downtown. Check out the Downtown Boise Association's Web site at **www.downtown boise.org.**

ILLINOIS

Evanston

Home to Northwestern University, downtown Evanston is vital and fabulous.

Peoria

Momentum is building along the riverfront, including restaurants, nightlife, festivals, and the beginnings of an urban residential neighborhood. Visit the Peoria RiverFront's Web site at **www.peoriariverfront.com.**

Rockford

Lagging behind in downtown development, Rockford is readying its River District for a wave of future commercial and residential development along the Rock River. Watch for Rockford success stories in the coming years. See the River District Association's Web site at **www.riverdistrict.com.**

Rock Island

Keep up with Rock Island's famous downtown Arts Entertainment District's progress by visiting Renaissance Rock Island's Web site at **www.ridistrict.com.**

Springfield

There are few residential opportunities today, but tomorrow is another story in downtown Springfield. See Downtown Springfield Incorporated's Web site at **www.downtownspringfield.org.**

Wheaton

A northwest Chicago suburb with an urbanizing historic downtown, Wheaton is worth watching. Check out **www.downtownwheaton.com.**

INDIANA

Indiana is one of the least-expensive states for downtown living, with high interest in center city revitalization.

Bloomington

Home to Indiana University, small-town Bloomington's center is the quin-tessential Main Street, with nearby housing opportunities. See the Uniquely Bloomington Downtown Association's Web site at **www.uniquelyblooming ton.com**.

Evansville

This regional river city offers inexpensive living and is growing its urban amenities. See Downtown Evansville, Inc.'s Web site at **www.downtown evansville.org** and click "**Live**."

Fort Wayne

With a new downtown plan in place, Indiana's second city is poised for revitalization. See Fort Wayne Downtown Improvement District's Web site at **www.downtownfortwayne.com** and click "**Living Downtown**."

Lafayette

On the eastern banks of the Wabash River and a pedestrian bridge away from downtown West Lafayette and Purdue University, this small city has major potential.

Muncie

Downtown Muncie, home to Ball State University, is working hard to build a thriving downtown. See the Muncie Downtown Data Center's Web site at **www.munciedowntown.com**.

IOWA

Iowa, like Indiana, is a top state for improving downtowns and inexpensive real estate.

Cedar Rapids

There's momentum in downtown Cedar Rapids—an inexpensive option for small-city urban living—but few residential opportunities exist now. Keep up with the city's progress at Cedar Rapids Downtown District's Web site, **www.downtowncr.org**.

Davenport

Take day trips to Chicago from this on-the-ball small city on the Mississippi River. See the Downtown Partnership's Web site at **www.downtowndaven port.com** and click "**Residential**" to explore what's available.

Des Moines

What a great downtown. Similar to Omaha, downtown Des Moines is clearly one to watch. Visit the Downtown Community Alliance's Web site at **www.knowdowntown.com** and click "**Housing**."

Iowa City

It's one of America's premier college towns with a fantastic, thriving, walkable downtown. Check out the Downtown Association of Iowa City's Web site at **www.icdowntown.com**.

Sioux City

This lovely, compact, and cozy Missouri River town offers small-town living with a big-town environment with a lot that's going on. Although off the radar, it's definitely worth researching. See the Downtown Partners' Web site at **www.downtownsiouxcity.com** and click "**Live Downtown**."

KANSAS

Lawrence

Home to the University of Kansas, Lawrence's downtown bustles with youth and is often packed with pedestrians. There are many surrounding historic neighborhoods. Check out what's there at Downtown Lawrence Inc.'s Web site: **www.downtownlawrence.com**.

Topeka

The state capital's downtown is residentially sparse, but Topeka has a plan for tomorrow's downtown. See Downtown Topeka Inc. at **www.downtown topekainc.com**.

Wichita

Wichita, Kansas' largest city, is often overlooked but is a runner-up on the "Downtowns to Watch" list. Consider this wonderful city's amenities at Wichita Downtown Development Corporation's Web site, **www.downtown wichita.org**.

KENTUCKY

Bowling Green

Small Bowling Green is taking advantage of its quaint downtown square. It's also home to big Western Kentucky University. Check out the Downtown Redevelopment Authority's Web site at **www.downtownbg.org**.

Covington

As a close runner-up for the "Distinctively Different" downtown category, Covington resembles the feeling of downtown Asheville. This small city also has excellent skyline views of downtown Cincinnati across the Ohio River. Incredible new skyscraper condos are popping up, and the city's historic districts are marvelous. See the City of Covington's Web site at **www.covingtonky.com**.

Lexington

It's a city and it's a small town, with excellent urban neighborhoods. See the Downtown Lexington Corporation's Web site at **www.downtown lex.com** and click **"Downtown Living/Housing"** for more information.

Louisville

It's the sixteenth-largest city with a new focus on revitalization and another downtown to watch. See the Louisville Central Area, Inc.'s Web site at **www.lca-inc.org** and click **"Downtown Living."**

LOUISIANA

Baton Rouge

With a new downtown plan and a new focus, watch for increasing signs of life in downtown Baton Rouge at Baton Rouge Downtown Development District's Web site: **http://brgov.com/dept/ddd**.

Lafayette

Visit Downtown Lafayette Unlimited's Web site at **www.downtownalive.org**.

New Orleans

Katrina's devastating blow has severely hurt downtown New Orleans. See the recovery efforts at the Downtown Development District's Web site: **www.neworleansdowntown.com**.

Shreveport

Tremendous efforts are underway in downtown Shreveport. See the Downtown Development Authority's Web site at **www.downtownshreveport.com** for more information.

MAINE

Portland

You can join in the revitalization of this water city. See Portland's Downtown District's Web site at **www.portlandmaine.com**.

MARYLAND

Baltimore

Baltimore's less expensive real estate prices here are luring urbanites away from nearby Washington, and much is happening in Baltimore's historic urban neighborhoods. See the Downtown Partnership's Web site at **www .godowntownbaltimore.com** and click **"Living."**

MASSACHUSETTS

Boston

On the short list of historic and dynamic downtowns, Boston provides one of America's most thriving urban living experiences. Check out Downtown Crossing's Web site at **www.downtowncrossing.org**.

Salem

Cute, quaint, historic, and revitalizing. See the Salem Main Street Downtown Initiative's Web site at **www.salempartnership.org**.

Springfield

See the Springfield Business Improvement District's Web site at **www .springfielddowntown.com** and click **"Real Estate"** for downtown living options.

Worcester

With a dead downtown mall and ever-compared to nearby Providence, Worcester is a city with something to prove, and a city to watch in the next decade.

MICHIGAN

Ann Arbor

Surrounded by the University of Michigan campus, downtown Ann Arbor thrives as a runner-up in the "Distinctively Different" category. See the Ann Arbor Downtown Development Authority's Web site at **www.ci.ann-arbor.mi.us/dda**.

Detroit

Downtown Detroit is making unusual progress with an infusion of urban living opportunities. Don't count Detroit out yet. See the Downtown Detroit Partnership's Web site at **www.downtownpartnership.org** and click **"Housing."**

Grand Rapids

Few living opportunities are here today, but downtown Grand Rapids is a lovely district that's certain to join the trend toward downtown housing. See its progress at Grand Rapids Downtown Alliance's Web site at **www .downtowngr.org**.

Kalamazoo

Kalamazoo has a very nice and increasingly vibrant small-city downtown. See the Downtown Kalamazoo Inc.'s Web site at **www.central-city.net** and click **"Downtown Living."**

MINNESOTA

Duluth

A beautiful Lake Superior setting and quaint surrounding neighborhoods surround downtown Duluth. See the Greater Downtown Council's Web site at **www.downtownduluth.com**.

Minneapolis

Downtown Minneapolis is growing, and vibrant, with the mammoth University of Minnesota campus just to the north. See the Minneapolis Downtown Council's Web site at **www.downtownmpls.com**.

Saint Paul

The smaller, more "homey" side of the Twin Cities is a great place to retire. See the Capital City Partnership's Web site at **www.capitalcity partnership.com**.

MISSOURI

Columbia

Columbia has a fun downtown with 7,100 residents, many of them students of the nearby University of Missouri. Keep this downtown on your shortlist if you want to stay young. See Columbia Special Business District's Web site at **www.discoverthedistrict.com** and click **"Living."**

Kansas City

Downtown is coming alive fast, bringing new condominiums and lofts and new residents. See the Downtown Council's Web site for more information at **www.downtownkc.org** and click **"Urban Living."**

St. Louis

Historic office buildings have been converted into thousands of urban lofts, grocery stores, and restaurants, bringing new vitality to downtown St. Louis. See the Downtown St. Louis Partnership's Web site at **www.downtown stlouis.org** and click **"Live."**

Springfield

The major city of the Ozarks, downtown Springfield boasts a successful art walk, new movie theater, great dining, and, now, big plans for downtown living opportunities. Retirees will soon have more options as the downtown continues to blossom. See the Downtown Springfield Community Improvement District's Web site at **www.itsalldowntown.com** and click **"Real Estate."**

MONTANA

Billings

See what's going on in downtown Billings at the Downtown Billings Partnership, Inc.'s Web site at **www.downtownbillings.com** and click **"Downtown Housing"** for more information.

Great Falls

Visit Downtown Great Falls's Web site at **www.downtowngreatfalls.com** for information on living, shopping, and entertainment.

Missoula

This mountain and college town is a great retirement destination. See the Missoula Downtown Association's Web site at **www.missouladowntown.com**.

NEBRASKA

Lincoln

Here's another big college town with the large University of Nebraska campus at Ruppies' disposal, with several quality residential development opportunities. See the Downtown Lincoln Association's Web site at **www.down townlincoln.org**.

NEVADA

Las Vegas

Downtown Las Vegas is growing skyward with thousands of new high-rise residential units. See the Las Vegas Chamber of Commerce's Luxury High-Rise Web page at **www.lvchamber.com/relocation/highrise.htm**.

Reno

Downtown Reno is positioning itself for residential growth. See the City of Reno's Web site at **www.cityofreno.com** and type in **"Downtown"** in the search box for more information.

NEW HAMPSHIRE

Manchester

The largest city in New Hampshire is now providing downtown living. See the Intown Manchester Management, Inc.'s Web site at **www.intown manchester.com** and click **"Real Estate"** for more information.

NEW MEXICO

Albuquerque

Phenomenal focus on downtown redevelopment is happening here. See the Downtown Action Team, Inc.'s Web site at **www.abqdowntown.com** and click **"Real Estate."**

NEW YORK

Albany

Find out what's available in downtown Albany by visiting the Central BID District Management Association, Inc.'s Web site at **www.centralbid.com** and the Downtown Albany BID at **www.downtownalbany.org**.

Buffalo

Although slow to redevelop, Buffalo remains one of the most beautiful cities in America with a stunning historic downtown. See Buffalo Place Inc.'s Web site at **www.buffaloplace.com** and click **"Live"** for more information.

Ithaca

Home to Cornell University, this is a perfect small-town downtown. **www.downtownithaca.com**.

Rochester

It's another very nice downtown in upstate New York and worth a look. See Rochester Downtown Development Corporation's Web site at **www.rochester downtown.com** and click **"Living."**

Troy

The neighborhoods in and around downtown are attracting artists and historic preservation enthusiasts. See the Troy Downtown Collaborative's Web site at **www.troydowntown.com**.

NORTH CAROLINA

Durham

Downtown Durham is fast redeveloping, especially near the Duke University campus and is finally coming into its own. See the Downtown Durham, Inc.'s Web site at **www.downtowndurham.com** and click **"Downtown Lifestyle,"** then **"Residential Options"** for more information.

Greensboro

As one of North Carolina's great cities, Greensboro also has one of the state's fastest emerging downtowns. See Downtown Greensboro, Inc.'s Web site at **www.downtowngreensboro.net** and click **"Living."**

Raleigh

This downtown has become very popular in the last ten years, with an ever-increasing number of housing opportunities. See the Downtown Raleigh Alliance's Web site at **www.downtownraleigh.org** and click **"Real Estate."**

Waynesville

It's a *fabulous* small-town downtown in the Smoky Mountains. See the Downtown Waynesville Association's Web site at **www.downtownwaynes ville.com**.

Wilmington

The East Coast's new film capital is the new place to be. Downtown Wilmington is in the center of the action. See the Wilmington Downtown, Inc.'s Web site at **www.wilmingtondowntown.com**.

Winston-Salem

Although more industrial-looking than other North Carolina cities, downtown Winston-Salem provides a more down-to-earth, yet wonderful urban living experience. Learn about the wildly successful art walks and fun festivals at the Downtown Winston-Salem Partnership's Web site at **www .dwsp.org** and click **"Living Downtown."**

NORTH DAKOTA

Fargo (and Moorhead, Minnesota)

It may be cold but downtown Fargo is emerging into an exciting community. It's inexpensive, and with downtown Moorhead, Minnesota, just across the Red River, residents get two for one. See the Downtown Community Partnership's Web site at **www.fmdowntown.com**.

OHIO

Akron

With 25,000 students at the University of Akron, and with the addition of residential opportunities, this downtown is worth considering. See the Downtown Akron Partnership's Web site at **www.downtownakron.com**.

Cincinnati

Hilly urban neighborhoods and a revitalizing center are waiting in downtown Cincy. See the Downtown Cincinnati, Inc.'s Web site at **www.downtowncincinnati.com** and click **"Downtown Living."**

Cleveland

Cleveland has received national praise for its downtown revitalization, particularly for its stadiums and Rock and Roll Hall of Fame, and almost $2 billion of investments in recent years. See the Downtown Cleveland Partnership's Web site at **www.downtownclevelandpartnership.com** and click **"Residential"**.

Dayton

Dayton is small but its downtown development is ambitious. See the Downtown Dayton Partnership's Web site at **www.downtowndayton.com** and click **"Living."**

Toledo

Tax-abated condominium units mean more money in downtown residents' pockets. See what's available at the Downtown ToledoVision, Inc.'s Web site at **www.downtowntoledoinc.com** and click **"Downtown Living."**

OKLAHOMA

Tulsa

See Downtown Tulsa Unlimited, Inc.'s Web site at **www.tulsadowntown.org** and click **"Downtown Development,"** then **"Residential"** to browse potential for sale and rental units.

OREGON

Eugene

This is a smaller city with an enthusiastic downtown development community. See the Downtown Eugene Inc.'s Web site at **www.downtowneugene.com**.

Medford

The best of both worlds—a growing downtown and a small town. Downtown Medford offers above-storefront apartments, town homes, and new condominiums. See the latest on the Medford Urban Renewal Agency's Web site at **www.downtownmedford.com** and click "**Living**".

Portland

Widely regarded as one of the best downtowns, and a close runner up for one of the "Dynamic Downtowns," Portland is A-plus urban living. See the Portland Business Alliance's Web site at **www.portlandalliance.com** and the Portland Development Commission at **www.portlanddev.org**.

Salem

Consider this small city's art hops on Wednesday nights and popular downtown mixers. Find out more at Salem Downtown Association's Web site at **www.downtownsalem.org**.

PENNSYLANIA

Erie

Here's a nice, very affordable small city with an exceptional historic waterfront downtown. See the Erie Downtown Improvement District's Web site at **www.eriedowntown.com** and click "**Downtown Living**."

Lancaster

This is a thriving small downtown in the middle of Amish country that offers urban living opportunities. See the Lancaster Downtown Development District's Web site at **www.downtownlancaster.com** and click "**Live and Work Here**."

Pittsburgh

Pittsburgh is one of America's most beautiful cities, and also one of the most affordable. See the Downtown Pittsburgh Partnership's Web site at **www.downtownpittsburgh.com**, click **"Real Estate,"** and then **"downtown living"** for more information.

State College

Wonderful small-town urban living with Penn State University as an education and entertainment anchor. See the Downtown State College Development District's Web site at **www.downtownstatecollege.com** and click **"Property for Sale/Rent/Lease."**

SOUTH CAROLINA

Charleston

Charleston's architecture and national reputation speaks for itself. There is no downtown Charleston Web site, but try **www.historiccharleston.org** for more information.

Columbia

This one of the southeastern's most exciting small cities, and a "Downtown to Watch" near miss. See more about what's happening at City Center Partnership, Inc.'s Web site at **www.citycentercolumbia.sc** and click **"Live Downtown."**

Greenville

Greenville is too close to Asheville not to understand what a great downtown can mean for a city. Downtown Greenville is on its way. See the City of Greenville's Web site at **www.greatergreenville.com** and click **"Neighbor hoods,"** then **"Living Downtown."**

SOUTH DAKOTA

Sioux Falls

If the 5,000 proposed residential housing units are actually constructed, the city will become a small dynamo of a downtown. It already offers a high-quality experience for such a small city. See what's planned at Main Street Sioux Falls, Inc.'s Web site at **www.dtsf.com**.

TENNESSEE

Clarksville

The 1999 tornado devastated downtown Clarksville, and the city is busy rebuilding downtown to represent the fifth-largest city in Tennessee. Downtown boasts Austin Peay State University's big plans for the future. See the opportunities at the Clarksville Downtown District Partnership's Web site at **www.clarksville.tn.us**, click **"Econonic Development,"** then **"Downtown District Partnership."**

Johnson City

Downtown Johnson City's development has finally arrived. This small mountain city is the largest of the tri-cities metro area of northeast Tennessee, and young—20,000 students attend East Tennessee State University just east of downtown. See Johnson City Development Authority's Web site: **www.downtownjc.org**.

Knoxville

Knoxville is perched on a ridge adjacent to the University of Tennessee. Construction is now revitalizing the downtown's historic area and new condominiums are also being built. See the Central Business Improvement District's Web site at **www.downtownknoxville.org** and click **"Live."**

Murfreesboro

Set on a lovely, vibrant courthouse square, downtown Murfreesboro's surrounding historic neighborhoods are within walking distance of this growing city of 80,000. See Main Street Murfreesboro's Web site for more information at **www.downtownmurfreesboro.com**.

Nashville

This capital of Tennessee and country music has been off the downtown-development radar. Suddenly, unexpectedly, downtown Nashville is exploding with new residential opportunities and urban revitalization. Not only is this a downtown to watch, its new amenities such as the symphony hall, upcoming rail system, 1,000-foot residential tower, and a long list of condominium projects in "SoBro" (South of Broad), "The Gulch," and nearby Midtown neighborhoods are particularly impressive. Although long behind others in the concept of city living, Nashville is poised to catch up quickly to become a dynamic international neighborhood destination for urban enthusiasts. See downtown Nashville Partnership's Web site at **www.nashvilledowntown.com** for proof!

TEXAS

Corpus Christi

With its premier gulf location, this is Texas's sleeper downtown that's about to take off with new residential development. Watch for the progress by visiting the Corpus Christi Downtown Management District's site at **www.downtowncorpuschristi.com**.

Dallas

About 1.2 million people live in the city, and its downtown population of 30,000 keeps growing. See the Downtown Improvement District's Web site at **www.downtowndallas.org** and click **"Live,"** then **"Intown Housing"** for more information.

El Paso

The weather is great and the downtown organizations are hard at work on urban redevelopment. See the El Paso Downtown Management District at **www.elpasodowntownmanagementdistrict.org**.

Fort Worth

As a candidate and near miss for a best sunbelt downtown, this is one of the most vibrant and interesting cities in Texas. See the Downtown Fort Worth, Inc.'s Web site at **www.dfwi.org** and click **"Downtown Living."**

Houston

America's fourth-largest city and one of the most sprawling now offers many options for quality urban living. Glance at the properties at Houston Downtown Management's Web site at **www.houstondowntown.com** and click **"Living Here."**

San Antonio

A near miss in the "Distinctively Different Downtown" category, San Antonio's delicious downtown Riverwalk and new residential development is worth considering. See the Downtown Alliance of San Antonio's Web site at **www.downtownsanantonio.org**.

UTAH

Salt Lake City

A big-city feeling with trains and fantastic shopping, downtown Salt Lake City, a runner-up for best four-season downtowns, is one of the nicest in America. See the Downtown Alliance of Salt Lake City's Web site at **www.downtownslc.org** for more information.

VERMONT

Burlington

Church Street, Burlington's celebrated downtown corridor, makes this small city's brilliant downtown stand out from all other cities its size (around 40,000). Limited living spaces in the center of downtown doesn't stop surrounding neighbors from taking advantage of the lively scene that's fueled by the students of the University of Vermont. Visit the Church Street Marketplace District Commission's Web site at **www.churchstmarketplace.com**.

VIRGINIA

Hampton

Although not very dense and with limited housing opportunities, downtown Hampton is filled with assets including a vibrant waterfront and

Hampton University. See the Downtown Hampton Development Partnership's Web site at **www.downtownhampton.com** for more information.

Norfolk

Downtown Norfolk is experiencing a wave of residential and commercial development along a revitalized waterfront. See the Downtown Norfolk Council's Web site at **www.downtownnorfolk.org** and click **"Commercial and Residential Real Estate"** for a listing of housing opportunities.

Roanoke

With its exceptional city market, the Star City's downtown also offers equivalent downtown housing choices of cities many times its size. See Downtown Roanoke, Inc.'s Web site at **www.downtownroanoke.org** and click **"Real Estate."**

WASHINGTON

Bellevue

Bellevue is an eastern suburb of Seattle with a vibrant, walkable downtown with an impressive 4,000 residents. See the Bellevue Downtown Association's Web site at **www.bellevuedowntown.org**.

Spokane

As eastern Washington's urban hub, downtown Spokane is poised for residential growth, and perhaps may begin by the time you retire. See the Downtown Spokane Partnership's Web site at **http://downtown.spokane.net**.

Tacoma

Hilly downtown Tacoma is a smaller alternative to nearby Seattle. See the Downtown Merchants Group's Web site at **www.downtowntacoma.com**.

Olympia

Delightful downtown Olympia is a fun arts and shopping district with adjacent urban neighborhoods. See what's going on at the Olympia Downtown Association's Web site at **www.downtownolympia.com**.

WISCONSIN

Eau Claire

Keep checking the Downtown Eau Claire Inc. Web site for new places for Ruppies to live in this clean and beautiful small city near the Twin Cities of Minnesota: **www.downtown-eauclaire.com**.

Green Bay

Green Bay is Wisconsin's sleeper downtown on the bay. See Downtown Green Bay Incorporated at **www.downtowngreenbay.com**.

Kenosha

The downtown of this small city on Lake Michigan is enjoying new condominium development with lake views, nearby marinas, great restaurants, and the novelty of restored electric streetcars, not to mention beautiful historic residential districts.

Racine

Racine has an ambitious downtown development plan and enviable location—on Lake Michigan and between Milwaukee and Chicago. It's definitely worth considering, especially if your retirement is still a few years away. See the Downtown Racine Corporation's Web site at **www.racinedown town.com**.

WYOMING

Cheyenne

Although very few downtown proper residential opportunities are available, check out the surrounding neighborhoods. See the Cheyenne Downtown Development Authority's Web site at **www.downtowncheyenne.com** for more information.

CANADIAN DOWNTOWNS

Canadian cities are innovative, efficient, and extremely clean. In many ways, downtowns in Canada are ahead of those in America and are definitely worth a look.

ALBERTA

Calgary

Calgary provides a pedestrian mall, shopping at the "Downtown on 8th Shopping Distrct," the Penny Lane Entertainment District, and a large Chinatown. To the west, the Rockies provide a year-round playground and day trip destination: **www.downtowncalgary.com**.

Edmonton

Edmonton is the most northern major city on the North American continent with a gem of a downtown. Join 4,000 neighbors around tree-lined MacKay Avenue or find a loft in the emerging Warehouse District. You can also hop on the light rail to travel around the city. Visit **www.edmontondowntown.com** and click **"More in the Core"** and then **"Living"** for more information.

BRITISH COLUMBIA

Vancouver

"Hollywood North" is arguably the best city in the entire world with a model downtown full of gleaming glass and steel high-rise condominium towers. The city boasts stunning water and mountain views, pedestrian-filled streets, world-class cultural amenities, and mammoth Stanley Park. Visit Downtown Vancouver Business Improvement Association and see for yourself: **www.downtownvancouver.net**.

MANITOBA

Winnipeg

Downtown Winnipeg, rising from the prairies, is a major cosmopolitan city in Canada that deserves more attention. See **www.downtownwinnipeg biz.com** and click **"Downtown Living Tour"** for more information. Also learn about the shops, restaurants, and nightlife by visiting the historic Exchange District's Web site at **www.exchangedistrict.org**.

NOVA SCOTIA

Halifax

A dynamo of a small city and a major cruise ship destination, downtown Halifax offers unique shopping, fabulous restaurants, and breathtaking water views. The commercial revitalization of the Barrington Street Historic District proves that this city loves its core. See **www.downtownhalifax.ns.ca** to learn more.

ONTARIO

Brampton

Although small, downtown Brampton provides a thriving farmer's market, eateries, museums, and Thursday night concerts. Visit **www.city.brampton .on.ca/downtown-brampton** and click **"Downtown Living"** to learn more.

Hamilton

Downtown Hamilton provides a major Canadian city complete with a symphony, opera, museums, and major league sports but without the hugeness of Toronto. See more at **www.downtownhamilton.org**.

London

The "Forest City" boasts an impressive downtown scene with many options for renting and buying. Visit Main Street London at **www.main streetlondon.ca** for additional information and click **"Live."**

Ottawa

The nation's capital's downtown is on fire with residential, shopping, and cultural opportunities. This place is definitely worth a look as you plan your retirement: See Downtown Rideau, Ottawa's Arts and Theatre District at **www.downtownrideau.com**, and the awesome ByWard Market at **www.byward-market.com**.

Toronto

This is Ontario's world city and Canada's largest, with downtown living opportunities far from the core similar to New York's vast urban living neighborhood choices. If you're interested in becoming a Toronto Ruppie, begin by exploring the following sites:

Bloor-Yorkville: **www.bloor-yorkville.com**

Downtown Yonge: **www.downtownyonge.com**

The Distillery Historic District: **www.thedistillerydistrict.com**

St. Lawrence: (St. Lawrence Market: **www.stlawrencemarket.com**)

Cabbagetown: **www.oldcabbagetown.com**

Corktown: **www.corktown.ca**

Other notable neighborhoods (not exhaustive) without Web sites include the Annex, Queen Street West Neighbourhood, Garden District, Financial District, Entertainment District, Little Italy, and South Annex (to name a few!).

QUEBEC

Montreal

Eyes on Paris? Montreal's exceptional Centre-Ville neighborhoods provide a close-to-home option for retirees seeking something truly unique— French culture and a big city lifestyle. Although no downtown Montreal sites are available, get a feel for the city's history and architecture by visiting Old Montreal's Web site at **www.vieux.montreal.qc.ca**.

Quebec

On the hilly banks of the St. Lawrence River, 400-year-old downtown Quebec is another "European" option for retirees seeking a life adventure. (No dedicated downtown Web site, but see **www.quebecregion.com** for a glimpse of what Quebec City offers.)

SASKATCHEWAN

Regina

The Provincial capital's downtown is growing and booming with new residents and 200 shops—extraordinary for a smaller city. Find out how you can become Regina's next urban dweller at **www.reginadowntown.ca** and click **"Downtown Living."**

Saskatoon

Another amazing downtown in the middle of Canada, Saskatoon has fully embraced the urban living movement. Get a lot more home for your money and live in an innovative smaller city by visiting the Partnership's Web site at **www.downtownsaskatoon.com**, then click **"Live."**

REFERENCES

Chapters 1–5
Downtown Miami "Citizens on Patrol"
Miami Herald
The Ohio State University's Continuing Education Department

Metropolitan Populations
United States Census, Annual Estimates of the Population of Metropolitan
and Micropolitan Statistical Areas: April 1, 2000 to July 1, 2003.

Downtown Populations Statistics
Who Lives Downtown?, by Eugenie L. Birch,
The Brookings Institution Metropolitan Policy Program, November 2005.

Census Zip Code Tabulation Areas for Asheville, Madison, Oklahoma City,
Omaha, and Providence.

General Real Estate
National Association of Realtors (**www.realtor.com**)
National Association of Realtors' Homefair (**www.homefair.com**)
National Association of Realtors' Homestore Inc. (**www.homestore.com**)
(January 2006 values used for "price snapshots")
Homestore Inc.'s RentNet Online Rental Guide (**www.rentnet.com**)

State Income and State Sales Tax
Federation of Tax Administrators

ABOUT THE AUTHOR

Kyle Ezell is the founder of "Get Urban America, Ltd.," a Columbus, Ohio–based urban planning firm dedicated to teaching the urban lifestyle to Americans. Kyle is a trained cultural geographer and a nationally known certified city planner who has been interviewed by numerous newspaper and television media as an expert on revitalizing cities. In his presentations across the country, Kyle demonstrates how retirees and empty nesters can find fun, freedom, and high-quality lives in the middle of town. Kyle invites you to become a Ruppie by visiting **www.retiredowntown.com**.